MODERN ENGENDERING

SUNY SERIES, FEMINIST PHILOSOPHY
JEFFNER ALLEN, EDITOR

MODERN ENGENDERING

CRITICAL FEMINIST READINGS
IN MODERN WESTERN PHILOSOPHY

EDITED BY

Bat-Ami Bar On

STATE UNIVERSITY OF NEW YORK PRESS

Susan R. Bordo's chapter is taken from her book,
*The Flight to Objectivity: Essays in Cartesianism and
Culture,* published by State University of New York
Press, 1987. Reprinted with permission of the publisher.

Cynthia Willett, "Hegel, Antigone, and the Possibility of a
Woman's Dialectic," taken from *Philosophy and Literature,* Spring 1991. Copyright
© 1987 by the Johns' Hopkins University Press. Reprinted by permission of the
publisher.

Published by
State University of New York Press, Albany

For information, address State University of New York
Press, State University Plaza, Albany, N.Y., 12246

Production by Diane Ganeles
Marketing by Fran Keneston

Library of Congress Cataloging-in-Publication Data

Modern engendering : critical feminist readings in modern Western
   philosophy / edited by Bat-Ami Bar On.
      p.   cm. — (SUNY series, feminist philosophy)
   Includes bibliographical references and index.
   ISBN 0-7914-1641-0 (alk. paper).—ISBN 0-7914-1642-9 (pbk. :
alk. paper)
   1. Philosophy, Modern—History and criticism.   2. Feminist theory.
I. Bar On, Bat-Ami, 1948–   II. Series.
B791.M64   1994
190'.82—dc20   92-36047
                                                                    CIP

10   9   8   7   6   5   4   3   2

This book is dedicated to my students and to my teachers.

Contents

Preface

The idea for an anthology of critical feminist readings in the history of modern Western philosophy developed from the idea for an anthology of critical feminist readings in Plato and Aristotle. The former idea was inspired by students' complaints about the irrelevance of a history of ancient Greek philosophy course that is gender-blind. Because a history of Western philosophy curriculum usually consists of courses in ancient Greek philosophy and Modern Western philosophy, and because the relevance of the latter may also benefit from integrating a gendered analysis, it seemed appropriate to develop not only a volume of critical feminist readings of the former but to go on and develop a volume of critical feminist readings of the latter.

As with the Plato-Aristotle volume, in the case of this volume too, Jeffner Allen coached the development of an idea into a proposal to the press, and an incredible network of women philosophers encouraged me to implement the idea and helped me do so by suggesting possible contributors to the anthology or by contributing to the anthology themselves. The contributors, of course, are the people who actualized the idea and I would like to thank each one—Susan R. Bordo, Lisa M. Heldke, Jane Kneller, Wendy Lee-Lampshire, Lynda Lange, Marcia Lind, Sarah A. Bishop Merrill, Margaret Nash, Amy Newman, Kelly Oliver, Elizabeth Potter, Robbin May Schott, Ofelia Schutte, Kristin Waters, and Cynthia Willett—for their work, for indulging my editorial requests, even the quirky ones, and doing so with a sense of humor, and for the generosity of their spirits.

Introduction

Bat-Ami Bar On

Whether we like it or not, we are within philosophy, surrounded by masculine-feminine divisions that philosophy has helped to articulate and refine. The problem is whether we want to remain there and be dominated by them, or whether we can take up a critical position in relation to them, a position which will necessarily involve the deciphering of the basic philosophical assumptions latent in discussions about women.

Michéle Le Doeuff[1]

I

I begin the introduction to this anthology with the same quotation from Michele Le Doeuff's "Women and Philosophy" with which I began the introduction to this book's sister volume about Plato and Aristotle. I do this since I believe that Le Doeuff captures well the situation of the feminist reader of the history of canonical Western philosophy. The feminist reader realizes that canonical Western philosophy has contributed to the production of the hegemonic system of interrelated gender differences. At the same time, it is far from obvious to her or him whether her or his thinking can become free from the influences of this system. Nonetheless, she or he takes a critical position toward this system in the hope that her or his work will contribute to a process of liberation.[2]

As I noted in the introduction to the Plato-Aristotle volume, the contribution of the feminist critique is not unproblematic because of the many ways in which it may reinscribe just what it attempts to criticize and deconstruct, hence, in the final analysis, contribute to the philosophical production of gender differences. This might be clearer when thinking somewhat differently about what it is that anthologies like this do.

Some time ago I saw a new anthology of readings of the Western philosophical canon, and looking at the contents, realized that all the essays were both about and authored by men. What that made perfectly clear to me is the extent to which the study of the history of canonical Western philosophy has been and to a great extent still is a form of male-bonding.

Every essay in this anthology, like every essay in its sister volume, has been written by a woman. If this anthology functions somewhat analogically to an anthology of essays by men, then it is a form of female-bonding. The analogy, however, is far from perfect. Men commenting on men bond both to the men they comment on and to each other. Because all the essays in this anthology are about men, while the women who authored them bond to each other by partaking in something that can be generally conceived as the same project, our bonding gets disrupted through the commentary—it bonds us to men. Though the bonding to men is also a disrupted bonding, ruptured by the bonding of women to women through the common project of a feminist commentary, it is because of it that a feminist criticism of a canon can and probably reinscribes the canon while criticizing it.

Problematic as an anthology like this is, I believe that it is extremely valuable. The least it does is challenge the philosophical claim that gender is marginal to a philosophy produced in a culture in which gender is significant. And gender has been shown to be particularly significant to modern philosophy by, for example, Evelyn Fox Keller, who has argued that contrary to ancient Greek philosophy and especially Plato's philosophy, modern Western philosophy, beginning with Bacon, more rigidly differentiates between the genders, valorizes masculinity and men and disvalues femininity and women, and legitimizes the domination of women by men as it legitimizes the domination of nature by men.[3]

II

In the U.S. the challenge of philosophy's claim that gender is marginal to philosophy was first put in print within the disciplinary boundaries of philosophy in 1973 when *The Monist*[4] published the first collection of essays written by U.S. academic philosophers that addressed feminist issues. This collection included one essay—Christine Pierce's "Equality: *Republic V*"[5]—that examined an argument by a person whose works are a part of the story of Western philosophy from a feminist perspective. The next collection of essays that addressed feminist issues philosophically formed the 1973–

1974 volume of *The Philosophical Forum*.[6] It included several feminist studies of positions of canonized philosophers, as well as Carol C. Gould's essay "The Woman Question: Philosophy of Liberation and the Liberation of Philosophy"[7] in which Gould argues for the possibility of studying woman philosophically.

Gould accepts the by now terribly contested claim that the proper subject of philosophical studies is the universal and that, therefore, philosophical examinations methodologically and necessarily exclude particular and accidental differences. According to her, it follows from this that woman as woman cannot be studied philosophically, if she is thought of as an accident of the universal human since, when thought of in this way, she would have to be studied not as woman but as human. Gould claims that, however, given an unessentialist conception of universality as concrete universality, woman could be studied philosophically. Her notion of a concrete universal is that of an ensemble of systematically related differences that are constituted by and constitutive of certain relations that are historically and socially, hence culturally, located. Woman is such a concrete universal. She says:

> Being a woman ... is ... a property whose definition depends on the relation between men and women in concrete social life. ... These relations or interrelations are ... not external relations between individuals who are already independently defined by some criterion ... Men become men, and woman become women, in the course of these interrelations.[8]

Gould, who believes that it is important and seems to be very optimistic about there being a way to philosophize about woman, does not address the role of canonical Western philosophy in the production of the hegemonic Western system of interrelated gender differences. Yet, like other Western disciplines, canonical Western philosophy has been contributing to this production along three lines.[9]

First, canonical Western philosophy provides claims and arguments about or descriptions and analyses of what it is to be a woman as distinguished from a man, what is appropriate for a woman as distinguished from a man, and what kinds of relations women and men should have. In addition, it deploys the feminine and the masculine as metaphysical principles or as metaphors, and it also deploys certain forms or styles of thinking. Finally, it uses both in such a way that claims and arguments about or descriptions and analyses of other things engender these things as it intertwines them with the conceptions of woman and man and our relations, consequently also expanding, though not necessarily enriching, the conceptions of woman, man and our relations.

The essays in this anthology criticize canonical modern Western philosophy's contribution to the production of the hegemonic Western system of interrelated gender differences. Some of them focus specifically on the ways in which modern Western philosophy constructs genders and analyzes gender relations. For example, Marcia Lind's "Indians, Savages, Peasants and Women: Hume's Aesthetics," Kristin Waters' "Women in Kantian Ethics: A Failure at Universality," and Ofelia Schutte's "Nietzsche's Psychology of Gender Difference" show how each of these philosophers creates idealized categories such as that of good normative evaluators, competent moral agents, and even philosophical mavericks and rebels by excluding and inferiorizing women.

A second group of essays provide a detailed analysis of the philosophers conceptions of masculinity and femininity or of concepts that are intertwined with them. Lynda Lange takes a critical look at Rousseau's dualism and its normative implications in "Women and Rousseau's Democratic Theory: Philosopher Monsters and Authoritarian Equality". Robin May Schott's "Rereading the Canon: Kantian Purity and the Suppression of Eros" examines the intersection of the feminine with the sensible for Kant. Cynthia Willett criticizes Hegel for failing to accord emotions a proper place in his aesthetics, and more generally, failing to accord desires a proper place in his dialectic. For Hegel both emotions and desire are associated with the feminine in "Hegel, Antigone and the Possibility of a Woman's Dialectic". Another look at Hegel is Amy Newman's in "Hegel's Theoretical Violence" where she argues that Hegel is not simply one-sidedly valorizing the masculine and inferiorizing the feminine but advocates the suppression of woman and the feminine.

A third group of essays calls attention to the intertwining of gender with conceptual schemas and networks. Thus, in "Marx and the Ideology of Gender: A Paradox of Praxis and Nature" Wendy Lee-Lampshire argues that it is only at face-value that ecofeminism could appropriate the Marxian conception of praxis in order to articulate its vision of an undestructive and unexploitative human to nature relation. According to Lee-Lampshire, the Marxian conception of praxis is actually unsatisfactory because it is situated within a conceptual network that valorizes reason as separate from nature which is associated with women. Similarily, in "Who is Nietzsche's Woman?" Kelly Oliver finds in Nietzsche a critic of dualism and an advocate of plurality who did not and could not break away from the tradition due to his commitments to masculine ideals. And, in "Interaction in a World of Chance: John Dewey's Theory of Inquiry", Lisa Heldke argues that Dewey's critique of the epistemological themes of modernity, despite its affinity to the feminist critique of the same, is problematic because it privileges science and manipulative inquiry which are intertwined with masculinity and masculine ways of doing things.

A special case of the third group are essays that situate the philosophical texts they read historically in ways that expose them as linked in many ways with the conceptual schemas of their time. One example of this is Susan Bordo's "The Cartesian Masculinization of Thought and the Seventeenth Century Flight from the Feminine" which situates Descartes' conception of thinking in his time, showing that Descartes, like others in the seventeenth century, masculinized the previously unmasculine concept of thought in response to the crisis of the time. Another example is Ellizabeth Potter's "Locke's Epistemology and Women's Struggles" which situates Locke's epistemology socio-politically showing that in a time of crisis Locke formulated an epistemology that responded to the needs of the English middle-class of his time, hence, an epistemology designed to refute both the conservative royalists and the radical populists.

While most of the essays in this anthology are very critical of modern Western philosophy, there are a few essays that suggest that some modern philosophers do have ideas that can be useful for feminists, ideas that I described as raidable in the introduction to the Plato-Aristotle volume. Thus, for example, Sarah A. Bishop Merrill's "A Feminist Use for Hume's Moral Ontology" argues that Hume has a non-essentialist view of persons that could be useful for the development of a feminist ethics. Similarly, Jane Kneller's "Kant's Immature Imagination" suggest that Kant's moral theory has both a sensible and a rational aspect which could be integrated and is, therefore, important for feminist ethical theorizing. And, in "Nietzschean Debris: Truth as Circe" Margaret Nash put forth the claim that there are important affinities between Nietzsche's critique of modernity, and particularly his emphasis on play and the disunity of the subject, and feminist insights about modernity and the possibility of overcoming it.

III

The possibility of finding raidable ideas in modern Western philosophical texts is in part a function of the fact that multiple inconsistencies are one of the properties of any canon. One would have to assume that a text or a corpus is totally unified by authorial intentions or subconscious designs, or is nothing but a symptomatic expression of a totalizing and invasively saturating hegemonic culture, or of a discursive practice or discursive mode, in order to believe that tensions are not a property of a text or a corpus, let alone a canon that is formed by many texts and corpuses.[10]

Still, the ambiguity and contradictory richness of canonical modern Western philosophy is also constituted by its interpretation and specifically its rational reconstruction, which, according to Richard Rorty, is a genre of historiographical philosophical studies that is motivated by historically located philosophical inquiry and driven by questions in such a way that rational reconstructionists "confine themselves to a relatively small portion of the philosopher's work"[11] and do not produce interpretations that converge. Rorty describes rational reconstructions as follows:

> They are written in light of some recent work in philosophy which can reasonably be said to be "about the same questions" as the great dead philosophers was discussing. They are designed to show that the answers he gave to these questions, though plausible and exciting, need restatement or purification—or, perhaps, the kind of precise refutation which further work in the field has recently made possible.[12]

In the case of this anthology, as in the case of the Plato-Aristotle volume, the influencing recent work is primarily feminist philosophical work in ethics, social and political philosophy, epistemology, philosophy of mind, and philosophy of science.[13] This work raises questions about and seeks alternatives to the philosophical construction of reality through a value-laden binary oppositional prism, the adequacy of moral theories that construe normative evaluations as a kind of a straightforward correct application of principles, and the idea of moral autonomy and agency, as well as scientific autonomy and agency, insofar as they are understood exclusively in terms of a general and unsituated reason.

By reading the canonical Western texts in light of current feminist philosophizing, the essays in this anthology contribute to the unique yet growing reinterpretation of the story of Western philosophy by groups whose voices have been excluded from this story. Because this interpretation is done by outsiders who are also insiders, both bound to the discipline and to each other yet in a disrupted way, it is particularly insightful about the ways canonized Western philosophy has contributed to the hegemonic dominant culture and about the ways it can perhaps, nonetheless, be useful to resistant readers.

Notes

1. Le Doeuff, Michéle, "Women and Philosophy" in Moil, Toril (ed.), *French Feminist Thought: A Reader.* Oxford: Basil Blackwell, 1987, p. 182.

2. See Bartky, Sandra Lee's introduction to her *Femininity and Domination, Studies in the Phenomenology of Oppression,* N.Y.: Routledge, 1990.

3. Keller, Evelyn Fox's *Reflections on Gender and Science.* New Haven: Yale University, 1985.

4. *The Monist* 57 (1973).

5. Pierce, Christine, "Equality: Republic V". *The Monist* 57 (1973): 1–11.

6. *The Philosophical Forum* 5 (1973–1974).

7. Gould, Carol C. "The Woman Question: Philosophy of Liberation and the Liberation of Philosophy." *The Philosophical Forum* 5 (1973–1974): 5–44.

8. Gould, pp. 28–29.

9. I believe that these three kinds of Western disciplinary contributions to the production of the Western system of interrelated gender differences, hence the Western cultural production of women are suggested by feminist criticisms of the disciplines. For some of these see: Caine, Barbara, Grosz, E. A., de Lepervanche, Marie (eds.) *Crossing Boundaries: Feminism and the Critique of Knowledges.* Sydney: Allen and Unwin, 1988, DuBois, Ellen Carol, Kelly, Gail Paradise, Kennedy, Elizabeth Lapovsky, Korsmeyer, Carolyn W. and Robinson, Lillian S., *Feminist Scholarship: Kindling in the Groves of Academe.* University of Illinois, 1985, Spender, Dale (ed.) *Men's Studies Modified: The Impact of Feminism on the Academic Disciplines.* Oxford: Pergamon, 1981.

10. On this, see LaCapra, Dominick, *Rethinking Intellectual History.* Cornell University, 1983, especially the first chapter "Rethinking Intellectual History and Reading Texts", pp. 23–74. See also, and somewhat in

contrast, MacIntyre, Alasdair, The Relationship of Philosophy to Its Past" in Rorty, Richard, Schneewind, J. B. and Skinner, Quentin (eds.). *Philosophy in History.* Cambridge University, 1984, pp. 31–48.

11. Rorty, Richard, "The Historiography of Philosophy: Four Genres" in Rorty, Richard, Schneewind, J. B. and Skinner, Quentin (eds.), *Philosophy in History.* Cambridge University, 1984, p. 57.

12. Rorty, p. 57.

13. A few very recent anthologies provide some excellent examples of current feminist philosophical work. See: Benhabib, Seyla and Cornell, Drucilla (eds.), *Feminism as Critique: On the Politics of Gender.* University of Minnesota, 1987. Code, Lorraine, Mullett, Sheila, and Overall, Christine (eds.) *Feminist Perspectives: Philosophical Essays on Method and Morals.* University of Toronto, 1988, Griffiths, Morwenna and Whitford, Margaret (eds.), *Feminist Perspectives in Philosophy.* Indiana University Press, 1988, Kittay, Eva Fedder and Meyers, Diana T. (eds.), *Women and Moral Theory.* Totowa, N.J.: Rowman and Littlefield, 1987. Other anthologies that address ethics are Claudia Cord (ed.) *Feminist Ethics,* Lawrence, KS: University Press of Kansas, 1991 and Eve Browning Cole and Susan Coultrop-McQuin (eds.), *Explorations in Feminist Ethics,* Bloomington, IN: Indiana University, 1992. An anthology that brings together a number of essays from different philosophical fields is Garry, Ann and Pearsall, Marilyn (eds.), *Women, Knowledge and Reality: Explorations in Feminist Philosophy.* Boston: Unwin Hyman, 1989. Two recent anthologies Goldren epistemology and the philosophy of mind Alcoff, Linole and Potter, Elizabeth (eds.) *Feminist Epistemologies.* NY: Routledge, 1993 and Louise M. Anthony and Charlotte Witt (eds.), *A Mind of One's Own,* Boulder, CO: Westview, 1993. Other sources for such examples are *Hypatia* and the Newsletter of *Feminism and Philosophy.*

PART ONE

BEGINNINGS: DESCARTES

The Cartesian Masculinization of Thought and the Seventeenth-Century Flight from the Feminine

Susan R. Bordo

[I]f a kind of Cartesian ideal were ever completely fulfilled, i.e., if the whole of nature were only what can be explained in terms of mathematical relationships—then we would look at the world with that fearful sense of alienation, with that utter loss of reality with which a future schizophrenic child looks at his mother. A machine cannot give birth.

(*Karl Stern,* The Flight From Woman)

Philosophical Reconstruction, Anxiety and Flight

If the transition from Middle Ages to Renaissance can be looked on as a kind of protracted birth, from which the human being emerges as a decisively separate entity, no longer continuous with the universe with which it had once shared a soul, so the possibility of objectivity, strikingly, is conceived by Descartes as a kind of *re-birth,* on one's own terms, this time.

We are all familiar with the dominant Cartesian themes of starting anew, alone, without influence from the past or other people, with the guidance of reason alone. The product of our original and actual birth, childhood, being ruled by the body, is the source of all obscurity and confusion in our thinking. As Descartes says in the *Discourse,* "since we have all been children before being men . . . it is almost impossible that our judgments should be as pure and solid as they would have been if we had had complete use of our reason since birth and had never been guided except by it." The specific origins of obscurity in our thinking are, as we have seen, the "prejudices" of childhood, which all have a common form: the inability, due to our infantile "immersion" in the body, to distinguish properly between subject and object. The purification of the relation between knower and known requires the repudiation of childhood, a theme

3

which was not uncommon at the time. The ideology of childhood as a time of "innocence" and the child as an epistemological *tabula rasa* had yet to become popular. Rather, childhood was commonly associated, as Descartes associated it, with sensuality, animality, and the mystifications of the body.

For Descartes, happily, the state of childhood *can* be revoked, through a deliberate and methodical reversal of all the prejudices acquired within it, and a beginning anew with reason as one's only parent. This is precisely what the *Meditations* attempts to do. The body of infancy is transcended. The clear and distinct ideas are released from their obscuring material prison. The result is a securing of all the boundaries which, in childhood (and at the start of the *Mediations*) are so fragile: between the "inner" and the "outer," between the subjective and the objective, between self and world.

It is crucial to recall here that what for Descartes is conceived as epistemological threat—"subjectivity," the blurring of boundaries between self and world—was not conceived as such by the medievals. Rather, the medieval sense of relatedness to the world, as we know from its art, literature and philosophy, had not depended on "objectivity," but on continuity between the human and physical realms, on the interpenetrations, through meanings, of self and world. But *locatedness* in space and time, by Descartes' era, had inexorably come to the forefront of human experience, and the continuities and interpenetrations which had once been a source of intellectual and spiritual satisfaction now presented themselves as "distortions" caused by personal attachment and "perspective." Objectivity, not meaning, became the issue, and "so long as the human being is embedded in nature and united with it, objectivity is impossible." By the time of Kant, this "condition" for knowledge—the separation of knower and known—is philosophically apprehended. Human intelligence, Kant discovers, is *founded* on the distinction between subject and object. The condition of *having* an objective world, on the Kantian view, is to grasp phenomena as unified and connected by the embrace of a discrete consciousness, capable of representing to itself its own distinctness from the world it grasps. But what Kant here "discovers," (and what came to be regarded as a given in modern science and philosophy) was a while in the making. For Descartes, the separation of subject and object is a *project,* not a "foundation" to be discovered.

. . . The Cartesian reconstruction has two interrelated dimensions. On the one hand, a new model of knowledge is conceived, in which the purity of the intellect is guaranteed through its ability to transcend the body. On the other hand, the ontological blueprint of the order of things is refashioned. The spiritual and the corporeal are now two distinct substances which share no qualities (other than being created), permit interaction but no merging, and are each defined precisely in opposition to the other. *Res cogitans* is "a thinking and unextended thing"; *res extensa* is "an extended and unthinking thing." This mutual exclusion of res cogitans and res extensa made possible the conceptualization of complete intellectual independence from the body, res extensa of the human being and chief impediment to human objectivity. The dichotomy between the spiritual and the corporeal also established the utter diremption—detachment, dislocation—of the natural world from the realm of the human. It now became inappropriate to speak, as the medievals had done, in anthropocentric terms about nature, which for Descartes is pure res extensa, "totally devoid of mind and thought." More important, it means that the values and significances of things in relation to the human realm must be understood as purely a reflection of how *we* feel about them, having nothing to do with their "objective" qualities.

"Thus," says Whitehead, in sardonic criticism of the "characteristic scientific philosophy" of the seventeenth century, "the poets are entirely mistaken. They should address their lyrics to themselves and should turn them into odes of self-congratulation . . . Nature is a dull affair, soundless, scentless, colorless; merely the hurrying of material, endlessly, meaninglessly." For the model of knowledge which results, neither bodily response (the sensual or the emotional) nor associational thinking, exploring the various personal or spiritual meanings the object has for us, can tell us anything about the object "itself." *It* can only be grasped, as Gillespie puts it, "by measurement rather than sympathy." Thus the spectre of infantile subjectivism is overcome by the possibility of a cool, impersonal, distanced cognitive relation to the world. At the same time, the nightmare landscape of the infinite universe has become the well-lighted laboratory of modern science and philosophy.

The conversion of nightmare into positive vision is characteristic of Descartes. Within the narrative framework of the *Meditations,* "dreamers, demons, and madmen" are exorcised, the crazily fragmented "enchanted glass" of the mind (as Bacon called it) is transformed into the "mirror of nature," the true reflector of things. But such transformations, as Descartes' determinedly up-beat interpretation of his own famous nightmare suggests, may be grounded in *defense*—in the suppression of anxiety, uncertainty, and dread. Certainly, anxiety infuses the *Meditations*, . . . *a cultural* anxiety, arising from discoveries, inventions, and events of the era which were major and disorienting.

That disorientation . . . is given psycho-cultural coherence via a "story" of *parturition* from the organic universe of the Middle Ages and Renaissance, out of which emerged the modern categories of "self," "locatedness," and "innerness." This parturition was initially experienced as *loss*, i.e., as estrangement, and the opening up of a chasm between self and nature. Epistemologically, that estrangement expresses itself in skepticism, and in an unprecedented anxiety over the possibility of reaching the world as "it" is. Spiritually, it expresses itself in anxiety over the *enclosedness* of the individual self, the isolating uniqueness of each individual allotment in time and space, and the arbitrary, incomprehensible nature of that allotment by an alien, indifferent universe. We may speak here, meaningfully, of a *cultural* "separation anxiety."

The particular genius of Descartes was to have philosophically transformed what was first experienced as estrangement and loss— the sundering of the organic ties between the person and world— into a requirement for the growth of human knowledge and progress. And at this point, we are in a better position to flesh out the mechanism of *defense* involved here. Cartesian objectivism and mechanism, I will propose, should be "read" as a *reaction-formation*—a denial of the "separation anxiety" described above, facilitated by an aggressive intellectual *flight* from the female cosmos and "feminine" orientation towards the world. That orientation (described so far in this study in the gender-neutral terminology of "participating consciousness") had still played a formidable role in medieval and Renaissance thought and culture. In the seventeenth century, it was decisively purged from the dominant intellectual culture, through the Cartesian "re-birthing" and re-structuring of knowledge and world as *masculine*.

I will begin by exploring the mechanist flight from the female cosmos (which Carolyn Merchant has called "The Death of Nature"). Then, I will focus on the specifically epistemological expression of the seventeenth century flight from the feminine: "the Cartesian masculinization of thought." Both the mechanist reconstruction of the world and the objectivist reconstruction of knowledge will then be examined as embodying a common psychological structure: a fantasy of "re-birthing" self and world, brought into play by the disintegration of the organic, female cosmos of the Middle Ages and Renaissance. This philosophical fantasy will be situated within the general context of seventeenth century attitudes toward female generativity, as chronicled by a number of feminist authors. Finally, the relevance of these ideas of current discussions about gender and rationality, and to current re-assessments of Cartesianism, will be considered in a concluding section.

The Death of Nature and the Masculinization of Thought

... The medieval cosmos whose destruction gave birth to the modern sensibility was a *mother*-cosmos, and the soul which Descartes drained from the natural world was a *female* soul. Carolyn Merchant, whose ground-breaking interdisciplinary study, *The Death of Nature,* chronicles the changing imagery of nature in this period, describes the "organic cosmology" which mechanism overthrew:

> "... minerals and metals ripened in the uterus of the Earth Mother, mines were compared to her vagina, and metallurgy was the human hastening of the living metal in the artificial womb of the furnace ... Miners offered propitiation to the deities of the soil, performed ceremonial sacrifices ... sexual abstinence, fasting, before violating the sacredness of the living earth by sinking a mine."

The notion of the natural world as *mothered* has sources, for the Western tradition, in both Plato and Aristotle. In Plato's *Timeaus,* the formless "receptacle" or "nurse" provides the substratum of all determinate materiality (... also referred to as "space"—*chora*—in the dialogue.) The "receptacle" is likened to a mother because of its receptivity to impression; the father is the "source or spring"—the eternal forms which "enter" and "stir and inform her." The child is the determinate nature which is formed through their union: the *body* of nature.

In this account, the earth is not a mother, but is itself a child of the union of "nurse" and forms. The notion that the earth *itself* mothers things, e.g., metals and minerals, required the inspiration of the Aristotelian theory of animal reproduction. In that theory, the female provides not only matter as "substratum," but matter as sensible "stuff": the *catamenia,* or menstrual material, which is "worked upon" and shaped by the "effective and active" element, the semen of the male. In the fifteenth and sixteenth centuries, this account of animal generation was projected onto the cosmos. A "stock description" of biological generation in nature was the marriage of heaven and earth, and the impregnation of the (female) earth by the dew and rain created by the movements of the (masculine) celestial heavens.

The female element here is *natura naturata,* of course—passive rather than creative nature. But passivity here connotes *receptivity* rather than inertness; only a living, breathing earth can be impregnated. And indeed, for Plato most explicitly, the world *has* a soul—a female soul—which permeates the corporeal body of the universe. In the seventeenth century, as Merchant argues, that female world-soul died—or more precisely, was *murdered*—by the mechanist re-visioning of nature.

This re-visioning of the universe as a *machine*—most often, a clockwork—was not the work of philosophers alone. Astronomy and anatomy had already changed the dominant picture of the movements of the heavens and the processes of the body by the time the *Meditations* were written. But it was philosophy, and Descartes in particular, that provided the cosmology that integrated these discoveries into a consistent and unified view of nature. By Descartes' brilliant stroke, nature became *defined* by its lack of affiliation with divinity, with spirit. All that which is God-like or spiritual—freedom, will and sentience—belong entirely and exclusively to *res cogitans.* All else—the earth, the heavens, animals, the human body— is merely mechanically interacting matter.

The seventeenth century saw the death, too, of another sort of "feminine principle"—that cluster of epistemological values, often associated with feminine consciousness, which apparently played a large and respected role in hermetic philosophy and, it might be argued, in the pre-scientific orientation toward the world in general. If the key terms in the Cartesian hierarchy of epistemological values are clarity and distinctness—qualities which mark each object off from the other and from the knower—the key term in this alternative scheme of values might be designated (following Gillespie's contrast here) as *sympathy.* "Sympathetic" understanding of the object is that which understands it through "union" with it, or, as James Hillman describes it, through "merging with" or "marrying" it. To merge with or marry that which is to be known means, for Hillman, "letting interior movement replace clarity, interior closeness replace objectivity". It means granting subjective or intuitive response a positive epistemological value, even (perhaps especially) when such response is contradictory or fragmented. "Sympathetic" thinking, Marcuse deems, is the only mode which respects the object "in its own right", that is, which allows the variety of its meanings to unfold without coercion or too focused interrogation.

Barfield's and Berman's discussion of medieval "participating consciousness," Bergson's notion of "intellectual sympathy," and Jasper's "causality from within" all contain elements of what I have called "sympathetic thinking." The deepest understanding of that which is to be known comes, each argues, not from analysis of parts, but from "placing oneself within" the being of an object, as Bergson puts it (at which point it ceases to be an "object" in the usual sense) and allowing *it* to speak.

An emphasis on the knower's *passivity* is shared by this ideal of knowledge and the Cartesian ideal. But whereas passivity for Descartes (and for Bacon) meant yielding to the authority of the object's "own" nature, for sympathetic thinking the objective and subjective *merge,* participate in the creation of meaning. The most inspired and articulate contemporary advocates of "sympathetic thinking" are Carol Gilligan and Evelyn Fox Keller, each of whom speaks forcefully to the need for integration of such thinking into our dominant conceptions of rationality. This does not mean a rejection, but a *re-visioning* of "objectivity." Keller's conception of "dynamic objectivity" is especially relevant here:

> "Dynamic objectivity is . . . a pursuit of knowledge that makes use of subjective experience . . . in the interests of a more effective objectivity. Premised on continuity, it recognizes difference between self and other as an opportunity for a deeper and more articulated kinship. The struggle to disentangle self from other is itself a source of insight—potentially into the nature of both self and other. It is a principle means for divining what Poincare calls "hidden harmonies and relations." To this end, the scientist employs a form of attention to the natural world that is like one's ideal attention to the human world: it is a form of love."

In contrast to the conception of "dynamic objectivity," Descartes' program for the purification of the understanding has as its ideal the rendering *impossible* of any such continuity between subject and object. The scientific mind must be cleansed of all its "sympathies" toward the objects it tries to understand. It must cultivate absolute *detachment.* Recognizing the centrality of such ideals to modern science has led writers like Sandra Harding to characterize modern science in terms of a "super-masculinization of rational

thought." Similarly, Karl Stern has said that "[What] we encounter
in Cartesian rationalism is the pure masculinization of thought."
The notion that modern science crystallizes masculinist modes of
thinking is a theme, too, in the work of James Hillman; " . . . the
specific consciousness we call scientific, Western and modern," says
Hillman, "is the long sharpened tool of the masculine mind that has
discarded parts of its own substance, calling it 'Eve,' 'female,' and
'interior.' " Evelyn Fox Keller's "Gender and Science" systematically
explores various perspectives (including developmental perspectives) on the connection between masculinity and modern science.

It must be stressed that descriptions of science as the "masculinization of thought" refer to what these authors view as characteristic cognitive and theoretical biases of male-dominated science,
not the fact of that male dominance itself. Science has, of course,
statistically excluded women, insisting that women cannot measure
up to the rigor, persistence, or clarity that science requires. It also
has its share of explicitly misogynist doctrine, as does its ancient
forefathers, Aristotle and Galen. But the most interesting contemporary discussions of the "masculinist" nature of science describe a
different, although related, aspect of its "masculinism": a characteristic cognitive style, an epistemological stance which is required
of men *and* women working in the sciences today. In the words of
Evelyn Fox Keller:

> "The scientific mind is set apart from what is to be known, i.e.,
> from nature, and its autonomy is guaranteed . . . by setting apart
> its modes of knowing from those in which the dichotomy is threat-
> ened. In this process, the characterization of both the scientific
> mind and its modes of access to knowledge as masculine is indeed
> significant. Masculine here connotes, as it so often does, autonomy,
> separation, and distance . . . a radical rejection of any commin-
> gling of subject and object."

It is in this sense that the dominant scientific and philosophic
culture of the seventeenth century indeed inaugurated "a truly
masculine birth of time," as Francis Bacon had proclaimed it. Similarly and strikingly, Henry Oldenberg, secretary of the Royal Society, asserted in 1664 that the business of that society was to raise
"a masculine philosophy." In her penetrating and imaginative study
of sexual metaphors in the history of epistemology, Keller pays very
serious attention to such historical associations of gender and "cognitive style," which we might have thought to belong to a peculiarly

modern mentality, but which in fact crop up frequently in Royal Society debates. As Keller reads them, the controversy between Bacon and Paracelsus becomes an explicit contest between masculine and feminine principles: head versus heart, domination over versus merging with the object, purified versus erotic orientation toward knowledge, etc., (pp. 43–65). Bacon's own deepest attitudes, Keller suggests, were more complicated and ambivalent than his oft-reproduced and notorious images of male seduction, penetration and rape of nature may suggest. But what emerges with clarity, despite any subtleties in the attitudes of individual thinkers, is that the notion of science as "masculine" is hardly a twentieth century invention or feminist fantasy. The founders of modern science consciously and explicitly proclaimed the "masculinity" of science as inaugurating a new era. And they associated that masculinity with a cleaner, purer, more objective and more disciplined epistemological relation to the world.

The emergence of such associations, in an era which lacked our heightened modern consciousness of gender as an issue, is remarkable. They suggest that the contemporary notion that thought *became* "super-masculinized" at a certain point in time is not merely, as some might argue, a new, fashionable way of labelling and condemning the seventeenth century objectivist turn—a turn, many would say, which has already been adequately described, criticized and laid to rest by Whitehead, Heidegger, and, more recently, Richard Rorty. Bacon's metaphor, rather, urges us in the direction of confronting a profound "flight from the feminine" at the heart of both Cartesian rationalism and Baconian empiricism. To appreciate the dimensions of that "flight," however, necessitates a return to the insights of developmental psychology.

The Cartesian "Re-Birth" and the "Father of Oneself" Fantasy

> Descartes envisages for himself a kind of rebirth. Intellectual salvation comes only to the twice-born.
>
> (Frankfurt, *Demons, Dreamers, and Madman*)

Psychoanalytic theory urges us to examine that which we actively repudiate for the shadow of a loss we mourn. Freud, in *Beyond the Pleasure Principle,* tells the story of an eighteen-month-old boy—an obedient, orderly little boy, as Freud describes him—who, although "greatly attached to his mother," never cried when she left him for a few hours.

> "This good little boy, however, had an occasional disturbing habit of taking any small objects he could get hold of and throwing them away from him into a corner, under the bed, and so on, so that hunting for his toys and picking them up was often quite a business. As he did this he gave vent to a loud, long drawn-out 'o-o-o-o', accompanied by an expression of interest and satisfaction. His mother and the writer of the present account were agreed in thinking that this was not a mere interjection but represented the German word *'fort'* ('gone'). I eventually realized that it was a game and that the only use he made of any of his toys was to play 'gone' with them . . . [T]he complete game [was] disappearance and return . . . The interpretation . . . became obvious. It was related to the child's great cultural achievement—the instinctual renunciation (that is, the renunciation of instinctual satisfaction) which he had made in allowing his mother to go away without protesting. He compensated himself for this, as it were, by himself staging the disappearance and return of the objects within his reach . . . Throwing away the object so that it was 'gone' might satisfy an impulse of the child's, which was suppressed in his actual life, to revenge himself on his mother for going away from him. In that case it would have a defiant meaning: 'All right, then, go away! I don't need you. I'm sending you away myself.' "

The 'fort-da' game and Freud's interpretation of it places the Cartesian facility for transforming anxiety into confidence, loss into mastery, in a striking new perspective. Within the context of the cultural separation anxiety described in this study, Descartes' masculine "rebirthing" of the world and self as decisively separate appears, not merely as the articulation of a positive new epistemological ideal, but as a reaction-formation to the loss of "being-one-with-the-world" brought about by the disintegration of the organic, centered, female cosmos of the Middle Ages and Renaissance. The Cartesian reconstruction of the world is a 'fort-da' game—a defiant gesture of independence from the female cosmos, a gesture which is at the same time compensation for a profound loss.

Let us explore the interpretation proposed above in more detail, turning again to developmental theory for insight. The project of growing up is to one degree or another (depending on culture and child-raising practice) a project of separation, of learning to deal with the fact that mother and child are no longer one and that gratification is not always available. Social and personal strategies for the child's accomplishing this are varied; every culture no doubt has its own modes of facilitating the separation of mother and child, to the degree that such separation is required by the culture. Psychoanalytic theory has focused on *internal* mechanisms, describing the different responses—longing, mourning, denial—that the child may have to separation. The mechanism of *denial* is of particular interest for my purposes. Although the dream of total union can persist throughout life, another, contradictory project may be conceived, psychoanalytic thinkers have suggested, centered around the denial of any longing for the lost maternal union. Instead, the child seeks mastery over the frustrations of separation and lack of gratification through an assertion of self against the mother and all that she represents and a rejection of all dependency on her. In this way, the pain of separateness is assuaged, paradoxically, by an even more definitive separation—but one that is *chosen* this time and aggressively pursued. It is therefore experienced as autonomy rather than helplessness in the fact of the discontinuity between self and mother.

One mode of such self-assertion is through the fantasy of becoming the parent of oneself, of "re-birthing" the self, playing the role of active parental figure rather than passive, helpless child. Such a notion of "re-birthing" or "re-parenting" the self figures in both Freudian and object-relations frameworks. Building on Winnicott's concept of the "transitional object" (a blanket, toy, or stuffed animal which eases the child's accommodation to and ultimate mastery over the process of separation from the mother), Ross argues that such objects function, symbolically, as the child. In cuddling, scolding the object, the child is actually playing at self-parenting, at being his or her own baby. Such self-parenting allows the child to feel less precariously at the mercy of the mother and more in control of his or her own destiny.

Working from a more Freudian framework, Norman O. Brown re-interprets the Oedipal desire to "sexually" possess the mother as a fantasy of "becoming the father of oneself" (rather than the helpless child of the mother.) Sexual activity here (or rather, the fantasy of it) becomes a means of denying the actual passivity of having been born from that original state of union into "a body of limited powers, and at a time and place [one] never chose", at the mercy of the now-alien will of the mother. The mother is still "other," but she is an other whose power has been harnessed by the will of the child. The pain of separateness is thus compensated for by the peculiar advantages of separateness: the possibility of mastery and control over that on which one is dependent. Melanie Klein (writing in 1928, much earlier than Brown) emphasizes the aggressive, destructive, envious impulses which may be directed against the mother's body—particularly against the organs of conception, pregnancy and birth—in the child's effort to achieve such control.

Certainly, the famous Baconian imagery of sexual assault and aggressive over-powering of a willful and unruly female nature (she must "be taken by the forelock" and "neither ought a man to make scruple of entering and penetrating these holes and corners," etc.) makes new psycho-cultural sense in the context of these ideas. More subtly, the Cartesian project of starting anew through the revocation of one's actual childhood (during which one was "immersed" in body and nature) and the (re)creation of a world in which absolute separateness (both epistemological and ontological) from body and nature are keys to control rather than sources of anxiety can now be seen as a "father of oneself" fantasy on a highly symbolic, but profound, plane. The sundering of the organic ties between person and nature—originally experienced, as we have seen, as epistemological estrangement, as the opening up of a chasm between self and world—is re-enacted, *this* time with the human being as the engineer and architect of the separation. Through the Cartesian "rebirth," a new "masculine" theory of knowledge is delivered, in which detachment from nature acquires a positive epistemological value. And a new *world* is reconstructed, one in which all generativity and creativity fall to God the spiritual father rather than to the female "flesh" of the world. With the same masterful stroke—the mutual opposition of the spiritual and the corporeal—the formerly female earth becomes matter and the objectivity of science is insured.

"She" becomes "it"—and "it" can be understood. Not through "sympathy," of course, but by virtue of the very *object*-ivity of the "it." At the same time, the "wound" of separateness is healed through the *denial* that there ever was any union: for the mechanists, unlike Donne, the female world-soul did not die; rather the world *is* dead. There is nothing to mourn, nothing to lament. Indeed, the new epistemological anxiety is evoked, not over loss, but by the memory or suggestion of *union:* "sympathetic," associational, or bodily response obscures objectivity, feeling for nature muddies the clear lake of the mind. The "otherness" of nature is now what allows it to be known.

The Seventeenth Century Flight from the Feminine

The philosophical "murder" of the living female earth, explored in the preceding section as a reaction-formation to the dissolution of the medieval self/world-unity, must be placed in the context of other issues in the gender politics of the sixteenth and seventeenth centuries. Thanks to the historical research of such writers as Carolyn Merchant, Brian Easlea, Barbara Ehrenreich, Dierdre English, and Adrienne Rich, we have been forced to recognize the years between 1550 and 1650 as a particularly gynophobic century. What has been especially brought to light is what now appears as a virtual obsession with the untamed natural power of female generativity, and a dedication to bringing it under forceful cultural control.

Nightmare fantasies of female power over reproduction and birth run throughout the era. Kramer and Sprenger's *Malleus Maleficarum,* the official witch-hunter's handbook, accuses "witches" of every imaginable natural and supernatural crime involving conception and birth. The failure of crops and miscarriages were attributed to witches, and they are accused both of "inclining men to passion" and of causing impotence, of obstructing fertility in both men and women, of removing the penises of men, of procuring abortion, and of offering newborns to the devil.

Such fantasies were not limited to a fanatic fringe. Among the scientific set, we find the image of the witch, the willful, wanton virago, projected onto generative nature, whose scientific exploration, as Merchant points out, is metaphorically likened to a witch trial. The "secrets" of nature are imagined as deliberately and slyly "concealed" from the scientist. (Easlea, p. 214) Matter, which in the *Timeaus* is passively receptive to the ordering and shaping masculine forms, now becomes, for Bacon, a "common harlot" with "an appetite and inclination to dissolve the world and fall back into the old chaos" and who must therefore be "restrained and kept in order". The womb of nature, too, (and this is striking, in connection with Melanie Klein) is no longer the beneficent mother but rather the *hoarder* of precious metals and minerals, which must be "searched" and "spied out."

There were the witch-hunts themselves, which, aided more politely by the gradual male take-over of birthing, and healing in general, virtually purged the healing arts of female mid-wives. The resulting changes in obstetrics, which rendered women passive and dependent in the process of birth, came to identify birth, as Bacon identified nature itself, with the potentiality of disorder and the need for forceful male control. So, too, in the seventeenth century, female sexuality was seen as voracious and insatiable, and a principle motivation behind witchcraft, which offered the capacious "mouth of the womb" the opportunity to copulate with the devil.

The ideology of the voracious, insatiable female may not be unique to the sixteenth and seventeenth centuries. But it is not historically ubiquitous. By the second half of the nineteenth century, medical science had declared women to be naturally passive and "not much troubled by sexual feeling of any kind." Peter Gay suggests that this medical fantasy was a reaction-formation to that era's "pervasive sense of manhood in danger," brought about by its own particular social disruptions in the family and gender relations. I would suggest, along similar lines, that key changes in seventeenth century scientific theory of reproduction functioned in much the same way, although in reaction to different threats and disruptions.

Generativity, not sexuality, is the focus of the seventeenth century's fantasies of female passivity. Mechanist reproductive theory ("happpily", as Brian Easlea sarcastically puts it) made it "no longer necessary to refer to any women at all" in its "scientific" descriptions of conception and gestation. Denied even her limited, traditional Aristotelian role of supplying the (living) menstrual material (which, shaped by the individuating male "form" results in the fetus), the woman becomes instead the mere *container* for the temporary housing and incubation of already formed human beings, originally placed in Adam's semen by God, and parcelled out, over the ages, to all his male descendants. The specifics of mechanistic reproductive theory are a microcosmic recapitulation of the mechanistic vision itself, where God the father is the sole creative, formative principle in the cosmos. We know, from what now must be seen as almost paradigmatic examples of the power of belief over perception, that tiny horses and men were actually "seen" by mechanist scientists examining sperm under their microscopes.

All this is only to scratch the surface of a literature that has become quite extensive over the last decade. Even this brief survey, however, yields striking parallels. The mechanization of nature, we see, theoretically quieted the "common harlot" of matter (and sanctioned nature's exploitation) as effectively as Baconian experimental philosophy did so practically. Mechanistic reproductive theory successfully eliminated any active, generative role for woman in the processes of conception and gestation. And *actual* control over reproduction and birth was wrested away from women by the witch-hunters and the male medical establishment. Something, it seems, had come to be felt as all too powerful, and in need of taming.

What can account for this upsurge of fear of female generativity? Many factors—economic, political, institutional—are crucial. But I would suggest that the themes of "parturition" and "separation anxiety" discussed in this study can provide an illuminative psycho-cultural framework within which to situate seventeenth century gynophobia.

The culture in question, in the wake of the dissolution of the medieval intellectual and imaginative system, had lost a world in which the human being could feel nourished by the sense of oneness, of continuity between all things. The new, infinite universe was an indifferent home, an "alien will," and the sense of separateness from her was acute. Not only was she "other," but she seemed a perverse and uncontrollable other. In a century (1550–1650) which had brought the worst food crisis in history, violent wars, plague and devastating poverty, the Baconian imagery of nature as an unruly and malevolent virago was no paranoid fantasy. More important, the cruelty of the world could no longer be made palatable by the old medieval sense of "organic" justice—justice on the level of the workings of a whole with which one's identity merged and which, while perhaps not fully comprehensible, was nonetheless to be trusted. Now there is no organic unity, but only "I" and "She"— an unpredictable and seemingly arbitrary "she," whose actions cannot be understood in any of the old "sympathetic" ways.

"She" is *Other*. And "otherness" itself becomes dreadful—particularly the otherness of the female, whose powers have always been mysterious to men, and evocative of the mystery of existence itself. Like the infinite universe, which threatens to swallow the individual "like a speck," the female, with her strange rhythms, long acknowledged to have their chief affinities with the rhythms of the natural (now alien) world, becomes a reminder of how much lies outside the grasp of man.

"The quintessential incarnation" of that which appears to man as "mysterious, powerful and not himself," as Dorothy Dinnerstein says, is "the woman's fertile body." Certainly, the mother's body holds these meanings for the infant, according to Klein. If Dorothy Dinnerstein is right, women (particularly the woman-as-mother, the original "representative" of the natural world, and virtually indistinguishable from it for the human infant) are always likely targets for all later adult rage against nature. Supporting Dinnerstein's highly theoretical account are anthropologist Peggy Reeves

Sanday's cross-cultural findings that in periods of cultural disruption and environmental stress, male social dominance—particularly over female fertility—tends to be at its most extreme. In the seventeenth century, with the universe appearing to man more decisively "not-himself" than ever before, more capricious and more devastating in her capacity for disorder, both the mystery of the universe and the mystery of the female require a more definitive solution than had been demanded by the organic world view.

The project that fell to both empirical science and rationalism was to tame the female universe. Empirical science did this through aggressive assault and violation of her "secrets." Rationalism, as we have seen, tamed the female universe through the philosophical neutralization of her vitality. The barrenness of matter correlatively insured the revitalization of human hope of conquering nature (through knowledge in this case rather than through force). But the mystery of the female could not be bent to man's control simply through philosophical means. More direct and concrete means of neutralization were required for that project. It is within this context that witch-hunting and the male medical take-over of the process of reproduction and birth, whatever their social and political causes, can be seen to have a profound psycho-cultural dimension as well.

The Contemporary Revaluation of the Feminine

My next focus will be on the recent scholarly emergence and revaluation of epistemological and ethical perspectives "in a different voice." That voice, which has been described as "feminine" in classical as well as contemporary writing (e.g., Carol Gilligan, Sarah Ruddick, Nancy Chodorow), claims a natural foundation for knowledge, not in detachment and distance, but in what I have called "sympathy": in closeness, connectedness and empathy. If finds the failure of connection (rather than the blurring of boundaries) as the principle cause of breakdown in understanding.

In the seventeenth century, when Paracelsus articulated the alchemical conception of knowledge as merger of mind and nature, the "female" nature of this ideal operated for him solely as a metaphor, as did Bacon's contrasting ideal of a virile, "masculine" science. In the second half of our own more sociologically oriented century, women themselves—not some abstract "feminine principle"—have been identified as cultural bearers of the alternative, "sympathetic" scheme of values. The research of Chodorow and Gilligan, in particular, has suggested that men and women (growing up within a particular cultural framework, it must be emphasized), *do* appear to experience and conceptualize events differently, the key differences centering around different conceptions of the self/world, self/other relation:

> "Girls emerge . . . with a basis for "empathy" built into their primary definition of self in a way that boys do not. Girls emerge with a stronger basis for experiencing another's needs or feelings as one's own (or thinking that one is experiencing another's needs or feelings) . . . girls come to experience themselves as less differentiated than boys, more continuous with and related to the external object-world and as differently oriented to their inner object-world as well."

Carol Gilligan has described how these developmental differences result, in men and women, in differing valuations of attachment and autonomy, and correspondingly different conceptions of morality.

The association of cognitive style with gender is in itself nothing new. We find it in ancient mythology, in archetypal psychology, in philosophical and scientific writings, and in a host of enduring popular stereotypes about men and women (for example, that women are more "intuitive," men are more "logical," etc.) In the second half of the nineteenth century, the celebration of a distinctively female moral sensibility was widely held by both feminists and sexual conservatives. What *is* new in the recent feminist exploration of gender and cognitive style is a (characteristically modern) emphasis on gender as a social construction, rather than a biological or ontological given. If men and women think differently, it is argued, that is not because the sexes inevitably embody timeless "male" and "female" principles of existence, but because the sexes have been brought up differently, develop different social abilities, have occupied very different power positions in most cultures. Using a psychoanalytic framework, Nancy Chodorow explores the origins of these differences in the differing degrees of individuation from the mother demanded of boys and girls in infancy.

An appreciation of the *historical* nature of the masculine model of knowledge to which the feminine "different voice" is often contrasted helps to underscore that the embodiment of these gender-related perspectives in actual men and women is a cultural, not a biological phenomenon. There have been cultures in which (using *our* terms now, not necessarily theirs) men thought more "like women," and there may be a time in the future when they do so again. In our own time, women may be coming to think more and more "like men". The conclusion is not, however, that any association of gender and cognitive style is a reactionary mythology with no explanatory value. For the sexual division of labor within the family in the modern era has indeed fairly consistently reproduced significant cognitive and emotional differences along sexual lines. The central importance of Chodorow's work has been to show that boys have tended to grow up learning to experience the world like Cartesians, while girls do not, *because* of developmental asymmetries resulting from female-dominated infant care, rather than biology, anatomy or "nature."

It is of crucial importance, however, that feminist scholars like Chodorow more explicitly and emphatically underscore the fact that they are describing elements of a social construction, characteristic of certain (though not all) forms of gender organization, and *not* the reified dualities of an "eternal feminine" and "essential masculine" nature. A great deal of current division among feminists rests on lack of clarity and understanding regarding this distinction. This is unfortunate, because the sociological emphasis and understanding of gender as a social construction is one crucial difference between the contemporary feminist revaluation of the "feminine" from the nineteenth century doctrine of female moral superiority. Too often, recently, the two have been conflated.

A still more central difference between nineteenth century and twentieth century feminism is the contemporary feminist emphasis on the *insufficiency* of any ethics or rationality that operates solely in one mode, "feminine" *or* "masculine." The nineteenth century celebration of a distinctively feminine sensibility and morality functioned in the *service* of pure masculinized thought, by insisting that each "sphere" remain distinct and undiluted by the feminine. This was, of course, precisely what the seventeenth century masculinization of thought had accomplished—the exclusion of "feminine" modes of knowing, not from culture in general, but from the scientific and philosophical arenas, whose objectivity and purity needed to be guaranteed. Romanticizing "the feminine" within its "own" sphere is no alternative to Cartesianism, because it suggests that the feminine has a "proper" (domestic) place. Only in establishing the scientific and philosophical legitimacy of sympathetic modes of knowing in the *public* arena (rather than glorifying them in their own special sphere of family relations) do we present a real alternative to Cartesianism.

Feminism and the "Recessive" Strain in Philosophy

The Cartesian ideals are under attack in philosophy today, and philosophers who subscribe to those ideals, whether in their analytic or phenomenological embodiment, are on the defensive. Because philosophy has been so dominated by the Cartesian standpoint, the erosion of Cartesianism has been interpreted by some as signalling the "death of philosophy," and many of the current debates among philosophers are couched in those terms. If anything is dying, however, it is the intellectual rule of a particular model of knowledge and reality. Philosophers who grew up under that rule, and who were taught to identify philosophy *with* it, may experience the end of that rule as portending the "end of philosophy." But in fact, philosophy has always spoken in many voices (although they have seldom been heard by the Cartesian "cultural overseer"), some of which are being revived and renovated today. More significantly, voices from those groups which philosophy has traditionally excluded are now offering the discipline the very means of its revitalization: the truths and values which it has suppressed from its dominant models. Those truths and values have been living underground, throughout the Cartesian reign, and are now emerging to make a claim on the culture.

This emergence cannot be adequately understood unless seen against the backdrop of the last several decades of social and political life. Philosophers may think that the widespread self-critique in which philosophy is currently engaged began with the publication of Richard Rorty's *Philosophy and the Mirror of Nature*. But (as Rorty would probably be the first to acknowledge), the impact of that work had much to do with its timely crystallization of historicist currents that had been gathering momentum since the 1960s. Those currents were themselves activated by the various liberation movements of that decade. There is a certain similarity here with the Renaissance, in the cultural reawakening to the multiplicity of possible human perspectives, and to the role of culture in shaping those perspectives. But in our era, the reawakening has occurred in the context of a recognition, not merely of the undiscovered "other," but of the *suppressed* other. Women, people of color, and various ethnic and national groups have forced the culture into a critical re-examination not only of diversity (as occurred for Renaissance culture) but of the forces that *mask* diversity. That which appears as "dominant," by virtue of that very fact, comes to be suspect: It has a secret story to tell, in the perspectives to which it has denied legitimacy, and in the historical and political circumstances of its own dominance.

Fueled by the historicist tradition in epistemology, psychoanalytic thought, *and* the political movement for women's rights, representation and participation in cultural life, feminist ethics and epistemology now appears as one of the most vital forces in the development of post-Cartesian focus and paradigm. The feminist exposure of the gender biases in our dominant Western conceptions of science and ethics—the revelation that the history of their development, the lenses through which they see the world, and their methods and priorities have been decisively shaped by the fact that it has been men who have determined their course—has come as a startling recognition to many contemporary male philosophers. Inspired by the work of Gilligan, Chodorow, and Keller, feminist theory has been systematically questioning the historical identification of rationality, intelligance, "good thinking," and so forth with the masculine modes of detachment and clarity, offering alternative models of fresher, more humane, and more hopeful approaches to science and ethics.

It is not only in explicitly feminist writing that these phenomena are occurring. Many of the "new paradigms" being proposed in the recent spate of literature on modernity and modern science are grounded in sympathetic, participatory alternatives to Cartesianism. (See Berman, Capra in particular) In philosophy, a whole slew of reconsiderations of traditional epistemological "problems" such as relativism, perspectivism, the role of emotions and body in knowledge, the possibility of ultimate foundations, etc., has brought the feminine perspective in through the back door, as it were. Without explicit commitment to feminism *or* "the feminine," philosophers are nonetheless participating in a (long overdue) philosophical acknowledgment of the limitations of the masculine Cartesian model, and are recognizing how tightly it has held most modern philosophy in its grip.

This is not to say that detachment, clarity and precision will cease to have enormous value to the process of understanding. Rather, our culture needs to re-conceive the status of what Descartes assigned to the shadows. Such re-evaluation has been a steady, although "recessive" strain in the history of philosophy since

Descartes. Leibniz's declaration that each monad is its *own* "mirror" of the universe, Hume's insistence that "reason is and ought to be a slave of the passions," and, perhaps most importantly, Kant's revelation that objectivity itself is the result of human categorization and structuring opened various doors that in retrospect now appear as critical openings.

Hume, for example, may now be seen as having a rightful place—along with Nietzsche, Scheler, Peirce, Dewey, James, Whitehead, and, more recently, Robert Neville—in the critical protest against the Cartesian notion that reason is a "pure" realm free from contamination by emotion, instinct, will, sentiment, and value. Within this protest, we see the development both of a "naturalist" *anthropology* over against the Cartesian ideals of precision, certainty, and neutrality (Nietzsche, Scheler, Dewey, James), and a complementary *metaphysics* (Peirce, Whitehead, Neville) in which "vagueness" as well as specificity, tentativeness, and valuation are honored as essential to thought.

In emphasizing the active, constructive nature of cognition, Kant undermined the Cartesian notion that the scientist "reads off" what is simply *there* in the world. The Kantian "knower" is transcendental, of course, and Kant's "constructionism" begins and ends, like most Enlightenment thought, with a vision of universal law—in this case, the basic, a historical requirements of "knowability," represented by the categories. But the "Copernican Revolution in Thought," in asserting the activity of the subject, opened the door, paradoxically, to a more historical and contextual understanding of knowing. The knower, not the known, now comes under scrutiny—and not, as Descartes scrutinized the knower, for those contaminating elements which must be purged from cognition, but for those "active and interpreting forces," as Nietzsche says, "through which alone seeing becomes seeing *something*." The postulation of an inner "eye" in which these forces "are supposed to be lacking . . . [is] an absurdity and a nonsense."

The articulation of the biological, social and epistemological determinants of what Nietzsche called "perspective" can be seen as a paradigm of modern thought. The main theoretical categories of that paradigm have been worked out by various disciplines: the "philosophical anthropology" of Max Scheler, Karl Mannheim's work on ideology, and, historically fontal, the dialectical materialism of Karl Marx. Marx, of course, was himself not primarily interested in epistemological questions. But he is, nonetheless, the single most important philosophical figure in the development of modern historicism, with his emphasis on the historical nature of all human activity and thought and our frequent "false consciousness" of this. It was Marx who turned the tables on the Enlightenment, encouraging suspicion of all ideas that claim to represent universal, fundamental, "inherent," or "natural" features of reality.

The Cartesian ideal of the detached, purely neutral observer is here viewed as a type of mystification, and the ideals of absolute objectivity and ultimate foundations seen as requiring *historical* examination. In the modern era, "universal" after "universal" has fallen, under the scrutiny of Marxists, anthropologists, feminists, philosophers of science, and deconstructionists. The various claims regarding human nature and human sexuality (the "naturalness" of competition, the "necessity" of sexual repression, the "biological" nature of gender differences) have been challenged. Rorty and Foucault, respectively, have argued that the "mind" and "sexuality" are "historical inventions." And Patrick Heelan has shown that our most basic perceptions of space have a cultural history.

None of this signals the end of philosophy. What it *has* meant, however, is that it is extremely difficult today for the Cartesian philosopher to sit comfortably on the throne of the cultural overseer, "neutrally" legislating "how rational agreement can be reached" and where others have gone astray. The ideal of absolute intellectual purity and the belief in a clear and distinct universe are passing, though not without protest, out of the discipline. It is too soon to tell what sort of impact feminist and other reconstructions will have on the intellectual and political life of our culture. But what does seem clear is that alternatives to Cartesianism are emerging out of Cartesianism's "shadow" itself. If a "flight from the feminine," as I have argued, motivated the birth of the Cartesian ideals, the contemporary re-evaluation of the feminine has much to contribute to the world that will replace them.

PART TWO

THEMES OF MODERNITY: THE ENGLISH TRADITION

Locke's Epistemology and Women's Struggles

Elizabeth Potter

Locke's political theory is a liberal one, understood to be liberating for the individual; it provides theoretical grounds for religious freedom, wide suffrage and other basic civil rights belonging to individuals.[1] The epistemology that serves as the basis for Locke's political theory is set out in his *An Essay Concerning Human Understanding*.[2] There one finds expressly stated the theory of knowledge implicit in his political works, especially in the political mandate that individuals should be free to follow the dictates of their own reason.

Locke worked out his political theory as he not only thought about but also participated in the struggle against absolute monarchy in seventeenth century England, basically a struggle for limited monarchy and religious toleration. What has not been adequately recognized is that Locke's epistemology, like the political philosophy which it supports, was formed in the context of this political struggle. Neither John Locke's epistemology nor his political philosophy were conceived in political innocence and as this essay will argue, his epistemology undercut the epistemology and political theory of many women and men engaged in class and gender struggles during the seventeenth century.

Locke's liberal epistemology and liberal political theory had definite implications for women; liberal, enlightenment feminists used Locke's arguments to express their own demands for the recognition that women have the same basic rights men have: the right to legal standing, suffrage and freedom of religion.

To see feminists as inheriting only strengthening tools from Locke, however, is to miss part of the picture. Most Locke students have not fully recognized that the political struggle in seventeenth century England was not a two-way struggle—between the king and the people—but a three-way struggle involving conflicting interests among classes of the people. Thus, the picture of that struggle as one between the Tories (who supported absolute monarchy) and the Whigs (who wanted a strong parliament) is not completely accurate. In fact, the Whigs represented the interests of middle and upper middle-class merchants, traders and investors, and fought not only against royalists and Tory attempts to suppress their claims to freedom and representation, but also alongside the Tories against the political aspirations and claims of a large group of poor and lower-class women and men. Christopher Hill has noted two revolutions in England during the seventeenth century, the one that succeeded, and *for* which Locke worked, and the one that "never happened, though from time to time it threatened. This might have established communal property, a far wider democracy in political and legal institutions, might have disestablished the state church and rejected the protestant ethic."[3]

The failed revolution, like the successful one, had its political theorists, its visions of how society should be governed, its hopes for the relations between religion and the state—and its underlying epistemology. It also offered women a measure of freedom from the political, religious and familial constraints upon them, relief from the rule that women must be chaste, silent and obedient. But Locke specifically argues against both the political theories and the epistemology of the unsuccessful revolutionaries. Thus, Locke's epistemology was not an isolated, abstract and politically neutral theory, but was rather a hybrid: a liberal response to a repressive epistemology—a response potentially liberating for middle-class women—*and* itself a repressive response to a more radical epistemology, liberating for lower-class women as well as lower-class men.

Is Locke's epistemology still both liberating and repressive for women? Yes. Women in liberal democracies around the world use his assumptions to argue for civil equality and freedom from oppression, for the right to abortion, equal pay, equal work and for many other specific rights. Yet these assumptions are not liberating for all women. The sort of epistemology put forward by the Quakers, Levellers, and others in the Seventeenth Century has even greater liberatory potential for those women (and men) who do not have the economic means to live in the world the way middle-class women and men do and so to see the world as they see it.

The following discussion does not adopt Locke's epistemology; for him, the political, economic and gender context in which knowledge is produced is not relevant to epistemology. Even today, the liberal epistemological tradition arising from Locke's work distinguishes the "context of discovery" from the "context of justification" of theories; this means that a good theory, whether of knowledge or of science, is neutral among competing political views. Because Locke's epistemology explains how the individual makes knowledge—by having ideas, compounding and abstracting from them and so on—it obscures the ways in which the political, economic or gender relations among individuals affect the production of knowledge. The influence of these relations upon epistemological and scientific theories is clarified only when one adopts an epistemology which reveals their relevance.

For example, the philosopher Mary Hesse argues that all good theories, including theories of knowledge, are constrained not only by empirical adequacy, simplicity and other "cognitive virtues," but also by "coherence conditions" including judgments about the goodness of certain analogies, models and so on. Other philosophers argue that these coherence conditions also include judgments about proper political, economic, gender or racial relations.[4] As will be shown below, Locke's theory of knowledge was constrained by such judgments.

Part I: The Historical Context of Locke's Epistemology

Anyone seeking to understand how Locke's work is both liberating and repressive must begin by looking at English history forty years before he began work on the *Two Treatises of Government* and on the *Essay Concerning Human Understanding*. In 1641, eight years before the King of England, Charles I, was beheaded in the most wrenching moment of the English Civil War, the House of Commons enacted legislation that reveals the interests of many of the people who later felt it necessary to overthrow the King. Charles I had often dissolved Parliament when it passed legislation he disapproved of or when it failed to vote him the money he felt he needed. (Because of changes in the economy, bad management and extravagance, the Stuart Kings were always deeply in debt). The legislation included acts that mandated regular meetings of Parliament with or without the King's consent and that prevented the dissolution of parliament without its consent. Parliament also declared all taxes that it did not itself impose illegal, and it declared illegal the special courts used to take the property of the nobility and other powerful Englishmen, and the High Commission, to excommunicate people from the church and to censor the press. Finally, the House of Commons refused to grant Charles the army he wanted to reconquer Ireland, which had just rebelled against

English rule. Charles tried to arrest the leaders of the House who opposed him; when he failed, he left London. The English Civil War had begun.[5]

These Parliamentary actions reveal some of the issues of struggle between the English monarchs and the Court party, on one side, and the rising capitalist class represented by Parliament—merchants, traders, investors—on the other. Throughout the seventeenth century, the Stuart Kings struggled for a return to an absolute monarchy, while the "middling sort of people" struggled against absolute monarchy and for absolute control of their own property, for a say in how their country was governed and for a measure of freedom of religion.

The beheading of Charles I was the culmination of the English Civil War, a revolution sometimes called the Puritan Revolution since the fight was religious as well as political and economic and because many of the political and economic issues were debated in religious terms. The very name Puritan Revolution tells who won: the Puritans defeated the Royalists, but *they also defeated the radicals.*

The radicals were included among several groups of "masterless men" (and women) comprised first, of rogues, vagabonds and beggers; second, of casual laborers in London, dock workers, watermen, building laborers and journeymen as well as fishwomen—all those people who made up "the mob" as it was called in Locke's time; third, of the rural poor, including cottagers and squatters on commons, wastes and in forests; and, finally, the protestant sectarians, townspeople, often immigrants, who were small craftsmen, apprentices and "serious-minded laborious men" who rejected the state church. Instead of the hierarchical society logically supported by the doctrines of the Church of England, the sectarians preferred a more democratic society, logically supported by their belief that God is in all his saints so they do not need priests of the established church to mediate between them and God. Each individual has access to God; each is responsible to God for his or her own soul.[6]

Sectarian emphasis upon the individual soul had important implications for sectarian women. The Seventeenth Century saw the development of the ideal woman as a bourgeois who was to marry and to stay at home minding the house; while married, she was not to own property. She had no voice in the Church or State. Puritan marriage manuals continually reinforced the view that "the man when he loveth should remember his superiority"[7] and William Gouge, in his popular manual *Of Domesticall Duties* of 1622 and 1634, flatly declared that "the extent of wive's subjection doth stretch itself very far, even to all things."[8]

But the rise of sectarianism, with its view that God is in everything and everyone, threatened the sexual status quo. The Leveller John Lilbourne remarked that "Every particular and individual man and woman that ever breathed in the world since [Adam and Eve] are and were by nature all equal and alike in power, dignity, authority and majesty, none of them having (by nature) any authority dominion or magisterial power, one over . . . another."[9] Thus, sharing at least spiritual equality, all members of sectarian congregations, including women, debated, voted, prophesied and even preached. Too, since the sectarians believed that the regenerate must separate from the ungodly, sectarian women were often allowed or encouraged to divorce or separate from their unregenerate husbands.

For the Quakers, the principle that the spirit of life is in all creatures found expression in the doctrine of the inner light. "An intimate effect of the experience of the Inner Light was that the recipient recognized the God-within and began immediately to operate out of the assumption that she/he now possessed a spark of divine life."[10] In London, the Spirit led many sectarian women to preach and to travel as preachers and missionaries to the University towns as well as to Ireland and America; Quaker women also travelled to Italy and to the eastern Mediterranean to spread their message. Thus, for example, "In 1653 Mary Fisher and Elizabeth Williams went to Cambridge, where they 'discoursed about the things of God' with the young theologians and preached publicly at the gate of Sidney College. Their behavior so upset the mayor of Cambridge that he ordered them to be taken to Market Cross, where they became the first of the Friends to be publicly scourged."[11] Elizabeth Fletcher, aged seventeen, and her friend Elizabeth Leavens received about the same treatment at Oxford in 1654.

At various times during the Civil War and the years before the Restoration of the monarchy, sectarians, Levellers and others called for a number of more or less revolutionary reforms. They wanted an end to enclosures, the practice of enclosing and developing waste land, a practice which required that the people living on the land, sometimes for generations though without any explicit property rights in it, be displaced and rendered homeless. They also objected to rent racking, sharp rises in the rent owed by tenant farmers to landlords. Landlords often justified rent wracking on the grounds that tenants would work harder and grow new crops to meet the

growing demand for food in London and other towns. Like enclosures, fen drainage also yielded more land for cultivation and was
justified by its forcing squatters "to quit idleness and betake themselves to . . . manufactures . . . ".[12] The people whose homes and live-
lihoods were lost by fen drainage and enclosures fought back by all
available means. As early as 1603, women led a revolt against the
drainage of Deeping Fen in Lincolnshire, and participated in the destruction of enclosures in Braydon Forest in the 1630s, at Buckden
in 1641, at York in 1642 and in other places. Unfortunately, these
economic struggles divided women by class. In Yorkshire, the upper-
class Margaret Eure complained about lower-class women in a letter to Sir Ralph Verney,

> I wish you would take heed of women for this very vermin have
> pulled down an enclosure, which some of them were put in prison
> for it by the justices[;] they had their pipe [of tobacco] to go before
> them and their ale and cakes to make themselves merry when they
> had done their feats of activity.[13]

The economic picture for landless workers, out-servants, pau-
pers and cottagers was very bleak throughout the second half of the
Seventeenth Century: their expenses exceeded their incomes. The
export of corn kept prices high and the loss of their small plots
meant that wage laborers no longer had that cushion for times
of unemployment. Hill notes that "at least one-third of the house-
holds of England were exempt from the Hearth Tax on grounds of
poverty."[14] In London, the "mob" grew, constituted in part by casual
laborers who had drifted into the city in the attempt to make a living. There they could hope to escape enforcement of the Poor Law
and the Act of Settlement (which provided that unwelcome newcom-
ers be sent back to their last place of residence). But "neither contemporary nor modern economists can explain how [wage laborers]
lived."[15] Off and on throughout the 1640s London women petitioned
and demonstrated at Parliament complaining of the "decay of
trade" and the high price of food due to the war. In 1642, about four
hundred women, having petitioned the day before concerning "their
wants and necessities by reason of the great decay of trading . . . ",
returned for an answer and roughed up the Duke of Lenox when he
cried, "Away with these women, we were best to have parliament of
Women."[16] And in 1649, about five hundred Leveller women brought
a petition, signed by ten thousand women, for the release of Leveller
leaders and complaining that "Trading is utterly driven away, all

kinds of Provision for Food at a most excessive rate, multitudes ready to starve and perish for want of work, employment, necessaries, and subsistence. . . ."[17]

During the Civil War, both the sectaries and "the mob" were called upon to aid in the revolution by those who opposed the King; for example, they were foot soldiers in the New Model Army used by Cromwell to defeat Charles I. Once called upon to act, however, these people of the "lower orders" began to think and to speak for themselves and discovered that their political and economic interests conflicted not only with those of the King and his party, but also with those of the "middling sort" who were running the revolution. One of the most controversial demands made by the rank and file of Cromwell's army was for manhood suffrage. This demand was immediately recognized as a threat to private property. One of Cromwell's generals declared that "If you admit any man that hath a breath and being . . . this will destroy property. . . . Why may not those men vote against all property?"[18] Even Cromwell and the revolutionaries he stood for wanted suffrage only for men of property (usually understood to mean landed property), and they recognized that men of no property outnumbered them and might vote to redistribute wealth.

For spreading just such levelling ideas, Leveller leaders were often jailed as dangerous subversives. And just as often Leveller women petitioned and demonstrated at Parliament for their release. In doing so, these women in effect claimed the legal right to petition for redress of grievances (which as women and especially as wives, they did not have). Though they never claimed the right to vote, they did argue that since they had an equal share with men in the church, so they were "assured . . . also of a proportionable share in the Freedoms of this Commonwealth." "Have we not," they asked, "an equal interest with the men of this Nation, in those liberties and securities contained in the Petition of Right, and other good Laws of the Land?"[19] Women's suffrage does not appear to have been on anyone's political agenda.

Charles II was restored to the throne in 1660–61, but none of the conflicts discussed above were resolved during his reign: he wanted a return to absolute monarchy, financial independence and a return to Catholicism instead of Anglicanism as the official religion. The liberals who opposed him wanted to prevent the reinstitution of absolute monarchy and did not want him to be financially independent since this would allow him to support a standing army and use it to repress dissent and wage unpopular foreign wars; the liberals also wanted religious toleration (within limits), but above all they wanted to prevent Catholicism from becoming the state religion, perhaps not least because its doctrines were used to support absolute monarchy.[20]

Charles II suspended Parliament for much of the period between 1674 and 1679 and relied during this time on financial subsidies from Louis XIV, the absolute monarch of France. These actions, along with rumors of a secret treaty between Charles and Louis, gave rise to a growing fear of the King's pro-French, Catholic sympathies and led to unsuccessful attempts by four successive Parliaments to pass a bill excluding Charles' Catholic brother, James, from the throne—Anglicans and Dissenters alike were horrified at the possibility of a Catholic monarch. Nevertheless, in 1685 Charles died, a professed Catholic, and was succeeded by his Catholic brother, now James II.

The Adventures of John Locke

Traditional historians of philosophy have admitted that this was the context in which Locke worked out his political philosophy and his epistemology, but they have claimed that, as a philosopher, he was above party politics and was not involved in or influenced by them. Recent studies have shown, however, that Locke was very involved in the political activities of the 1670s and 1680s.[21]

In 1666, Locke served as secretary to Anthony Ashley-Cooper, later the Earl of Shaftesbury, and became his most trusted advisor and intimate friend. Although Shaftesbury became a staunch opponent of Charles II, he nevertheless served as Chancellor of the Exchequer and as Lord Chancellor of England. His opposition to Charles grew sharper when, apparently in 1673, he learned of the secret clauses in the Treaty of Dover whereby Charles pledged allegiance to Louis XIV and to make Catholicism the English religion in return for French subsidies; thereafter, Shaftesbury worked incessantly to prevent the reinstatement of the "tyranny of popery" in England. Locke worked with him in these efforts, writing in 1675 an expose of the popish plot,[22] which was publicly burned by the hangman in London. The next day, Locke hastily packed his bags and escaped to France, where he travelled for three years.

Ashcraft suggests that, while in France, Locke engaged in intelligence activities for Shaftesbury, trying to find out whether France was supporting Charles' pretensions to absolute monarchy. During this period, Shaftesbury became a central figure in the organization of the Whig party and in efforts to force Charles II to dissolve Parliament and hold new elections—activities for which in

1677 he was imprisoned in the Tower. Locke returned to England two years later, in time to participate both in the petition drives to get the King to reassemble Parliament and in the Exclusion Crisis. There were three elections during the Exclusion Crisis—the Whigs won them all—and in each Parliament, the Commons attempted to force the government to exclude James from the throne. The Exclusion Bill passed the Commons in 1680 but was defeated in the Lords, with Charles II himself present for the debate. Thereafter, Shaftesbury and his group decided that stronger measures were called for and in the abortive six-day Oxford Parliament, they presented a bill for a "Protestant Association," ostensibly to protect the King from papist assassination, but really to prevent James from becoming king. When Charles suspended the Oxford Parliament, the group of men around Shaftesbury began plans for an armed insurrection, later known as the Rye House Plot.

Meanwhile, Charles had received his subsidies from France, allowing him independence from Parliament; he continued removing Whigs from public office and began proceedings to pack Parliament with his own supporters. In July 1681, Shaftesbury was arrested, to be charged with treason for bringing the bill to form the Protestant Association. With others, Locke worked to secure his release, working all the while under surveillance by government spies. As a counter-measure, Locke and the other Whig activists began to use ciphers, mail drops, pseudonyms and "canting" letters—ostensibly innocent letters that carried a hidden meaning. They also developed a network of "safe" houses for people like Shaftesbury, wanted by the government after he was aquitted by a sympathetic London Grand Jury.

By the summer of 1682, Shaftesbury and others were deeply involved in plans for an insurrection: a general uprising in the country and seizing of the king's guards in London to be followed by a Scottish uprising. When the attempt aborted in October 1682, Shaftesbury fled to Holland and died soon after. Plans for another attempt proceeded apace, but with discovery near, Locke left Shaftesbury's house in May 1683, went into hiding in Whig "safe" houses, and left for Holland the next Fall. Through an examination of Locke's correspondence, his journals and his financial transactions, Ashcraft reveals that Locke "continued to play a role in the political activities of the revolutionary movement during his six years in exile."[23] In 1683 and again in 1684, the Scots met in Utrecht with the Earl of Argyll to discuss a rebellion along the lines of Shaftesbury's original plan, and historians know that Locke was in Utrecht in September 1684 in time for the second meeting. Soon after, Locke was expelled—at the King's command—from his studentship at Christ Church, Oxford for behaving himself "very factiously and undutifully to the government. . . ."[24] After the death of Charles in February 1685, and the succession of James to the throne, Charles's bastard son Monmouth, defeated in his hopes to gain the throne, joined the rebellion. Ashcraft notes that in May 1685, the sum of £500 passed through Locke's hands, probably to help buy arms for Monmouth. Finally, in 1685, the Earl of Argyll invaded Scotland and Monmouth invaded England from the south. Both were defeated.

The rebellion led Parliament to grant James II funds for a standing army. He cashiered three hundred officers, in what must have seemed a purge of Protestants, and waived the Test Act (passed by Parliament precisely to insure that only Anglicans held public office) so that he could replace most of the officers with Catholics. He began to replace Justices of the Peace, sheriffs and magistrates with pro-government men and changed the terms for judges from life to so long as he pleased to keep them. Finally, he issued a Declaration of Indulgence allowing both Catholic and Protestant Dissenters to worship publicly as they wished. This was the last straw. Seven Anglican Bishops petitioned the King to withdraw the Declaration on the grounds that he had no right to dispense with the Test Act. They were sent to the Tower. Most people in England did not want another Civil War and hoped, since James was an old man, that he would die peacefully—without an heir—and that the throne would return to a Protestant. But when James' son was born in 1688, this hope proved futile and seven English nobles sent a letter to William of Orange inviting him to invade England. James escaped to France in the summer of 1688 and the throne passed to William and Mary (James' Protestant daughter).

All the while, Locke was corresponding from Holland with friends in England, reading English news sheets, participating in political discussions with other exiled Englishmen and finishing the *Two Treatises of Government* and the *Essay Concerning Human Understanding*. These works were published in 1689.

Part II: Epistemology and Politics

Epistemological and political ideas do not occur in a vacuum; epistemological views often occur in response to one another, but they may also arise out of opposing political views. Locke and other

Dissenters held political and epistemological views clearly opposed to those of the Royalists. Generally, Royalists held that political authority arises either from divine right or the natural right of paternal authority, that is, the natural ruler of the family is the father and civil society is comprised of families of which the king is "father". Royalists thought it a Law of Nature that subjects must obey their sovereigns; individuals cannot have any obligations that allow them to challenge the will of the Sovereign and may never resist the will of the sovereign. Against this understanding of government, Dissenters such as Locke held that political authority is originally in the people who establish government through a social contract; Parliament makes law on behalf of the people, while the king is an executive holding office as a trustee and a servant of the people. If he breaks the social contract, he may be resisted as a tyrant.

One should not be surprised to find that the epistemologies of the Royalists and the Dissenters were directly related to their political views and so were also opposed. The major epistemological issue over which they disagreed was the nature and scope of rationality, and the connection between this epistemological issue and political issues is to be found in the religious debates of that period.

Since the time of Henry VIII, the state church in England under the monarchies was the Anglican church, whose doctrines, not surprisingly, agreed with the Royalist theory of political authority, while religious Dissenters held the opposing political view. Therefore, the ostensibly religious question of whether people had the right to dissent from Anglican church doctrine was also a political question about the origin of political authority and the right of subjects to disobey the sovereign. Dissenters thought that the Law of Nature imposes obligations on individuals which a magistrate such as the king cannot contradict; if he does, individuals must disobey him and obey a higher law.

Toleration of religious differences was, therefore, a very hot issue in seventeenth century England, and John Locke contributed significantly to the debate. He wrote the *Letter On Toleration* in the winter 1685–86, but as Ashcraft indicates, many of the epistemological issues with which Locke was concerned in the *Essay Concerning Human Understanding* were related to the toleration debate. Locke took extensive notes on Samuel Parker's *Discourse of Ecclesiastical Polity,* a vehement polemic setting out the Royalist view of rationality and objections to toleration, and it is possible to see many of the arguments in Locke's *Essay* as responses to Parker.[25] To the question whether ordinary individuals are rational

and therefore capable of making decisions about religion and morality, Parker and others on his side answered "no"; they referred to
the common people as "the rabble," as "wild and savage" or as "wild
and unreasonable," and argued that ordinary people should be told
what to do by those who are rational.[26] Against these claims, Locke
and other Dissenters worked out very sophisticated accounts of reason designed to show that reason is universal and can be used to
understand the obligations and rights imposed by Natural Law. In
Book IV of the *Essay Concerning Human Understanding,* Locke
stresses the universality of reason. God, he says, "has not been so
sparing to Men to make them barely two-legged Creatures, and left
it to Aristotle to make them Rational, i.e., those few of them that he
could get so to examine the Grounds of Syllogisms. . . . God has been
more bountiful to Mankind than so. He has given them a Mind that
can reason without being instructed in Methods of Syllogizing. . . ."
Nor is reason limited to men; women also have the power to
reason.[27] Everyone, therefore, can arrive at, among others, the
truths of morality.[28]

Locke's claim that reason is universal had, among others, a political meaning; it is a response to the ultimately political question
whether ordinary people can rationally decide to resist the sovereign. And although he never explicitly discusses the political implications, because he read Parker's *Discourse,* Locke's readers can
take it for granted that he understood the political meaning of the
assumption during the time he was writing the *Essay.*[29] The political meaning was made clear by Parker, who, with other Restoration defenders of absolute monarchy, argued that the "private
judgment" of individuals leads naturally to "a state of war" remi-
niscent of Hobbes' state of nature characterized by the war of all
against all and, to late seventeenth century English readers, remi-
niscent of the recent Civil War. According to Parker, private judgment or conscience is just self-interest. And since the self-interest of
different individuals differs, the natural outcome is the Hobbesian
war of all against all. Parker agreed with Hobbes that, to prevent
this war, "it was necessary there should be one supreme and public
judgment to whose determination the private judgment of every
single person should be obliged to submit himself," and this person
was, ultimately, the sovereign.[30]

Against this unhappy picture of human nature, the Dissenters
offered the view that an individual's conscience, or private rational
judgment, is the faculty by which he discovers for himself the objective moral law. Moreover, rational individuals can, when they differ,
work out their differences and live in peace.

There are, of course, epistemological problems for both sides in this dispute, but for the Dissenters, a major difficulty concerned just how the individual reason can arrive at universal, objective moral truths without resorting to the theory of innate ideas put forward by the French Catholic, Descartes. In the *Essay*, Locke states clearly that the truths of morality are self-evident and that we can know them with certainty; moreover, he spends the whole of Book I refuting the theory of innate ideas. But he never tells his readers *how* to be certain that any particular moral judgment is objectively true.[31] As Parker argued, a claim's merely appearing self-evident to one's (subjective) reason does not make it objectively rational or true.

But even if individuals can discover objective moral truths, a second problem arises immediately: will the individual then *act* morally? Parker was certain that they would not unless they were forced to by the magistrate. On this view, the magistrate (ultimately, the king) has absolute power over the actions of his subjects and the duty of the subjects is to obey the magistrate. But to salvage the individual's freedom of conscience before God, Parker and other monarchists argued that there is a sharp distinction between opinion and action. Thus, although a subject was duty-bound to obey the sovereign, he was free to disagree with the sovereign, to hold opinions the sovereign might not approve of. This distinction between opinion and action belonged with the doctrine of passive obedience—the view that a subject might think whatever he wished so long as he acted in obedience to the sovereign.

Against Parker's view of the relationship between opinion and action, or understanding and will, Dissenters claimed that action follows in an unbroken way upon understanding; therefore, the magistrate should not control a person's actions because in doing so, he interferes with the person's freedom of conscience. Many Dissenters held views similar to the one set out by Locke in II:21 of the *Essay*. There no chasm appears between understanding and will; instead Locke tells his reader that freedom properly characterizes agents; therefore the term "free will" is nonsense; it makes the will look like an agent whereas only people can be agents.[32] Moreover, Locke argues, if a free agent has a preference or desire for an action (which is the same for Locke as willing the action), the action "certainly follows" the preference.[33] Locke also argues that "the determination of the Will immediately follows the Judgment of the Understanding."[34] Taken together, these claims clearly deny Parker's distinction between the judgment and action; here, volition "immediately follows" judgment and the action "certainly follows" volition. Thus, if the magistrate interferes with a man's action, he not only interferes with the individual's freedom, he also necessarily (contra the Royalist doctrine of passive obedience) interferes with the individual's private judgment or conscience.

Against the epistemologies of both Parker and Locke, the sectarian epistemologies stand out as quite radical. Whereas Parker and Locke argued over whether all humans are rational, they agreed in principle that reason is necessary for the discovery of truth; the radical sectaries, however, had very different views about reason. Gerrard Winstanley claimed that reason is in everything. In his tract, *Truth Lifting Up Its Head,* Winstanley says that Reason is another name for God[35] and is not limited to humans but can be found in all creatures:

> Qu. Is Reason to be seene in every creature?
> Ans. Yes.
> Qu. What Reason is to be seene in a Horse?
> Ans. Reason carries him along to eate his meat, that he may doe worke for the use of man.[36]

The Quakers, on the other hand, did not believe that reason was very important; they certainly did not believe it necessary for finding the truth. For example, in Isaac Penington's account of meditation, he holds that

> . . . the creaturely activity which would search [the meaning of the scriptures] merely in its own understanding is to be repressed. Nor must the understanding have the handling of the key when it is given. The Divine Hand that gave can alone turn it aright. It is not the understanding that is to be fed by the scriptures but the heart. Nor is any fruit of the tree of life to be grafted upon the tree of knowledge. The life within and not the intellect is the treasury in which knowledge is to be stored. . . . [37]

Thus the Quakers and many other sectarians rejected reason in favor of divine inspiration.

Part III: Implications for Women

Locke argues in the *Essay Concerning Human Understanding* that everyone is rational and able to reach moral and religious truths; in the *Two Treatises of Government,* he argues that because they are rational all men have civil rights including the right to resist tyranny and the right to elect their legislative representatives. One can see, then, why Locke's thought has been liberating for people the world over who have sought intellectual grounds for their own struggles for basic human and civil rights. In his own time, and thereafter, Locke's thought justified these rights against attempts to deny them and to replace them with the arbitrary will of an absolute monarch or tyrant.

Soon after Locke wrote, women began to use his arguments in what might be characterized as a feminist way; that is, they used his arguments in their own attempts to win recognition of their rationality and of their rights to education as well as to suffrage and the redress of their grievances through legislative representation. Once Locke's natural rights doctrine was institutionalized, for example by means of the Declaration of Independence and the Constitution of the United States of America, the task of feminists working to end the oppression of women seemed obvious: argue that women have the same natural rights men have. This has been the strategy of liberal feminists from Mary Wollstonecraft to Susan B. Anthony to Molly Yard, the current president of the National Organization for Women. All share the fundamental enlightenment assumptions that rationality is the same for all people; that education, especially training in critical thinking, is necessary for the proper exercise of reason; and that having rationality is the basis for having natural rights. Like Locke, these liberals also believe that rational people are isolated individuals, ontologically and epistemologically independent of one another. This last belief, sometimes dubbed epistemological individualism, is central to liberal epistemologies and stands in marked contrast to the communitarian epistemologies of the Quakers and others discussed below.

These assumptions are clearly stated by Wollstonecraft in her book, *A Vindication of the Rights of Women.* There she says,

> Reason is . . . the simple power of improvement . . . of discerning truth. Every individual is in this respect a world in itself. . . . The nature of reason must be the same in all, if it be an emanation of divinity, the tie that connects the creature with the Creator.[38]

Wollstonecraft argues here that everyone has reason, the ability to discern truth, and that it is the same for all humans because it is what humans share with God. Her belief in epistemological individualism is expressly stated in her comment that every individual is a "world in itself" with respect to finding the truth. Moreover, Wollstonecraft argues that proper education, proper training in critical thinking, is most important if women are to become self-determining, to participate in public affairs. "How many women," she laments, "thus waste life away the prey of discontent, who might have practised as physicians, regulated a farm, managed a shop, and stood erect, supported by their own industry, instead of hanging their heads surcharged with the dew of sensibility."[39] One must note here Wollstonecraft's concern that women be in the middle-class; they should be doctors, not hospital janitors; regulators, not farm workers; managers, not shopgirls.

In the arguments of Elizabeth Cady Stanton and Susan B. Anthony for women's suffrage and equal rights, one finds clear appeal to Locke's doctrine that reason is universal and entails natural rights. Stanton argued on behalf of women that "We have every qualification required by the Constitution, necessary to the legal voter, but the one of sex. We are moral, virtuous, and intelligent, and in all respects quite equal to the proud white man himself."[40] Because "[t]he sexes are alike," women deserve equal rights.

The words of Susan B. Anthony at her trial 1873 expressed the grievances of women and echoed the grievances expressed in the Seventeenth Century, addressed by Locke in *The Two Treatises of Government* and, finally, by the United States Constitution:

> One half of the people of this Nation today are utterly powerless to blot from the statute books an unjust law, or to write there a new and a just one. The women, dissatisfied as they are with this form of government, that enforces taxation without representation,— that compels them to obey laws to which they have never given their consent—that imprisons and hangs them without a trial by a jury of their peers—that robs them, in marriage, of the custody of their own persons, wages, and children—are this half of the people left wholly at the mercy of the other half, in direct violation of the spirit and letter of the declarations of the framers of this government, every one of which was based on the immutable principle of equal rights to all.[41]

These Lockean arguments have been used effectively in the United States and elsewhere to secure for middle-class women the (admittedly limited, but nonetheless essential) rights to legal standing, property, access to some jobs, equal pay for equal work, abortion, etc. They have not secured "equal" work, decent jobs for poor women, paid abortions, freedom from sterilization abuse, decent child care or other rights important to poor women.[42]

Unfortunately, then, even though Locke's ideas were liberating for some people, they were not liberating for all. To understand why, the reader must return to the seventeenth century debates Locke participated in. Throughout his *Discourse* Parker repeatedly charged that all religious dissidents were "enthusiasts," irrational people guided by "inspiration." Because enthusiasts and enthusiasm were understood to have been the major cause of "the late tumult"—the Civil War—it was crucial, as Ashcraft points out, for the Dissenters to defend themselves from the charge of being enthusiasts.[43] In the imagination of men like Parker, anyone who advocated disobedience of the established church or the sovereign was *ipso facto* a violent revolutionary of the sort who took up arms against Charles I. Thus Locke and others who dissented from the established church and who objected to an absolute monarchy were forced to emphasize the rationality of their religious and political views and to show that they were "sober" men, not enthusiasts. Both Locke's later work on religion and his *Essay Concerning Human Understanding* stressed the necessity to sound faith of reason. Such accounts of the connection between reason and faith distinguished the Dissenting view from that of the sectarian enthusiasts.[44] Locke makes it clear that he understands a Christian to be a rational agent, "whose will must be guided by the light of his understanding" and who adheres to religion the more steadfastly as he understands the "evidences and true reasons" demonstrating its truth.[45] Reason can lead not only to knowledge of the world through sensory experience, but also to knowledge of God's existence and to knowledge of our moral obligations. Ultimately, all matters of faith must accord with reason.[46]

The emphasis on reason, however, opened Locke and other Dissenters to the charge of Socinianism, the heretical belief that salvation can be achieved through reason and knowledge rather than through the grace of God. To defend against this charge, these thinkers had to return revelation to a central position in the account of the relation between reason and faith—without reopening themselves to the charge of enthusiasm! Revelation had somehow to be distinguished from the inspiration or natural light of the enthusiasts. In the section of the *Essay* entitled, "Of Faith and Reason," Locke takes the line that only faith and not reason can discover the truths of Christianity, for example, "that the dead shall rise, and live again," but that faith cannot contradict reason and that reason alone can determine whether a proposition is in fact a revelation from God.[47] And in the next section, fittingly entitled "Of Enthusiasm," he deflects the charge of enthusiasm by attacking enthusiasts as irrational.[48] Moreover, the way he formulates his attack shows that he is familiar with the epistemological practices of Seekers and Quakers, among others. When he attacks "frequent communications from the divine Spirit," "this internal Light" and "this way of immediate Revelation; of Illumination without search; and of certainty without Proof," Locke is referring to the belief, held for example by the Quakers, that individuals are equally beloved of God, each has "that of God within," the Spirit of God or "the Inner Light" and so each individual has access to the Truth and may receive an inspiration or revelation of the Truth.

In his attack on this belief, Locke raises a problem the Quakers themselves dealt with: how can the individual and the group be sure that what the individual feels to be a revelation really is one and not just the individual's own idea? Locke argues that such people have no way to make this distinction and that they are psychologically disturbed; they are, he says, subject to melancholy, and their Enthusiasm rises "from the conceits of a warmed or over-weening Brain."[49]

Locke does not mention the Quaker solution to the problem, which is to submit the "leading" or "opening," as it was (and still is) called, to the group. The early Quakers were quite clear that they were not trying to reach the truth by majority vote, but by what came to be called "consensus" or the "sense of the meeting." In 1662 Edward Burrough described the Quaker method of consensus in the following directions:

> Being orderly come together . . . proceed in the wisdom of God . . . not in the way of the world, as a worldly assembly of men, by hot contests, by seeking to outspeak and overreach one another in discourse, as if it were controversy between party and party of men, or two sides violently striving for dominion . . . not deciding affairs by the greater vote . . . but in the wisdom, love and fellowship of God, in gravity, patience, meekness, in unity and concord . . . all things to be carried on; by hearing and determining every matter coming before you, in love, coolness, gentleness, and dear unity;—I say as one only party, all for the Truth of Christ . . . and to determine of things by a general mutual concord, in assenting together as one man in the spirit of truth and equity, and by the authority thereof.[50]

A clear difference between the epistemology of the Quakers and that of Locke was (and is) that the Quakers were not interested in doctrine, a set of closely reasoned beliefs, but in experience, both the experience of God and the experience of daily life. One should not expect to find and does not find, therefore, Quaker discussions of reason such as Locke's in Book IV of the *Essay*. Although most Quaker writers did not believe that the revelations of God could conflict with reason, they concerned themselves with "walking in the Light," not with working out rational theology. This is not to say, however, that the Quakers were not producing knowledge; indeed, both the inspirational "openings" encouraging, exhorting or chastising members, and the "openings" regarding specific actions to be taken by the group were forms of knowledge. And they were forms of knowledge reached by consensus in meetings in which Quaker women participated. They stand in marked contrast to decisions about doctrine and behavior made by hierarchical authorities: by an all-male clergy, or by councils, synods and debates of Anglicans, Presbyterians and other all-male Puritan groups as well as by all-male scholars and University dons.

The most important differences, then, between the consensus model of epistemology advocated by the "Enthusiasts" (and by many twentieth century Feminists) and the liberal epistemology Locke sets out in the *Essay* is that, on a consensus model, knowledge is not an individual affair; rather, it is produced by the group. In Book II, Locke shows how a single, isolated individual can have ideas and thus construct what has come to be called a "private language." Not until he sets out his philosophy of language in Book III does the society or community of speakers of English appear. But when he turns, in Book IV, to explain the various ways an individual connects his ideas in order to produce knowledge, the community disappears again. The individual mind alone can produce knowledge. On the other hand, the Enthusiast's model, to which Locke objects, is characterized by radical inclusion; theoretically everyone— women and men, rich and poor together—has the "inner Light" and can participate in producing the "sense of the meeting," and thereby helps to produce knowledge.

The epistemological and religious doctrine of the inner Light was authorizing for sectarian women; based on their belief and confidence in the Inner Light, they prophesied, preached, travelled and sometimes left their husbands. And although there was a division of labor in sectarian religious communities—women were in charge of looking after the poor and imprisoned—nevertheless, women spoke

out in meetings and participated in consensus. Thus, Locke's attack
on "Enthusiasm" was, in effect, an attack on an epistemology which
was liberating and authorizing not only for middle and upper-class
women, but for lower-class women as well.

Conclusion

Until recently the history of philosophy has been understood to
belong to an old-fashioned history of ideas according to which historians should attend only to the relationship between ideas themselves, because the social and political context in which ideas occur
is irrelevant to their truth. In the past, the only historians who vi-
olated this rule for good history were supposed "vulgar Marxists,"
offering only simplistic economic causes of intellectual ideas. One of
the assumptions behind the old-fashioned history of ideas is that
sound ideas are not influenced by the dirty world of politics and economics and that if politics or economics does influence ideas, the
ideas will probably be unsound. This assumption appears most
clearly as applied to science: good science is uninfluenced by its political and economic context. However, attention to the context in
which a good scientific theory is worked out may reveal that the
theory is determined not only by the data and by such "cognitive virtues" as simplicity and generality, but also by "coherence conditions" including social constraints. These social constraints do not
necessarily make a scientific theory a bad theory.[51] In the same
way, the discovery that Locke's epistemology is a response to other
epistemologies and other ideas with political implications does not
entail that Locke's epistemology is without merit. It merely entails
that Locke's epistemology is not politically innocent.

But the recognition that one of the paradigms of good epistemology takes sides in a political struggle gives great urgency to the
question what counts as a good epistemology. Of course, if one assumes in advance that Locke's epistemology gives the criteria for
good epistemology, one will dismiss the communal, Quaker epistemology immediately. Locke assumes without discussion that knowledge is made by the individual, and that a good epistemology
accounts for how the individual mind, among other things, connects
its atomic sensory ideas. He does not assume that knowledge is produced through complex interactions between people; therefore, a
good epistemology need not pay attention to how people interact to
produce knowledge.

Feminism has always been concerned to struggle against the hierarchical gender relations obtaining among people, and more recently, academic feminists have struggled to uncover the distortions in knowledge caused by unequal gender relations. Feminist scholars have successfully uncovered androcentric assumptions in theoretical concepts underlying history, literature, arts and sciences. But technical philosophical theories have appeared to be—like good scientific theories—immune from gender politics, hermetically sealed off and politically innocent. I suggest that philosophical theories as well as scientific ones only appear this way through the lens of old-fashioned history of ideas and of the epistemology supporting it. The production of Locke's theory of knowledge was not immune from gender politics, but one sees this only when one adopts another epistemology which assumes, *pace* Locke, that knowledge is produced through complex interactions between people and that a good epistemology should pay attention to how people interact to produce knowledge. Philosophers have been loathe to collapse the distinction between sociology of knowledge and epistemology as it has traditionally been conceived, but feminists require a new epistemology to struggle against the sort of suppression Locke practiced of women's contributions to knowledge production.

Notes

1. Cf. *Two Treatises of Government,* 2nd ed., ed. Peter Laslett, Cambridge: Cambridge University Press, 1967.

2. Cf. *An Essay Concerning Human Understanding,* ed. Peter H. Nidditch, Oxford: Clarenden Press, 1975.

3. Christopher Hill, *The World Turned Upside Down,* New York: Penguin Books, 1982, p. 15.

4. Cf. my "Modeling the Gender Politics in Science," *Hypatia* 3:1 (Spring 1988); Mary Hesse, *The Structure of Scientific Inference,* Berkeley and Los Angeles: University of California Press, 1974; W. V. O. Quine, *The Web of Belief,* New York: Random House, 1978; and David Bloor, "Durkheim and Mauss Revisited: Classification and the Sociology of Knowledge," *Studies in the History and Philosophy of Science* 13:267–297.

5. Christopher Hill, The Century of Revolution: 1603–1714, London: Thomas Nelson and Sons, Ltd., 1961, p. 111ff.

6. Hill, 1982, p. 40ff.

7. J. Dod and R. Cleaver, *A Godly Forme of Household Governement* . . . (London, 1614), sig. L₅r–v. Quoted in Keith Thomas, "Women and the Civil War Sects," *Past and Present* Vol. 13, 1958, p. 43.

8. William Gouge, *Of Domesticall Duties* (London, 1622), p. 268. Facsimile by Walter J. Johnson, Inc.; Theatrum Orbis Terrarum, Ltd.; Amsterdam, 1976.

9. Quoted in Thomas, 1958, p. 44.

10. Elaine C. Huber, " 'A Woman Must not Speak': Quaker Women in the English Left Wing," in *Women of Spirit, Female Leadership in the Jewish and Christian Traditions,* eds. Rosemary Ruether and Eleanor McLaughlin, New York: Simon and Schuster, 1977.

11. Ibid., p. 163.

12. Quoted in Hill, 1961, p. 203.

13. Quoted in Patricia Higgins, "The Reactions of Women," in *Politics, Religion and the English Civil War,* ed. Brian Manning. New York: St. Martin's Press, 1973, p. 183.

14. Hill, 1961, p. 206.

15. Ibid., quoted on p. 206.

16. Higgins, 1973, p. 185.

17. Ibid., p. 201.

18. Quoted in H. N. Brailsford, *The Levellers and the English Revolution,* ed. by Christopher Hill, Nottingham, England: Spokesman Books, 1976, p. 276.

19. Quoted in Higgins, 1973, p. 217.

20. I will use the anachronistic term "liberal" here because, although they are sometimes referred to by modern historians as "radicals", I wish to reserve "radical" for the group of people and ideas far more "levelling" than those of Cromwell and later of Locke and other Whigs.

21. The following discussion is indebted to Richard Ashcraft, *Revolutionary Politics and Locke's Two Treatises of Government,* Princeton, NJ: Princeton University Press, 1986 and to Hill, *The Century of Revolution.* For a bibliography of recent critiques of the view that Locke was politically innocent, cf. Ashcraft, p. 86n.

22. The Popish Plot was alleged to be a plot by Catholics to assassinate the King, kill English Protestants and return the country to Catholicism. It was used as a reason to continue the repression of Catholics in England and to execute Papists suspected of participating in it.

23. Ashcraft, p. 408ff.

24. Ibid., quoted on p. 431.

25. Ibid., p. 105.

26. Ibid., pp. 42 and 49n.

27. *ECHU,* IV:17, §4.

28. *ECHU,* IV:11, §8; cf. also IV:3, §18.

29. Ashcraft, 1986, p. 105.

30. Ibid., quoted on p. 50.

31. In his *Essays on the Law of Nature,* Locke does say that "[s]ince man has been made such as he is . . . there necessarily result from his inborn constitution some definite duties for him, which cannot be other than they are." Thus, natural law "is a fixed and permanent rule of morals . . . so firmly rooted in the soil of human nature" that "human nature must needs be changed before this law can be either altered or annulled" (quoted in Ashcraft 1986, p. 58n). These remarks could be construed to mean that the natural law is innate, but Locke's mature view, as set out in the *Essay Concerning Human Understanding,* is clearly that innate ideas are not necessary to explain universal, objective truths.

32. Cf. esp. *ECHU,* II:21, §11, 14–20.

33. *ECHU,* II:21, §23.

34. *ECHU,* II:21, §71).

35. Among the many considerations that led him to change the name of God to Reason, he says, is "because I have been held under darknesse by that word, as I see many people are. . . ." (Sabine, Works, p. 105)

36. George H. Sabine, ed., *The Works of Gerrard Winstanley,* Ithaca: Cornell University Press, 1941, p. 110.

37. Summarized by W. C. Braithwaite, in *The Second Period of Quakerism,* Cambridge: Cambridge University Press, 1961, p. 382.

38. Quoted in Josephine Donovan, *Feminist Theory: The Intellectual Traditions of American Feminism,* New York: Frederick Ungar Publishing Co., 1935, p . 10.

39. Ibid., quoted on p. 11.

40. Ibid., quoted on p. 17.

41. Ibid., quoted on pp. 19–20.

42. Against arguments that the oppressions of women will end if we just fix the list of rights to include the necessary ones, many feminists have agreed with Critical Legal Theorists that rights theories cannot in principle solve the problems facing women. For feminist critiques cf. Frances

Olsen, "Statutory Rape: A Feminist Critique of Rights Analysis," *Texas Law Review,* 63:3 (November 1984), pp. 387–432; Freeman, "Violence Against Women: Does the Legal System Provide Solutions or Itself Constitute the Problem?" *Canadian Journal of Family Law,* Vol. 3 (1980), p. 377; Catherine MacKinnon, "Feminism, Marxism, Method and the State: Toward Feminist Jurisprudence," *Signs,* Vol. 8 (1983), p. 635; Rifkin, "Toward a Theory of Law and Patriarchy," *Harvard Women's Law Journal,* Vol. 3 (1980), p. 83. For general critiques of rights theories cf. Mark Tushnet, "An Essay on Rights," *Texas Law Review,* 62:8 (May 1984), pp. 1363–1403; Roberto Unger, *Knowledge and Politics,* New York: Free Press (1975); Unger, *Law in Modern Society,* (1976); and Unger, *Passion: An Essay on Personality,* (1984). The great controversy over whether rights theory is bankrupt has generated a vast literature.

43. Ashcraft, 1986, p. 54.

Indians, Savages, Peasants and Women: Hume's Aesthetics

Marcia Lind

" . . . *we have to return to confrontation with 'the' canon, examining it as a source of ideas, themes, motifs, and myths . . . The point in so doing is not to label and hence dismiss even the most sexist [literary] classics, but to enable all of us to apprehend them, finally, in all their human dimensions."* "Treason Our Text," Lillian Robinson[1]

" . . . *The starting point of these reflections was usually a feeling of impatience at the sight of the 'naturalness' with which newspapers, art and common sense constantly dress up a reality . . . I wanted to track down, in the decorative display of* what goes without saying *the ideological abuse which, in my view, is hidden there."* Mythologies, *Roland Barthes*

Introduction

Feminists who work on texts within the philosophical canon are caught in a bind: we want to draw on the insights contained in canonical works but must, at the same time, acknowledge that those insights were often bound up with views which defined as 'universal' things like interests, needs, capacities, or conditions for the flourishing of 'mankind', which clearly were not. And when a supposedly universal generalization in fact has been only partially true, it has too often been the case[2] that those not covered by the (supposedly universal) generalization have interests and needs—both theoretical and practical—which are obscured, delegitimated, and ultimately denied.

One way of viewing the task of feminist philosophy in the face of this problem is that it ought to (a) locate the place(s) within a particular text where a limited set of interests or reactions is presented as a universal one and (b) assess the extent to which those false universal claims have affected the theory in which they are lodged. In this way it is possible to understand which insights in a theory can be appropriated for contemporary purposes—and also see more clearly where contemporary work that draws on traditional sources has inherited the biases of those traditional texts along with their insights.[3]

In this paper I examine David Hume's essay "Of the Standard of Taste," focusing mostly on locating places where Hume makes universal generalizations which are not, in fact, universally valid. I have chosen to look at this essay because it brings into sharp relief the problem of illegitimate universal generalization. I will also go on to suggest, in very broad terms, how this problem may show up in Hume's other texts and thus affect Hume's larger theoretical claims. And finally, I want to note that for purposes of feminist theory it is timely to explore this issue now, since there is currently some dispute about using Hume's views as grounding for feminist philosophy.[4]

Overview of the Argument

Central to Hume's aesthetics—and his ethics—is an 'impartial observer'—a figure who represents the uncorrupted 'natural' reactions of the human species; that is, who demonstrates how anyone, free of bias and simply in virtue of being human would respond. In Hume's aesthetics such a figure is called the 'good critic'. Hume thinks we can come to know what people's natural reactions are by finding 'uniformity' or 'near uniformity' among good critics. My argument will be that: (1) Hume has not succeeded in showing the existence of such uniformity; (2) that Hume's impartial spectator figure, in his aesthetics, and I will suggest, his ethics, in fact was 'partial', with reactions influenced by class, race and gender; and that (3) therefore, Hume cannot, even on his own terms, make the inferences he did make about which reactions were part of the nature of the human mind. Further, I will suggest that Hume was able to believe that these partial responses were indeed representative of the whole, and that he therefore had legitimately uncovered empirical uniformity, because of views he held about the underlying similarity of all people, and where that underlying similarity best showed up.

1. Responding to the Skeptic

In "Of the Standard of Taste," Hume sees himself as providing a response to someone who believes there are no right or wrong answers to ethical or aesthetic questions. This "skeptic" [ST 6] sees

ethics and aesthetics, unlike other domains, as governed by sentiment, and thinks radical relativism is the consequence of this fact.
Hume imagines such a person saying: " . . . a thousand different
sentiments, excited by the same object, are all right . . . " [ST 6] And
the same person might go on: "Beauty is no quality in things themselves; it exists merely in the mind which contemplates them and
each mind perceives a different beauty. One person may even perceive deformity, where another is sensible of beauty; and every individual ought to acquiesce in his own sentiment, without
pretending to regulate those of others . . . To seek the real beauty, or
real deformity, is as fruitless an inquiry, as to pretend to ascertain
the real sweet or real bitter." [ST 6] Hume's response to the skeptic
is that indeed he can ascertain "real beauty", that he can tell us
which sentiments are correct and which incorrect. I will argue here
that this response to the skeptic is badly flawed.

Hume thinks he can respond to the skeptic by finding universal
truths about the structure of the human mind. He believes he can
find: " . . . certain general principles of approbation or blame . . .
Some particular forms or qualities from the original structure of
the internal fabric are calculated to please, and others to dis-
please . . . " [ST 9] But why would finding such universal truths
about the structure of the mind—assuming he could—help Hume
to answer the skeptic above ? And how could he ever find such
truths ? An important clue to Hume's answer to both of these questions can be found in his use of the following story from Cervantes
(which will be quoted at length because it provides the 'key' to what
Hume thinks he is doing): "It is with good reason, says Sancho to
the squire with the great nose, that I pretend to have a judgment in
wine: this is a quality hereditary in our family. Two of my kinsmen
were once called to give their opinion of a hogshead, which was supposed to be excellent, being old and of a good vintage. One of them
tastes it, considers it; and, after mature reflection, pronounces the
wine to be good, were it not for a small taste of leather which he
perceived in it. The other, after using the same precautions, gives
also his verdict in favor of the wine, but with the reserve of a taste
of iron, which he could easily distinguish. You cannot imagine how
much they were both ridiculed for their judgment. But who laughed
in the end? On emptying the hogshead, there was found at the bottom an old key with a leathern thong tied to it." [ST 11]

Hume goes on to spell out for the reader the analogy with the
issue at hand: "The great resemblance between mental and bodily
taste will easily teach us to apply this story. Tho it be certain that
beauty and deformity, more than sweet and bitter, are not qualities

in objects, but belong entirely to the sentiment, internal or external, it must be allowd, that there are certain qualities in objects which are fitted by nature to produce those particular feelings." [ST 11][5]

What Hume thought he needed to do then, was to find those qualities in objects—those natural qualities—which are "fitted by nature" to produce the feeling that the object is beautiful or ugly. And the way to do this, Hume thinks, is to find the "universal rules of composition", those things which have been "universally found to please in all countries and in all ages". This would then allow him, Hume thought, to *justify* some aesthetic claims. For "to produce those general rules or avowed patterns of composition is like finding the key with the leathern thong, which justified the verdict of Sancho's kinsmen." [ST 11]

2. *Good Critics*

Hume thought he could find such qualities and the ideal—and universal—responses to them, by looking at what he called 'good critics'. People who are good critics are supposedly judged within their own cultures to have the ability to perceive the presence of such rules of composition—the objective quality involved—even when such qualities are present only in very minute amounts.[6] Thus, it is not unreasonable to expect good critics to be present in every culture. What seems to be the case, however, is that Hume is (illicitly) supporting a hierarchy among and within cultures so that only some cultures will be taken to have good critics. But before getting to that claim, I want to first look at what Hume says about critics and their abilities.

When Hume is describing the good critic, the analogy he uses is to health ; "A man in a fever would not insist on his palate as able to decide concerning flavors ; nor would one affected with the jaundice pretend to give a verdict with regard to colors. In each creature there is a sound and a defective state ; and the former alone can be supposed to afford us a true standard of taste and sentiment." [ST 9] In other words, Hume believes that some people are in a 'sound state', and that such people are healthy. They thus will respond 'properly' to various stimuli—in a way which goes beyond any particularly culture-bound reaction—just as (supposedly) physical diseases are distortions in a universal, not culture-bound way. And 'good critics' are such (healthy) people.

Hume gives five characteristics which characterize these people (the critics) who are in such a state: (1) They have delicacy of taste [ST 11–12]; (2) They have sufficient practice in judging [ST 13]; (3) They have made adequate comparisons [ST 14]; (4) They are unprejudiced or impartial [ST 15]; (5) They use their "good sense" to check that they have, to the best of their abilities, engaged in (1)–(4) (above) [ST 16]. Lacking these five, one will be blocked from perceiving what, from the "original structure" of humans, is "calculated to please."

How can such ideal reactors help Hume answer the skeptic ? By looking at the way they uniformly react. Hume says, for example: "If in the sound state of the organ, there be an entire or considerable uniformity of sentiment among men, we may thence derive an idea of the perfect beauty." [ST 10] And he also says: " . . . the joint verdict of such [good critics] wherever they are to be found, is the true standard of taste and beauty." [ST 17] Thus uniformity among critics across all cultures is very important, Hume thought, for answering the skeptic. For only armed with such a "joint verdict", such "entire or considerable uniformity" could Hume infer, as he wants to, which qualities we are "fitted by nature" to react to as if they are beautiful or ugly.[7]

Hume had no doubt that such uniformity existed. He believed (along with many of his contemporaries)[8] that without distorting influences, all people were very much the same. He says, for example:

> "Mankind are so much the same, in all times and places, that history informs us of nothing new or strange in this particular. Its chief use is to discover the constant and universal principles of human nature, by showing men, in all varieties of circumstances and situations and furnishing us with material from which we may form our observations and become acquainted with the regular springs of human action and behavior." [I 55]

Therefore it is not surprising that Hume would think that what all humans find beautiful, for example, would be fairly uniform; uniform enough to make inferences about what was built into the structure of the mind. I want to go on to see if the uniformity that Hume thought he had established, and which played such an important role within his argument, was established legitimately.

3. Uniformity

I believe that Hume did not legitimately establish that such uniformity existed. As a matter of empirical fact, such uniformity did not exist among the general population, even if one could some-

how subtract the 'distortions' to which the general populace is subject. And given the relation that the critics are said to have held to
the general populace, it follows that such uniformity of response
will not exist among the critics either. Since the lack of agreement
among the critics is, then, derived from the lack of agreement
within the general population, the most direct way of arguing that
there is no uniformity of response would be to argue that there is no
such uniformity at the level of the general population. The problem
with this approach is that Hume thinks that whatever is examined
at the level of the general population is always riddled with what
appear to be deep differences, but are really only reflections of distortions or biases—and therefore do not undermine the claim of underlying agreement in reaction. He says, for example: "The Rhine
flows north, the Rhone south; yet both spring from the same moun-
tain, and are also actuated, in their opposite directions, by the same
principle of gravity. The different inclinations of the ground on
which they run cause all the difference of their course." [D 150] And
so showing lack of agreement at the level of the general population,
would for Hume, just represent more of the Rhine/Rhone case. It
would not invalidate the claim that when superficial differences, or
distortions, are taken away, there is indeed general agreement, one
way in which that all people do indeed respond to certain natural
qualities.

Because of this manoever of Hume's, it seems that the only way
to refute his claim to uniformity of reactions is to show that there is
not sufficient uniformity at the level of the critics. For were someone
to show this, Hume could not respond by saying that such lack of
uniformity is simply a result of bias or distortion, whereas he could
respond this way were someone to show this lack within the general
populace. Further, if there is no uniformity of response at the level
of the critics, it follows that there is also no uniformity of response
at the level of the general population—since the critics are the ideal
form of that population—that is, subject to less distortions. Therefore the strategy here is to show that what looks like uniformity of
reactions among critics is not legitimately derived.

As stated previously, Hume thought critics were distinguished
by five factors. One of those factors was making 'adequate comparisons', and this is what shall be focused on here. When speaking of
adequate comparisons, Hume says that "Indians", "savages", or
"peasants", could not possibly have made such comparisons. Why ?
Their experience, Hume says, is not wide enough. The way he puts
it is this: "a man who has had no opportunity of comparing the dif-

ferent kinds of beauty is indeed totally unqualified to provide an opinion . . . " [ST 14] For, as he goes on to say, even though, "the coursest daubing contains a certain lustre of colors and exactness of imitation . . . which would affect the mind of a peasant or Indian with the highest admiration . . . " [ST 14], and "even vulgar ballads are not entirely destitute of harmony or nature . . . " [ST 14], it is nonetheless the case that; "none but a person familiarized to *superior beauties* would pronounce their members harsh, or narration uninteresting." [ST 14, my emphasis]

But who sets up the criterion for "superior beauties"? For surely the Indian has one range of experiences, one sort of basis for comparisons, and other people, for example, eighteenth century critics, another. Why is one sufficiently broad and the other not ?

4. Bias

My hypothesis is that Hume was artificially constructing agreement among critics by limiting who was party to the agreement. And that further, he was using this (artificially derived) agreement to prove that there was agreement at the level of the general populace, were they somehow to be relieved of their biases and distortions. And he used this claim, in turn, to infer which reactions were built into the structure of the human brain.

Adequate comparison, for Hume, necessarily includes an exposure to 'superior beauties'. The supposed justification for including superior beauties is that a critic needs a certain amount of breadth to make informed judgments. A critic ought to be someone who has been exposed to all sorts of art. In order to get such exposure, a (potential) critic must be someone who is educated. But I want look a bit harder at the stipulation that it be the sort of education containing exposure to *superior* beauties.

What are superior beauties? The most likely possibilities are either: (a) something requiring more skills to understand ; or (b) beauties which prior critics, through the ages, and across cultures, have chosen as superior. If 'superior' here means the former, Hume needs to give us an account of the ways in which some beauties are indeed superior. He didn't give us such an account. But if 'superior' means the latter, then it is important to note that Hume seems to have looked at only a very small subset of the choices of all such critics ; that is, only those choices of critics from familiar cultures. Therefore what Hume is talking about when he is talking about exposure to 'superior' beauties is not just *any* sort of education, with any sort of range, but a *classical* education.[9]

But the effect of this is that certain people will be left out of the group of potential critics, namely all those who could not get classical educations. As a matter of empirical fact in the eighteenth century (as Hume himself says) Indians, savages, and peasants did not have access to a sophisticated (university) education. And in all likelihood, women, even of the upper-classes and certainly in the above named groups, would be left out as well. For even upper-class women were not allowed in universities and so they couldn't get such an education there. However, what the claim that women were excluded turns on—and what scholars don't yet know enough about—is the extent to which women were being educated at home and what they were being taught.[10]

The exclusion of these people has very serious implications for Hume's argument. But before saying exactly why, there is one obvious objection to the way my claim is proceeding which needs to be dealt with. Someone might say that although I have pointed to exclusions from Hume's group of potential critics, they are not exclusions which matter because they are only *de-facto* and not in-principle ones. It is true that these are *de-facto* exclusions. At whatever point that Indians, savages, peasants or women (of whatever class) got the sort of education required, Hume would let them into the group of potential critics.[11] But my claim is that even this *de-facto* exclusion is a serious problem.

Hume argued that critics needed exposure to superior beauties for them to have sufficient breadth to judge properly. That is, supposedly the critic has experienced what Indians, savages, peasants, (and whatever women) have experienced as beautiful *and* the 'superior' beauties as well. And supposedly, that would make such a person more qualified—on the grounds of breadth alone. But part of what I have been arguing is that 'breadth' here is not *mere* breadth—for were it mere breadth, there are certainly other domains across which the Indian, peasant or savage, is as broad as the critic.[12] Rather, Hume is talking about breadth which necessarily includes exposure to a certain sort of beauty—classical beauty— and probably does not include (although granted, I have not argued this here) exposure to the sort of thing the Indian or savage or (classically) uneducated woman considers beautiful as well. So under the cloak of mere breadth Hume is really insisting on only a certain kind of breadth.

And this in turn is problematic because insisting on a certain kind of breadth could be justified only if Hume could argue that this sort of breadth, and thus this sort of education, is the one which sufficiently frees people of their biases so that they can judge, as Hume thinks critics must, from the stance of "a man (sic.) in general". But there is no argument for that. And if there is no such argument, then the exclusion is not justified, and then, in turn, Hume is not doing what he thinks he is doing. For if he is limiting who is agreeing in a way which cannot be justified, Hume can't say, as he does, that this is (a manifestation of) how *all* people, when they are unbiased, would respond. Rather, it is, at best, how all people, when they are educated in a certain way, would respond. That is why the exclusion—*de-facto* or not—matters.

Hume can respond to this objection if he can justify his limit on who is agreeing. But his only justification for the sort of exclusion he is advocating—an exclusion via a certain kind of education—seems to be a (suppressed) thesis about the hierarchy of certain cultures and cultural values. That is, it has already been noted that Hume believed that in the absence of distorting influences, all people were essentially similar. Further, he believed (again, along with many of his peers) that this absence of distortion was better manifested by "civilized" cultures than by others. For he held that most of what appeared to be legitimate differences among people and cultures were really only varying stages of development, with high European and classical culture and cultural values as the most developed point. That point was what 'savages', 'Indians', and 'peasants' were on their way towards. And once humans were all "civilized", Hume thought their needs and interests would be very similar.[13] Thus, given the above beliefs, Hume could also believe that via education in the cultural values which supposedly represented lack of distortion and the apex of human culture, people could get to be 'truly human' and to operate 'correctly'. But there is no reason—or certainly not sufficient reason—to believe that the way in which a classical education works frees people of their biases, so that their judgments are merely human ones, rather than inculcations of cultural values.

The point is this : the agreement among critics cannot be artificially derived by constructing a group of critics who will agree because they share biases. And as Hume's description of who is to count as a good critic—at least regarding what is considered "adequate comparisons"—now stands, I believe this is the case. For Hume needs, as he himself put it, "considerable uniformity" in judgment to infer, even on his own grounds, how the human mind is structured to work, and thus to answer the skeptic. And since I have argued above that he did not legitimately demonstrate the existence of such uniformity, but instead, narrowed his group of critics so that it excluded those who might be most likely to disagree, then

Hume can't infer—as he needs to to answer the skeptic—that there is a way all humans, were they free of bias, would react.

Before going on to see whether and how this conclusion does or does not matter, I want to briefly examine a possible parallel problem in Hume's ethics.

5. Reverberations and Implications

(A) One Possible Parallel. One possible parallel between Hume's aesthetics and his ethics, and therefore a possible parallel problem, might be this: in his aesthetics Hume constructs a path to 'natural' aesthetic reactions by supposedly reporting on agreement among critics. But (if the above argument is correct) he is not really reporting, but narrowing down who counts as a critic in order to get agreement. Therefore, insofar as he is reporting, he is reporting on only a narrow, unrepresentative sample. Similarly, in his moral theory, Hume constructs a path to 'natural' moral reactions by supposedly reporting on what all people, when they are free of prejudice, that is, in the stance of the impartial observer, do universally.

But my concern is that there too, as in the aesthetics, there is a presumption of uniformity in reactions across the species when people are 'operating properly', and a presumption of what sort of subclass of people operates 'properly' that informs Hume's construction of the impartial spectator. I will not argue for this claim here, for it clearly merits a separate discussion. However, I believe it is obvious from only a brief glance at the history of ethics, that Hume's claims about what universally characterizes moral psychology when we are 'operating correctly' are problematic. He says, for example, that:

> "Every quality of the mind is denominated virtuous, which gives pleasure by the mere survey; as every quality, which produces pain, is called vicious. This pleasure and this pain may arise from four different sources. For we reap a pleasure from the view of a character, which is naturally fitted to be useful to others, or to the person himself, or which is agreeable to others, or to the person himself." [T 591]

But is it the case, for example, that everyone agrees, or that it is obviously correct that, as Hume says (above), a character judged virtuous is one that has the disposition to produce great pleasure or happiness ? Surely on a (crudely) Kantian picture, it would *not* be the case that a person judged virtuous—a person with a "good will"—has such a disposition. [Gr. 394, 398ff] And while some have claimed[14] that it is exactly this which marks Kant's theory as un-intuitive and incorrect, Kant thought that he was properly captur-ing the notion of morality by ideas of duty and not happiness. [Gr. 397]

Once again, the point is that if this parallel is correct, then just as the good critic does not capture the way people respond just in virtue of being human, neither does the impartial observer. Rather, this may well be another case of Hume's imposing his own (or his cultures') views about what counts as correct responses onto his data, and calling those responses 'natural'.

(B) Implications. I argued above that Hume has an overly narrow data base for identifying what is supposedly built into the mind, and that this leads to a skewed view—at least in the aesthetics—of the 'correct' reaction. But why does this criticism matter, and to what extent doesn't it matter ? As said earlier, this question shall be addressed here only in the most general terms. Therefore, I will try, in such terms, to explain both why the problem of bias in the impartial spectator is a serious but not disastrous one and, why, de-spite this problem, there is a core to Hume's account that feminist theory would do well to continue to draw on. But in order to do this, a brief general account of Hume's larger project is necessary.

Hume's larger project[15] was to create a non-rationalist, sentiment-based foundation for moral, political and aesthetic the-ory which was informed by a "scientific"[16] non-mythological view of human nature. Hume also wanted to establish that such a theory could avoid radical relativism. For he was concerned, in his ethics, his political philosophy, his aesthetics and his treatment of the passions, with having a theory in which someone could both iden-tify and justify appropriate and inappropriate reactions in all the above domains.

I have been focusing on this latter part of Hume's project, that is, his claim to objectivity. I have argued that his argument for ob-jectivity, at least in his aesthetics, is flawed because of a bias which allowed him to substitute a partial generalization for a universal one. And, as already indicated, it is a flaw that may run through his other texts as well. For in each area mentioned above, Hume must legitimately demonstrate the uniformity he thinks can ground his account of objectivity. And to the extent that he cannot, his account of what is the correct response in each of these domains is biased as well.

And to the extent that this is true, it would mean, in turn, that Hume's attempt to ground his philosophy on a 'scientific' view of human nature—a non-mythological one—had failed. For Hume as a *modern* philosopher believed that he was different from his predecessors in that: " . . . the moral philosophy transmitted to use by Antiquity, [was] . . . entirely Hypothetical, and depend[ed] more upon Invention than Experience. Every one consulted his Fancy in erecting Schemes of Virtue and of Happiness, without regarding Human Nature, upon which every moral Conclusion must depend." And he went on to say that: "This [the 'scientific' study of human nature] therefore I resolved to make my principle study, and the source from which I would derive every Truth in Criticism, [i.e., in regard to literature and the fine arts] as well as Morality." (from Hume's "Letter to a Physician", cited in Burton *Life and Correspondence of David Hume* p. 36) Thus Hume was trying to get away from the stories, the mythologies, the 'inventions', that philosophy had been subject to. But I believe, at least in his aesthetics, that Hume was simply substituting his own 'modern' mythology or 'invention'—that the responses of one group of people represented 'unbiased' and 'natural' reactions—for the inventions of his predecessors. This then, the attempt of philosophy to get away from its mythologies and ending up by re-inventing more—and, even more to the point, reinventing mythologies that delegitimize the experience and normative judgments of whole groups of people—is why the distortion in the impartial spectator matters.

But as serious as I think that failure is, it is *not* a failure which necessitated abandoning the larger Humean vision of an emotion-based normative theory, a vision which much of feminist theory, and especially feminist moral and political theory, shares,[17] and is trying to take further. For although Hume was wrong in claiming that his impartial spectator figure was the repository of 'natural' reactions, reactions universal among the species, there is no reason why future attempts to create an emotion-based theory must repeat this sort of mistake, and must include biases about which cultures, or parts of cultures, are 'pure' and have people who are working as they 'should'. And it is when a theory says those sorts of things, and goes on to correlatively say that 'flourishing' only occurs, or is most likely to occur, under a system which incorporates those biases, that the sorts of problems discussed here arise.[18]

To construct a viable emotion-based normative theory philosophers may well have to give up any claims to universality for any sort of idealized reactor—but for this we should be grateful to Hume for showing us what the problems might be with such a theory. Indeed to construct an emotion-based theory without making Hume's sort of mistake, the mistake of substituting partial generalizations for universal ones is, even within the feminist community, the really difficult task.[19] Thus the part of Hume which does not work—his substitution of cultural mores for what was supposed to be 'natural', is a failure which is sad—but useful. For it allows us to isolate the point at which Hume's project became doomed to fail. And it is exactly that point about which, as contemporary theorists—even contemporary feminist theorists—we need to be most careful.

Hume said, as cited above, that the importance of history is to uncover the natural, universal facts about human beings. But I believe that as philosophers, and as feminist philosophers, we would do well to make sure something else is done as well. And that is—in order to avoid making the mistake ourselves—to uncover the different things that people, at different points in history, have *needed to believe* were universal—universal and natural. Thus we must (to use Barthes' phrase), "track down, in the decorative display of *what-goes-without-saying,* the ideological abuse which . . . is hidden there."[20]

Notes

*David Hume's works will be referred to in this paper in the following way: ST = "Of the Standard of Taste", in *Of The Standard of Taste and Other Essays* (Indianapolis, Library of Liberal Arts, 1965); D = "Of the Dignity of Meanness of Human Nature", in *Of The Standard of Taste and Other Essays* (Indianapolis, Library of Liberal Arts, 1965); I = *An Enquiry Concerning Human Understanding,* ed. Eric Steinberg (Indianapolis, Hackett Publishing Co., 1977); T = *A Treatise of Human Nature,* ed., L. A. Selby-Bigge, 2nd edition (Oxford, Clarendon Press, 1978).

1. Thanks to Carol Hilles for telling me about Robinson's article.

2. For good illustrations of this point, see Susan Okin's *Women in Western Political Thought* (Princeton University Press, 1979).

3. In this task I take myself to be following in the footsteps of other feminist theorists—especially Okin, in her excellent book cited above.

4. See, e.g., Virginia Held's "Non-Contractual Society", in *Science, Morality and Feminist Theory,* edited by Hanen and Nielson (Calgary, The University of Calgary Press, 1987) p. 120, for one version of the view suspicious of Hume, and any number of articles by Annette Baier, most explicitly "Hume, The Women's Moral Theorist?" in *Women and Moral Theory,* edited by Kittay and Meyers (Totowa, N.J., Rowman and Littlefield, 1986), for the view which says Hume can be of help to feminists. I also consider

myself in the latter category. See my "Hume and Moral Emotions", in *Morality and Psychology,* edited by Rorty and Flanegan (Cambridge, Mass., MIT Press, forthcoming) and "Hume and Feminist Ethics" read at the Conference on Feminist Ethics, October 1988, Duluth, Minnesota.

5. Michelle Farrell has pointed out to me how interesting it is that Hume should use a literary text to help his philosophical argument—especially when the philosophical argument is about the value of literary texts.

6. Thanks to Joshua Cohen for making this point clear.

7. This is important despite Hume's claims (p. 19–24) that there is some allowable deviation; notice he still thinks there is a core of judgments in ethics and aesthetics running across all time and culture. He says, for example: "But where ideas of morality and decency alter from one age to another, and where vicious manners are described, without being marked with the proper characters of blame and disapprobation, this must be allowed to disfigure the poem and to be a real deformity." (ST 21)

8. See, for example, Christopher Berry's *Hume, Hegel and Human Nature* (Boston: Martinus Nighoff, 1982)—especially chapter 4, where he talks about the eighteenth century quest for a universal human nature.

9. That is, at least as that would have been understood in the eighteenth century.

10. For the cultural and educational situation of eighteenth century women, see *Woman in the 18th Century and Other Essays,* edited by Fritz and Morton (Toronto, Samuel Stevens Hakkert & Co., 1976), especially the essays by Robert Halsband, and Jean E. Hunter. See also L. Marcil-Lacoste, "The consistency of Hume's position concerning women", and S. Burns, "The Humean Female", both in *Dialogue* 15(3) (1976), pp. 414–424 and 425–40. And finally, Annette Baier's piece, *Hume on Women's Complexion* (manuscript), is informative on educational opportunities for women (and Hume's views on them) in Hume's time.

11. All I am arguing for in this paper is *de-facto* exclusion. And as regards gender (at least for those white and upper-class) that may be all that is going on. But regarding "Indians" and "Savages"—I want to underscore that my interpretation of Hume is a very generous one. For Hume says, for example (in "Of National Characters"): "I am apt to suspect the negroes and in general all the other species of men . . . to be naturally inferior to the whites. There never was a civilized nation of any other complexion than white, nor even any individual eminent either in action or speculation. No ingenious manufactures amongst them, no arts, no sciences . . . Such a uniform and constant difference could not happen in so many countries and ages, if nature had not made an original distinction betwixt these breeds of men . . . "

For an excellent paper on racism in Hume and other empiricists, see Harry Bracken's "Essence, Accident and Race", *Hermathena* 116, winter 1973, pp. 81–96.

12. There are a number of ways to argue for this claim when it is about the 'Indians, savages and peasants' that Hume is speaking of—and to do that well would be to argue from social historical or anthropological evidence. I won't do that here—but want to be merely suggestive. I am saying that 'breadth' is interest-relative. And one way to see that is through examples in contemporary culture. For example, urban American working-class children are more likely to have a broader grasp, say, of the varieties and subtleties of grafitti or rap music than are upper-class American children. Or that women who don't have a certain kind of education, in America, at least, may well know much more about a whole variety of phenomena in popular culture—romances, gothic novels, etc.,—than other sorts of people. And my point is that however one fills in the content of what is known by those people who may not have educations in 'high culture', it is begging the question to say that what they do know about this sort of aesthetic phenomena shouldn't count—and shouldn't count as being a sort of breadth—a breadth which people who do know about 'high culture' often do not have.

13. See, for example, where Hume says: ("Of Refinement in the arts")

" . . . every man would think his life or fortune much less secure in the hands of a Moor or a Tartar, than in those of a French or English gentleman, the rank of men the most civilized in the most civilized nations." or, " . . . Not to mention, that all ignorant ages are infested with superstition, which throws the government off its bias, and disturbs men in the pursuit of their interest and happiness . . . When the tempers of men are softened as well as their knowledge improved, this humanity appears still more conspicuous, and is the chief characteristic which distinguishes a civilized age from times of barbarity and ignorance . . . the combatants divest themselves of the brute, and resume the man."

It might also be worthwhile to mention that this is the point at which my paper comes closest to the McIntyre argument in his "Hume on Is and Ought" in *Against the Self-Images of the Age* (Notre Dame, University of Notre Dame Press, 1984). This article has been very influential on the argument I present in this paper—especially when MacIntyre says:

"We have moral rules [Hume thinks] because we have common interests. Should someone succeed in showing us that the facts are different from what we conceive them to be so that we have no common interests, then our moral rules would lose their justification.

Indeed the initial move of Marx's moral theory can perhaps be best understood as a denial of the facts which Hume holds to constitute the justification for social morality, Marx's denial that there are common interests shared by the whole of society in respect of, for instance, the distribution of property meets Hume on his own ground."

14. See, for example, Phillippa Foot's "Morality as a System of Hypothetical Imperatives" in her *Virtues and Vices* (Berkeley, University of California Press, 1978), for arguments which I consider extremely powerful as to why this aspect of Kant is indeed unintuitive.

15. For an extended account of how one could come to see this as Hume's larger project, see my dissertation *Emotions and Hume's Moral Theory*, Massachusetts Institute of Technology, 1987.

16. For a good account of the ways in which Hume took himself to have a "scientific" (not scientistic) account, see Kemp-Smith *The Philosophy of David Hume*, London, Macmillan and Co., 1964, chapter 3.

17. See, for example, Amelie Rorty's excellent paper "Pride Produces the Idea of Self: Hume on Moral Agency" (typescript) for an account of Hume without the 'flaws' I mention here.

18. Besides the Baier pieces mentioned earlier, see Gilligan, *In a Different Voice*, Harvard University Press, 1983; Jaggar; "Love and Knowledge: Emotion as an Epistemic Resource for Feminists", in Jaggar and Bordo, *Gender, Body, Knowledge*, 1989; Ruddick, *Maternal Thinking*, Beacon Press, 1989; Moi, "Patriarchal thought and the drive for knowledge" in Brennan, ed., *Between Feminism and Psycholanalysis*, London, Methuen, 1988, among many others.

19. See, e.g., Elizabeth Spelman's *Inessential Women*, Princeton University Press, 1989, as well as Fraser and Nicolson, "Social Criticism without Philosophy: An Encounter between Feminism and Postmodernism" in *Feminism/Postmodernism*, ed., Nicolson, Routledge, New York, 1990.

20. This chapter is a much-revised version of chapter 5 of my Ph.D. thesis (op. cit.). It achieved its present state in part through my reading of Susan Okin's *Women in Western Political Thought*. Barbara Herrnstein Smith's *Contingencies of Value* (Cambridge, Harvard University Press, 1988), which I read after finishing my thesis, makes some of the same critical points regarding Hume as I did both in the thesis and in this paper, and was very useful in convincing me that I really am committed to the criticisms of Hume made here.

I want to thank Jonathan Adler, David Auerbach, Bat-Ami Bar On, Joshua Cohen, Michelle Farrell, Owen Flanagan, Alison Jaggar, Alice Kaplan, Helen Longino and Lynre Tirrell for comments on some version of this paper. Josh was especially helpful on the thesis version, and I am very grateful to Alison for repeated readings of the current version. I also want to thank Robert Brandon, Barbara Hernnstein Smith and Jane Tompkins for helpful conversations about issues raised by this paper.

A Feminist Use for Hume's Moral Ontology

Sarah A. Bishop Merrill

In this essay, I do two things: in Part I), I clarify what kind of ontological foundations a moral philosophy that is acceptable to feminists should have;[1] and in Part II) I show that David Hume's concept and treatment of personhood provide such foundations.

Part I. Women and Ontology

In the common language of ancient Greece, and still today, *ontology* means the 'Logos', logic, or study, and the 'way', of 'Ontos' or being. Ontology is the theory and use of systematic assumptions about who or what exists, "has" being, and thus "who counts" or "matters" in a given universe, community, practice, or discussion. At the bottom of things in the history of oppression is an ontological error: human beings have often failed to include those "others" who are different from themselves.[2] So the ontologies supporting what were thought to be universal moral claims are not universal, but rather apply only to those who "count" or whose specific existence was referred to, experienced, or assumed.

Ontologies expressed in language and other social practices are always based on and limited by the experience and imagination of peoples and cultures in particular social and historical contexts. As such they usually are more exclusive than inclusive. And so an acceptable, accurate, and valid moral ontology used in the language of any universal ethical claims must often come under questioning by its users concerning who counts or is included in the moral universe spanned by ethics, just as people in the seventeenth century were urged by the questions of the Papal Bull of 1627 to consider the people called Native Americans as having souls like white people and thus counting among those who deserve respect, have rights, dignity, responsibilities, and can be "saved" for all eternity. "People" [meaning those exercising racial, gender, class, or species privilege] in all the centuries since have encountered resistance from those with darker skins than theirs, who ask to be included in concepts and practices of personhood. But change in regard and respect for persons does not occur until ordinary racist, classist, or sexist practices change. Differences and discrimination cannot merely be thought away.

It has been well-established that women did not "count" as public social and political persons, legal persons, or even human beings in the fully developed sense for Aristotle, for most theorists throughout history, and even within Hume's era, in the theories of the eighteenth century founding "fathers" of the United States Constitution. The systematic ruling out of women from the realm of those who count (e.g., among those who vote in Switzerland until quite recently), continues to this day in some cultures. This failure to consider women full persons occurred because women were thought to lack in quality (entirely) or quantity (in part) the necessary feature or capacity of authoritative "rationality" which has for most of five millennia been thought to be the essence of being a person, whether divine or human. Women often "bought" this story of their natures, and neither resisted nor expressed effective resentment in terms men could understand. But most crucially, after the death of cottage industries during the industrial revolution, their "worlds" became separate, so that practices of peer cooperation and recognition were unlikely between "private" and "public" spheres.

It is not an exaggeration to say that women, and certain others who are only now specifiable, literally did not exist as people in the world of male-dominated practices and thought. And yet, it is from those exclusive patriarchal practices and reflections that all of the modern moral theories have emerged. Although Carol Gilligan and many critics now discuss a "different voice" of the morality of care in women, which is however not exclusive to women, no distinctly feminist, women-oriented or woman-authored moral theory exists in the history of philosophy. The work of philosophers such as Mary Estell have been largely lost to us, though they offered cogent critiques of their contemporary male philosophers. They do not count among works of philosophical persons, being catalogued instead, in the very library where Hume was once librarian, under "Letters" and the like.[3] In spite of this fact, a feminist undercurrent in moral ontology can be seen, I think, as early as the eighteenth century, when Mary Wollstonecraft initiated the first wave of modern feminism and David Hume discussed morals and human nature with, among others, many women friends and companions. Undercurrent Ontology, of course, throws in a few new beings who were not counted, recognized as "one of us," or attended to before. This undercurrent begins in the nineteenth century in the unlikely space of Hegel's dialectical method and logic, and extends through Wittgenstein, the American pragmatists, and beyond into the rapidly emerging feminist moral theory that will begin the twenty-first century of this era.[4]

David Hume's method offers a long-ignored way of approaching ontology in providing a foundation for ethics. Hume's useful contribution for feminists, who think women "count" as people in the moral and ontological universe, lies in the fact that he refuses to see morality as ontologically rooted in some abstract and fixed "essence" without which one does not count as a person. Rather, the basis of Hume's ethics and epistemology is pragmatic, consisting in the practices of recognizing others and being recognized as people with existence and important features in the moral universe; such recognition occurs through: 1) the moral sentiments and the corrections of reason; and 2) the use of language by people, which he recognizes as a practice of moral and ontological significance in its very nature, and in its created and evolved uses.[5] Actual, different, contextualised people, not abstractions, ground morality for David Hume.[6] Similarly, feminists argue that women and those whose moralities transcend abstractions typical of Lawrence Kohlberg's "stage" theory of moral development, particularize and contextualize actual personhood, to resolve moral complexity. Hume's view has been ignored until now because the standard interpreters[7] see him from essentialist standpoints defined below.

The above claims about Hume's view of personhood will initially seem bizarre to those whose only acquaintance with Hume is through the famous passage in Section IV, Part IV, Book I of the *Treatise,* where Hume says that he cannot find through perception alone that thing called the self. Hume reports that when he is using what is called "the way of ideas," he finds merely a "bundle" or collection of perceptions. The Humean report above has been called, informally, the "bundle theory of the self." In fact, there is, however, no such theory, or thing, in the philosophy of David Hume.

Rather, Hume presents a variety of relationships among the "different states and episodes of the self" in Book I of the *Treatise.*[8] None of these aspects of perceived selfhood unify it "over and above these" diverse perceptions. Hume's presentation in Book I, of a concept of the self which is inadequate, is merely intended as a clear picture of human fallibility, and to prepare the reader for the description of the intentionality or motivating directedness of the idea-laden passions in Book II, which in turn lays the groundwork for the full-fledged social and realist (though not essentialist) view of the person in Book III. David Fate Norton, in *David Hume: Common Sense Moralist, Sceptical Metaphysician* has argued thoroughly for this conclusion as well. Unlike Alasdair MacIntyre, I disagree with Norton that Hume is skeptical metaphysically, preferring to maintain that Hume is skeptical in his epistemology, which yields modest, particular, but realistic common sense claims in metaphysics, especially in the clearly person-based ontology of his moral theory.

In other words, Hume does not claim that certain "furniture of the world" does not exist; he claims, like Locke and later Kant, that limited human reason can see very little of it, and that not at all clearly. Hume would of course grant that there is a great epistemic distance between, on the one hand, what can be *rationally known* of this world within which the knowers are situated, (a world which limits both the continuity and wholeness of perceptions and the rest of knowledge,) and, on the other hand, what *in fact is the case* about this world, viewed as it were, from outside by an ideally reasonable observer.

But people are as "active" as they are reasonable, Hume says, and have as much moral sense as reason. So people first *act as if* others existed. Early social practices imply the mutual recognition of personhood. Only later, when schooled by insecure essentialist groups in bigotry, hate, fear, or xenophobia, do people examine or want to "rationalize" what is made of them in terms of essences and perceived ways of being.[9]

Since in the *Treatise* Hume is not explicitly building a theory about personhood, but rather, laying the epistemic groundwork, and because many interpreters read and probe no further in Hume than the passage in Book I of the *Treatise*, expecting an essentialist sort of definition of 'self' and 'person,' it is not surprising that most find Hume's "view of personhood" disappointing, shallow, or without substance.[10] But because of his method, I think Hume's view of personhood will become increasingly interesting to feminists and others concerned with foundations in moral theory.

Hume avoids the traditional essentialist traps of the ontologies of patriarchal or phallist[11] moral theory, which fail to notice both the existence and the experience of women or do not take their embodied and socially contextualised existence seriously for moral theory.[12] Due to human limitations in experiencing, knowing about, or sympathizing with the lived situations of others different from ourselves, it has often been the case in human history that an abstract "essence" has been posited in place of the actual, experienced existence of the other. Making such perceived "essences" into a philosophical system has sometimes strengthened, and usually vastly weakened the ability of human beings to experience solidarity and to share their burdens and lives. ("All men [or women/ Sandinistas/Communists/Capitalists/Palestinians/or Jews/] are like that: [they]/he'll never change," and "Women are by nature irrational and made for the care of children and others," or "Blacks and Native Americans are basically different from whites," "They are animals: "we" people are human, and therefore, we people can use animals however we want to," are evidence of ontological essentialism at work in private and public realms.)

"Essentialism" Defined

"Essentialism" might be defined as the belief, usually assumed rather than stated, that every entity capable of having an abstract name or general characterization has an unchangeable or unexchangeable essence, which cannot be compromised without making that entity into a non-entity, that is, without changing its ontological status and taking it out of *being as an object* for those who define it from the outside, or externally. This is so for conceptual or intentional objects,—the objects of belief, fictions (e.g., unicorns), propositions, and qualities such as greenness, for instance,—as well as for more ordinary physical objects. It serves as an often useful vestige of that stage in our psychological development when we first began to have a sense of "object permanency,"— a stage when considerable anxiety about the seemingly arbitrary disappearance and reappearance of our first caretaker was relieved by seeing her and other objects as separate from ourselves, and enduring without our watching or willing it. Knowing that something has a fixed being and that it does not change at its core, gives us a sense of security.

An essentialist asks others to provide necessary and sufficient conditions, or a *test*, so that people can all know and agree on who or what "counts" as whatever it is that is being defined. This makes decisions less stressful for those in charge of administering the test: some people can easily rule out merely purported entities or those claiming to have important features of personhood (e.g., rationality, autonomy, the capacity for suffering, etc.) without further ado, based on the fact that they flunked the test specially constructed by those in charge.

This sort of thing was happening in a crude form in South Africa in this century, where skin color was evaluated as the essential criterion of membership in a political class, and, based on a single necessary (though not a sufficient) condition, certain people in South Africa are given full status as citizens, and others are labeled "Bantu" or, worse, "Kaffir," and relegated by force through the profoundly resented "Bantustan" policy to the "tribal homelands," without any choice about even what languages they are educated in. It certainly happened in Nazi Germany, where clear policies favoring euthanasia and downright extermination of the "defective" people of Jewish descent, and many others, were based on a very clear sense of what the test was, and who passed it. That exceptions were made in the cases of some "exceptional Jews" with influential patrons only made the policy's essentialism less subject to rejection and scrutiny.

Now it appears at first blush as if the problem with such practices is just that the test-makers made a "mistake" in the test, and asked about the "wrong" essential criteria of personhood. But what I infer from insights in David Hume's ontology and epistemological theory and methodology, is that the very notion of a test for something like personhood, and the basic ontology and methodology of a test were fundamentally misguided and based, instead of on truth about essences, upon practices of domination and oppression of those who were never intended to pass the test, or upon a culture- or gender-bound failure to see who or what exists. This phenomenon only first began to drop away from philosophy visibly in the eighteenth century, when liberation movements became a part of the experience of some sensitive philosophers who were also people. "Be a philosopher: But first," Hume said, in the sexist generic sense of his era's language, "be a man." [person][13]

Part II. Hume's Particularized Ontology
Of Actual Existence

A more detailed exploration of arguments supporting my claim that non-essentialist views of personhood are more acceptable to feminists than essentialist ones is a topic for another large discussion. All I intend to establish here in the second part of this essay is:

A.1. That Hume indeed holds a non-essentialist view of personhood, which is nonetheless realistic in ontology; [he holds that there really ARE people in the world, but that people don't know exactly what ultimate essence or necessary features if any make them real]; and

A.2. That Hume's view of personhood has been misinterpreted and that his method or argument for an acceptable, even good, ontological foundation for moral theory has been ignored, because interpreters have seen Hume's work from the standpoint of an understandable essentialist bias, which Hume explicitly disavows.

A.1. Realism Without Essentialism: The Limits of Ontoepistemics

Although David Hume was doubtful about the extent to which people can actually know things for sure, being, as philosopher, an "epistemological skeptic", he was quite commonsensical, being a "moral realist" about what in fact or "really" exists, and that reality can be found in the actual shared, particular experiences different people have of a constantly changing but nonetheless common world. So although Hume wants to show us that people ought never to be arrogant about exactly how much people *know,* he never doubts one thing: that diverse, particular people exist in and through reciprocal recognition with others; and as such, people, not intentions, virtue, and good will or the abstract right, are the first and the only ultimate proper objects of moral concern.

According to Hume's epistemologically informed way of doing moral philosophy, people exist in their concrete complexity, with feelings and reflections. People are not the unified abstractions which are assumed in claims that "The Self" exists and is meaningfully discussable or operative in isolation from context, history, society and place in a culture. In contemporary philosophy the legacy of this Emptiness of Abstraction is the ontological despair in such arguments as Derek Parfit's that philosophy can do away with selves and persons altogether in moral theory. While some moral theorists hang their moral ontologies on such abstract entities as virtue, character, the good, the right, the just, or even (in a Hegelian mode) World Spirit working itself out in the world as self-consciousness and freedom, Hume continues to be fascinated by real people, in all the complexity of their feelings, reasoning, and life projects. It is on people that his theory "hangs," and those who try it out against practice and experience say it fits.

While avoiding "final" definitions of the person in terms of necessary and sufficient conditions, Hume offers numerous insights into the existence and function of personhood, moving beyond a narrow, abstract focus on any posited essence of 'person' as useful theoretical fiction, to what I take to have been a fundamentally new way of approaching personhood.

Drawing on Locke's emphasis on the social nature of the existence of persons, Hume holds that people actually exist through being recognized, recognizing others, or resisting others until they are noticed and recognized. On Hume's analysis[14], the recognition of people occurs through two factors: i) the capabilities of various creatures and peoples for i) a) *resistance* and i) b) *effective expressions of resentment;* and ii) the "natural progress of human sentiments," by which the "boundaries of justice still grow larger."

Rationality is not included here, in Hume's account of how personhood actually works in the world. And it is also difficult to see how i) or ii) could be used as oppressive or exclusive measures or essences, since Hume does not present them as necessary conditions of personhood. Their presence singly or together in a candidate for personhood could be seen as sufficient conditions for the recognition of personhood, but since people do not ordinarily wonder about whether someone is a person, or propose someone as a candidate for personhood, such features merely characterize personhood contingently and variably, and are in some basic sense existentially redundant. That is, people already were open to treating the person as a person when they choose to notice i)a) or i)b) in the behavior or character of the other. They may have found this recognition easier if they perceived the other as like, rather than unlike, themselves. Hence, Hume worries about "too much partiality" in even the finest moral sentiments such as sympathy.

Furthermore, even sufficient condition status for i) or ii) is counter-intuitive, since it is highly doubtful that one person would discount the existence or personhood of another on the basis that they lacked sufficient resistance, resentment, or progress in moral sentiments. On the contrary, having too much resistance, like a hard object or unmovable underground boulder, make something not a person but a thing. Too much sympathy with others, Hume's cardinal moral sentiment, makes us more like a dog or a sentimentalized toy.

In a case of too little sympathy with others, people either try harder to educate the person and persuade them through offering better experiences in life, trying to influence them through role models, or people imprison them or mete out other punishment appropriate to persons. And yet, Hume is correct to describe personhood in terms of i) and ii), since the practice of recognizing personhood can best be characterized in such terms. Hume gives examples of resistance and resentment as well as of degrees and kinds of progress in human sentiments, being especially fascinated by women in not a small percentage of his examples. Usually however, his women friends had property and education, an unusual advantage which Hume recognized as such.

Unlike other male philosophers of his era, Hume observes that in many nations, women are reduced "to like slavery," and are rendered "incapable of all property," as opposed to their masters who, "when united," maintain their severe tyranny by bodily force. With what is apparently over-optimistic zeal born of his limited experience, Hume says in the second *Enquiry,* that in spite of the tyrannical situation in which women find themselves, "such are the insinuation, address, and charms" of men's "fair companions, that women are commonly able to break the confederacy, and share with the other sex in all the rights and privileges of society." In fact, in his essay "Of Moral Prejudice," Hume tells a story of a woman of strong spirit and an uncommon way of thinking, who, possessing property and education, sees herself not as a companion of men but as her own person. Her body becomes a source rather than a resource; and she thus exercises her right, responsibility, and resolve to conceive and educate a child on her own, without the "Tyranny, Inconstancy, Jealousy, or Indifference" of a husband, about which her friends complain. Hume's friend calls her "our philosophical heroine;" and Hume himself indicates that conventional judgment against her counts as moral prejudice. The difficulty is that she is seen as having departed "too far" from the bounds of custom.

In this example and numerous others, the personhood of women and girls is of explicit interest in Hume's ontology, a fact which I take to be neither coincidental nor an exceptional use of examples. Hume makes it clear that women *do* possess the means of expressing resentment and effectively resisting oppression. This is important to his general approach to moral practices because according to Hume, any creature with both rationality and a capacity to "make us feel the effects of their resentment" engages with us in a practice which involves not merely "gentle usage," (the natural virtue of benevolence to other animals[15] or things), but also considerations of "justice", which presuppose personhood.

The unstated systematic exclusion, and upon challenge, *the deletion of women, Blacks, and Native Americans from the ranks or confederacies of standard persons,* is the kind of practice Hume had in mind when he advised that women could overcome "the confederacy" their brothers formed against them, with "such" . . . "insinuation, address, and charms," which would prohibit the "testing" of some by others, for the artificially-created criterion, or the required essentialist criterion of personhood.

If **'person'** is neither an arbitrarily, conventionally used concept or term, nor an entity existing by virtue of a single, exclusive, specifiable essence or set of necessary and sufficient qualities, *without which people do not count or exist as such, what* then *is* **personhood** for Hume? Clearly, since personhood depends upon recognition (or claims to recognition through resistance), personhood exists only in being known by other persons. Knowledge is only worth something if it is based on experience, and reflection in language occurs *after* the fact of initial valuing of experiences and persons enough to name or predicate about them. Thus, the knowledge of persons, and their very existence, occurs only pragmatically, through social interaction, the use of language and imaginative projection, and the reflection on common need.

Personhood requires reciprocity and recognition. It requires an epistemology and a morality, together in practice. Although Hume occasionally talks about a fixed human nature, he clearly does not think human beings can ever adequately know what this nature is, as a whole, or from the outside. Only the contentless laws of reason are knowable in a sense that does not change, for Hume.

In the *Dialogues Concerning Natural Religion,* Hume has one of his characters hypothesize that "the structure of human thought" is similar to "a rotting turnip," a humorous reminder that indeed human minds and persons wane, die, and decompose. But even the variable parts of human nature, or the virtues and qualities, classes, categories, relations, and circumstances of actual people, have no *value* for moral judgment without the introduction of the perceptions and moral sentiments of "intelligent agents" who are "susceptible to those finer sensations."[16]

Like his description of the responses of the architects Palladio and Perrault to queries about descriptions of a building's beauty based on its parts, (viz., that the beauty results only **"when that complicated figure is presented to an intelligent mind," or "spectator,"**) Hume's description of the self or person implies that people are, in some sense, valuable wholes with moral beauty. People exist only through the recognition of other people or a sensitive spectator who can value in the general sense of the second variety of benevolence. And sometimes this recognition must come through vigorous assertion, expressions of resentment and effective resistance by those whom certain biased (by gender or numerous other factors) spectators have not recognized, or do not want to. Hume sees people, today's proper common language plural of "person," as inherently social beings who want to recognize and engage others, regardless of gender, and who want to evaluate their "internal *sentiments*"[17] about people in particular terms not by their property or wealth, but by the sympathetic qualities and virtues of their characters. But this does not imply relativism, since Hume stressed strongly the extent to which people are all similar in having certain moral and other varying sentiments, and the importance of searching for universal principles.

Wanting to found morality on empirical investigations or information concerning what really is the case about different particular people, Hume eschewed abstract essences, but not reality. Although such an approach always runs the twin dangers of being too open-ended, and of ignoring some important particulars, thus drawing at least tentative conclusions which exclude part of reality through an ineluctable ignorance, an approach which insists on universal abstractions as necessary for existence is even more dangerous, since on such a view, one could not even admit that one had left out certain particulars. The omitted particulars simply would not exist, which is something stronger and more exclusive than not being seen. So there are two ways of not seeing. Hume's is correctable. But if people think someone does not exist, then they can, in principle, neither look for her nor see her, except as a mirage or a flight of fancy.

In a Humean world, where liberty can thrive, it is true that while neither men nor women can move around the furniture of the world (prescribe a metaphysics, or whatever fixity exists in nature) members of both genders, all races, and nearly all circumstances have no essence, and, where taken to have significant existence as they assert it and find uptake from the recognition of others, are thus in principle capable of governing their affairs and allegiances, by means of language and mutual recognition, through mutual reflection and assertions of personhood. Because personhood is not a mere fiction or imagined being, but involves sympathetic, experiential, and normative belief in active existence, conceptions of the self and other people are ontologically discussable, real, sensitive, creative, and even revolutionary.

If people can never be known as wholes, completely externally and without any identification or sympathy on the part of the knower, as *mere* objects of study in a science, then to what whole-ness do people belong as selves? One is led to suspect that the only whole entity specifiable is not the individual person at all, since even "mine and thine" make sense logically only against a back-ground assumption of a common or shared good, according to Hume. Rather, the whole which is most real relative to the issue of ontology of personhood is either the whole perception of common people about what is important about personhood, the sort of thing the empirical study I conducted was designed to address,[18] or rather, as a bold conjecture, begging for testing or refutation: per-haps the whole to which human personhood belongs is the commu-nity of all persons, human and otherwise, connected even beyond their deaths [Hume's idea, in the *Treatise*] and possessing remark-ably uniform moral sentiments which are expressed using devices in various languages which signal the universally present judg-ments of moral praise and blame, even amidst great diversity.

Hume's Use of Person In A Refusal To Give A Definition. To charac-terize is not to define: one gives an explicitly tentative or partial pic-ture; the other limits and restricts reference. In a famous passage of the *Enquiry Concerning Human Understanding,*[19] Hume care-fully describes and illustrates, but refuses to *define* the important term "belief":

> Provided we agree about the thing, it is needless to dispute about the terms. The imagination has the command over all its ideas, and can join and mix and vary them, in all the ways possible . . . But its true and proper name . . . is *belief;* which is a term that ev-ery one sufficiently understands in common life.

It is noteworthy that Hume uses illustrations of people reflecting on the existence of other people in two places in this section.

In the instance giving rise to the passage quoted just above, a person believes that another person exists and indeed is present nearby. Hume is illustrating how belief, with the advantage added by a basic sentiment, feeling, or sense of pragmatic value, "distin-guished the ideas of the judgment from the fictions of the imagina-tion," and "gives ideas more weight and influence," "makes them appear of greater importance; informs them in the mind; and ren-ders them the governing principle of our actions." The belief Hume uses is, not coincidentally, the belief that another person is present:

> I hear at present, for instance, a person's voice, with whom I am acquainted; and the sound comes as from the next room. This im-

pression of my sense immediately conveys my thought to the person, together with all the surrounding objects. I paint them out to myself *as existing* at present, [emphasis added] with the same qualities and relations, of which I formerly knew them possessed. These ideas take faster hold of my mind, than ideas of an enchanted castle. They are very different to the feeling, and have a much greater influence of every kind, either to give pleasure or pain, joy or sorrow.[20]

For Hume, as for Bertrand Russell a century and a half later, knowledge by acquaintance is prior to knowledge by description. Ideas of persons have vastly more complexity than those of inanimate objects, and include reciprocity, along with a more complete dependence or interaction with context, which Hume calls "all the surrounding objects." It appears that experience in living with others is what gives this sort of idea a greater "hold" on the mind,—but for all that, it still deserves no more rigid a definition.

This modesty in ontological claims, which Hume called a "mitigated skepticism" is what guided Hume in his misunderstood claims about the "self," that special stand-in for personhood which he makes clear never actually exists without the other. Hume shows us something very important about the limits of language in guiding reason and emotion in moral education or improvement of culture and the common world; namely that what people as individuals or privileged groups call something is of limited ontological validity, just as what people call some entity encountered in ordinary living and in scientific investigation and theorizing alike, and thus infer it to "be," is limited by perceptions, experiences, loves, and languages.

"Self" and "person" are not separable from the language used in the practices of living together and recognizing morally significant features of other human beings, as people attend to the actual projects, feelings, reasoning, and reflections of others. Since language, ontology, and morality are inextricably linked through their mutual development in people, no study of ontology can be prior to the coloring and coding, the shaping and continual re-shaping of morality by language.

If personhood provides the essential (in the sense of "felt-to-be-most-important") element of the ontosophia of moral theory, then attention to language (and translation from natural language into logic, and its many quasi-languages), as it names, recognizes, and manipulates people, is its medium. For all human beings, and especially for women, this attending[21] is a source of liberation and mutual support. Morality is built as people construct, use, and teach the language used in living together. Just as in the Humean metaphor, the building only has value when a spectator is present, so it is only by _attending_ to the connected ontology and morality of personhood and power in language that people can clarify values, reflect on feelings, construct new forms of ontosophia in "insinuation, charms, and address," and generate social action.

A.2. Where Would Essences Be Found In Hume's Moral Ontology?

If a listing of the "essential" features of personhood, those which qualify an entity for just or equal treatment in considerations of justice, (or as "counting," in contemporary talk)[22], can be found anywhere in Hume's great body of work, it would be in places where the term "essential" is used in talk about justice in the _Enquiry Concerning the Principles of Morals:_

> All the laws of nature, which regulate property, as well as all civil laws, are general, and regard alone some essential circumstances of the case, without taking into consideration the characters, situations, and connections of the person concerned, or any particular consequences which may result from the determination of these laws . . . They deprive, without scruple, a beneficent man of all his possessions, if acquired by mistake, without a good title; . . . [_Appendix III._]

Note above that the "case," or legal and civil focus, (not the personhood or character, "situations," and consequences,) is what has "essential circumstances."

At the end of this paragraph, Hume balks at the injustice of legalism in contrast to a person-oriented morality with an outright admission that such general laws, like "even the general laws of the universe, though planned by infinite wisdom, cannot exclude all evil or inconvenience, in every particular operation." He thus admits that although it cannot always be avoided, such _legalism in fact does introduce some "evil or inconvenience," with respect to "the person concerned."_ He goes on to question the assertion that justice arises from conventions, to talk rather about practices from common interest "without any promise or contract," and to comment on the "loose signification" of the word, '_natural._'[23]

It is here that Hume's non-essentialist concept of the self can be used to solve a problem: Peter Winch recently pointed out[24] that unlike social contract theorists, e.g., Locke and Hobbes and Rousseau, Hume did not believe that a common or absolute consent is given to the sovereign or representative sovereign government. And Winch further asked why Hume grounds political allegiance in the same way he grounds personal fidelity: through the morally important social sentiments of people in their practices. Habit, social, economic and political practices, feelings and reasons of actual individual people, not a single agreement once and for all, determine a social order or political commitment.

If it is seen as only the first step, the Humean concept of self in the *Treatise*, (as not immediately presenting a meaningful unity to the same perceiving self), contributes much toward a fuller, socially reciprocal method of exposing and exemplifying the ways in which personhood works in the world: namely, only through mutual recognition and reflection on nearly universal moral sentiments and the correction of reason; and only in a context where human beings live and are aware of their common life together. The Humean approach to personhood might be called, then, a precursor of both existentialist and communitarian thought. The existence of people in a shared life is prior to any essence or contract or right. Certainly this model of lived personhood is close to the actual experience of women in being other-directed, more involved in issues of relatedness and dependency, and having deliberately weaker ego-boundaries, the experience that give rise to much recent feminist thinking on behalf of a morality of care.

In "On Justice," Hume is skeptical about finding "any foundation for the difference made by moral sentiment." It is this "foundation" which might in, say, Kantian and Aristotelian systems, be though to reside in some purported "essence" of the person: in the passion or in reason. Hume is quietly but firmly revolutionary, both about persons and political allegiance, when comparing only the formal, not the material similarities between some sorts of justice and mere superstition about methods of deciding what belongs to whom: [Justice is not frivolous, and is "absolutely requisite to the well-being of mankind and existence of society."]

> The same species of reasoning, it may be thought, which so successfully exposed superstition, is also applicable to justice; nor is it possible, in the one case more than in the other, to point out, the object, that precise quality or circumstance, which is the foundation of the sentiment. [*Enquiry Concerning the Principles of Morals*, Section III. Part II.]

Here, Hume is trying to express the fact that even though justice has a practical necessity and reality where superstition does not, the basis of reasoning about justice and all the rest of moral theory is not a "precise quality or circumstance" which can, in principle, be pinpointed. Rather, the moral sentiments and reasons governing just practices reside in people themselves, and in their community with each other. Truth, condemning superstition and promoting justice, is non-essentialist and non-objective. No one can "point out" that "precise quality or circumstance" which founds the often-shared sense that justice is due. Thus on this view, people cannot point out that someone possesses the essential features of personhood and *for that reason* alone is to be considered as covered by principles under the artifice of justice.

Hume On Practices and Human Nature: Not Essential But Contingent.

> Man is a reasonable being; and as such, receives from science his proper food and nourishment . . . [The human being] is a sociable, no less than a reasonable being . . . [and] an active being; . . . [N]ature has pointed out a mixed kind of life as most suitable to the human race, and secretly admonished them to allow none of these biases to *draw* too much, so as to incapacitate them for other occupations and entertainments.[25]

Human people are reasonable, social, and active (or in contemporary language, have dispositions to be pragmatic and proactive), by nature. But no one human quality ought to dominate exclusively.

Balance and complementarity among features, and not the "subordination," for instance, "of reason to passion," currently disputed by male-gendered philosophers, is what Hume sees and desires to make clear about human nature. And such balance characterizes the eclectic theory of a mature person, not a youth seeking to forge singleness or identity out of the normal *anomie* of young adulthood. Hume did in fact reconcile personal identity "as it regards our thought and imagination, and as it regards our passions and the concern we take in ourselves," (which he appeared to sunder forever in the *Treatise*) in his mature work, into a view of exceptional subtlety and with a much-ignored method which provides a morally adequate ontology of the person upon which to base future moral theories. However, since he was not an essentialist, Hume never laid out a unified theory of personhood.

This fact is a source of great frustration to those who think they have caught in a nutshell Hume's exact theory of the self or the person. Hume thus serves as the precursor of the Wittgensteinian movement which would assert that theories and systems, especially those in thrall to the "bewitchment" of language, are illusory and do not remove the puzzlement philosophers ought to have about such terms as "person." Hume offers only a method for ontological thinking.

It is, above all, the absence of certain assumptions which makes Hume's method attractive: although he is a naive or common sense realist about the world, including people, and although he has what could be called an educated view of nature, including human nature, he is not an essentialist about any of the qualities, features, virtues, conventions or laws which he observes in other people and himself. In a remarkably modern scientific or empirical stance, he does not assume that whatever virtues, qualities, powers, strength, or regularities he finds are eternal or essential, or that, without context or reflection, these features determine or explain all human behavior and moral judgments.

Conclusion

A non-essentialist method and ontology provides the only acceptable foundation for an adequate feminist moral theory[26], given two factors: human fallibility in knowing essences, and the systematic oppression of women and others which is inextricable from an essentialist moral ontology used by those in positions of power to shape language and legality in any society.[27] As Hume first suggested, personhood is not the sort of thing which is subject to a test for an "essence." Any adequate moral theory should take account of this.

Such a non-essentialist approach as Hume first offered gives up rigid, essentialist, and grossly incompatible exemplars of personhood used on at least two opposing and non-communicating sides of the abortion debates whose proponents cannot live together peaceably: For example, 1) an embryo or conceptus having merely an "essential" human genetic code and on that basis alone a purported positive right to life,—and somewhat implausibly to the resources needed to continue a life not yet recognizable as that of a person or capable of mutual recognition or reciprocal altruism,—versus 2) an adult human being with reason, emotion, and verbal communication, demanding negative rights "to be left alone:" to the privacy and exercise of her reproductive rights and responsibilities. Because of essentialism on both sides, the abortion debate is insoluble as it stands, without assistance from such alternative approaches to personhood as Hume's way provides.

In exchange for forcing us to give up the rigidly contentious paradigms of personhood which fuel the nastiness and insolubility of current debates on reproductive rights and responsibilities, feminist, pluralist, or Wittgensteinian approaches to personhood based on Hume's method perform a crucially important task: they maintain the importance of the essentially contested concept of personhood and its foundational role in moral theory, as the place-holder for both passive and pro-active sympathy and revolt, the necessary and liberating resistance and expressions of resentment due to oppression. The most singular advantage of this approach and the implied practices is that like good parents, they are firm but not dogmatic. The Humean view of personhood is fallibilist in the best sense, resisting pre-judgment of the content or test of personhood in terms of deterministic biological or social essences, functions, or roles.

Notes

1. I am grateful to my editor, Bat-Ami Bar On, for close criticism of several drafts of this work. Marilyn Frye, Alison Jaggar, Marilyn Friedman, Linda McAlister, Terry Winant, Ruth Ginsberg, Sandra Coyner, and numerous other members of the Midwest and Eastern Regions of the Society for Women in Philosophy attended presentations of early versions of this work, and to each of them I am grateful for stimulation and constructive feminist critiques of the whole project of the critical historical grounding of my study of the definition and use of concepts of personhood. John Exdell and Anita Superson devoted considerable time to reading my longer manuscript on Hume and made many helpful suggestions. Lois Bassett Pineau read and commented on an abstract of this paper, providing valuable insights. Annette Baier and Alise Carse are heartily thanked for encouraging comments.

2. This ontological problem, clearly seen in tendencies in any language using noun phrases or expressions which signify an existence claim, causes oppression unavoidably, since language must use ontologies which are rarely fully specifiable in discourse. The term "ontology" is derived directly from koine Greek, in what appears to be an unbroken line, through medievals and continental philosophers, as well as those who used the term "ontosophia" to designate experienced wisdom about ontos or what is. "Essences," in such approaches to ontology as Husserl's, are acceptable en-

tities because they are not *de re,* but concern the human *concept* of, e.g., personhood, after eidetic variations occur. I thank Linda Patrik, who chaired the session of the Eastern Division of the Society for Women in Philosophy in the Fall of 1989 for reconfirming the validity of my position that Husserlian essences are of the right sort, not essentialist in the negative sense which I employ here.

3. I am grateful for information and interesting insights gleaned from research on location in Scotland, provided by Patricia Ward Scaltsas of Edinburgh University, who was visiting at Rutgers and presented her paper "Women as Ends—Women As Means In the Enlightenment" at the same session at which I presented my paper on the "Three R's in Hume's Moral Ontology": at the Fall Meeting of the Society for Women in Philosophy, Eastern Division, University of Massachusetts at Amherst, October 21st, 1989. Any errors resulting from my interpretation of Scaltsas' careful reports concerning the cataloguing of Estell's work are entirely my own.

4. An important articulation of difficulties with essentialism, both in feminism and in phallist Western philosophy, has been achieved by Elizabeth V. Spelman in *Inessential Woman,* (Boston: Beacon Press, 1988). Although I do not say this "as a woman,"—the phrase Spelman calls the Trojan Horse of feminist ethnocentrism, a woman gendered member of the academic proletariat will find something different to be essential to her well-being and that of her community than any ontological essence can express. It is in becoming, recognizing differences with respect but not always merging, and questioning who and what is real, that any intelligent, truly alive creature survives.

5. The definition of "nature" is a wonderful philosophical problem which deserves much attention. It will have to suffice here to define "nature" as I find Hume used it, as "created and evolved uses." Thus the term "nature" mixes realist and operational definition, avoiding fixity or a static meaning, but denoting something real and not of human making. Our natures as human beings thus were both created, or given, and also changing or changeable by us, through reconceptualization or a change in practices, sentiments, and reasoning. Like our personhood in Hume, nature is real but does not need to be conceived in essentialist terms (as having fixed or eternal necessary and sufficient conditions), being strongly influenced in its existence by the perceptions and uptake or recognition of others.

6. Considerable support exists for this view of Hume, for instance in Alasdair MacIntyre's *Whose Justice: Which Rationality?,* (Notre Dame, Indiana: University of Notre Dame Press, 1988) where MacIntyre argues that what was important to Hume was the existence of particular individuals in a distinctive social order, and not merely a generic individual in a loose abstract or modern classical "liberal" sense. The person is for Hume inherently a particular, and it is with these particulars that Hume is preoccupied rather than with fixed, universal and context-less essences.

People have unique histories or contexts, as well as shared and reciprocal but particular social and cultural beliefs. When those taking "the standpoint of the forums of modern liberal culture" presuppose "the irrelevance of one's history to one's status as a participant in debate," they fail to attend to the importance of individual differences and individual people, confronting one another, as MacIntyre says, "in such forums abstracted from and deprived of the particularities of our histories." See especially pages 400 and 290–297.

7. A good example of the symptoms of essentialism is the title applied by Editor John Perry to three excerpts from Hume: "The Abandonment of Personal Identity," in Perry's *Personal Identity,* (Berkeley: University of California Press, 1975), pp. 157–176. In work of noted and respected commentators on Hume, for instance those in Amelie Oksenberg Rorty's *The Identities of Persons,* (Berkeley: University of California Press, 1976), and in particular in the work of Terence Penelhum, such statements as "Hume says three times what the self is," are characteristic of essentialist expectations. [Terence M. Penelhum, University of Calgary. "The Self in Hume's Philosophy. *in David Hume: Many Sided Genius,* Kenneth R. Merrill and Robert W. Shahan, Eds., Norman: University of Oklahoma Press, 1976.] That Penelhum says the following shows that, like many others, he seeks an essence: that which is by "nature" "the same" in each person: "for the mechanism of sympathy . . . to operate, each of us has to be aware that every other person is a person like himself; but the theory does not help us to spell out the nature of that which is thought to be the same in each one." [Penelhum, in Perry, Ed., p. 258.]

8. Again see MacIntyre, whose words are quoted here, from *Whose Justice? Which Rationality?.*

9. This view is consistent with recent research findings in the experimental social and psychological sciences which would have interested Hume. Indeed, ordinary people rarely question who counts as a person, or how to apply the various philosophical candidates for necessary and sufficient conditions of personhood. They consider it a "strange question" to ask. See my *Concepts of Personhood and the Quality of Care in Clinical Practice.* (unpublished manuscript as of 2/90, available from the author or through Dissertation Abstracts International, Ann Arbor, Michigan. June, 1987.)

10. The same sort of critic discounts Hume's whole theory of morality as well, of course, leaping in to swim in vain after the moral ontology which I maintain Hume's moral theory presupposes, never seeing that they have seen only the tip of the ontological iceberg, as it were. Thus they also miss the fullness of his emphasis on reason and the complexity of personal relations, the passions, and moral judgment. Such people are "merely sympathetic" with what they take to characterize Hume's moral theory sufficiently: only that it is, they think, "based on sympathy and benevolence;" and so they search in the moral theories of those better-read moral philos-

ophers who appear to them to provide "fuller" theories, ones which "see morality as involving an astute management of less attractive feelings." But Hume was already far beyond these concerns in his moral development, and indeed has a full blown theory of moral psychology and a moral ontology which is more than adequate, and more adequate than that of his contemporaries who read Hume and wrote after him, e.g., Kant, who appears to stress personhood but never gives us any help beyond a stipulative, abstract definition in term of "rationality," in deciding who counts as a Kantian person.

11. "Phallist" is the term coined by Marilyn Frye for the tendency to mistake one part of the human race for the whole. See pages 155 ff. of Frye's *The Politics of Reality:* Essays in Feminist Theory, (Freedom, California: The Crossing Press, 1983), for a very clear account of "Phallocentric Reality" and men's conceptions of women as "not authoritative perceivers." Epistemology [how people see things] and ontology [what people see or think they are seeing] are connected, if people have enough self-consciousness to distinguish their tools and means from the realities beyond their touch, and then enough courage or experience to reconnect a tool and that which was beyond its touch. But that women are "seeing something from a different point of view, and hence simply seeing something he cannot see," is a hypothesis many men and women ignore.

12. It is not merely coincidental that Hume often used autonomous women in his illustrations and examples at important places in his discussions. Although he fell victim to a mild version of "exceptionalism" in knowing and portraying rather exceptional or "Superwomen" in his examples, he appears to have been fully cognizant of the fact that most women of his time has neither the leisure nor the wealth to have careers outside the home. And yet he appeared to respect and explicitly praised nurturant work such as child care by both parents, often referring to the moral sentiments and nurturant practices of men as well as women. Hume was raised by a single mother and her friends.

13. For a somewhat outdated collaboration on feminist views of Hume, see Steven A. Macleod Burns and Louise Marcil-Lacoste, "Hume on Women: I. The Humean Female; and II. Hume's Moral Method," in *The Sexism of Social and Political Theory:* Women and Reproduction from Plato to Nietzsche, Edited by Lorenne M. G. Clark and Lynda Lange. (Toronto: University of Toronto Press, 1979), pp. 53–73. The authors have a slight tendency to quote Hume out of context, pointing out sexist assumptions in what Hume was clearly reporting descriptively about his times, often with implied protests against legalism.

14. At the end of Section II, Part I of Hume's *Enquiry Concerning the Principles of Morals,* "On Justice," Hume discusses human nature. Here, if anywhere, would be found "the essence" that in virtue of which people have

moral standing. Justice is after all not meted out to non-existent people, but always and only to those who have certain modes of legal or social existence.

15. The clear contrast that emerges when one refers to human beings, and/or the non-equivalent "persons" as opposed to "other animals" is interesting. Something like Janice Moulton's argument about the mythical gender neutrality of "man" could be developed concerning the mythical (but perhaps desirable) species-neutrality of "person" in most of its uses, as well as the objectivity of claims about human beings, who cannot properly be judged or viewed "from outside."

16. [*Concerning Moral Sentiment,* Appendix I to the second *Enquiry,* III.] Note that this term, "intelligent agent" is also Locke's. Daniel Dennett unlike other contemporary writers on Locke, Hume, and personhood, cites in his "Conditions of Personhood," (anthologized in several places, including his *Brainstorms*), the most significant portion of Locke's text; in that most expressive of Locke's passages, on what Dennett calls the moral and metaphysical aspects of Lockean persons, is found the discussion of what is now called "moral ontology," after David Fate Norton. The Locke passage characterizes "person" as a forensic term, {having to do with legal or civil debate}, which "applies to intelligent agents, capable of a law," and of happiness and misery.

17. It is not the *people* who are valued or ranked in the relativistic or ordinal ranking, according to wealth or position; but rather, the spectator's own "internal sentiments," are reflexively evaluated "regulated by the personal characters of men" more than by "the accidental and capricious favors of fortune." See the end of Section VI, Part II, "Of Qualities Immediately Agreeable To Ourselves," *Enquiry Concerning the Principles of Morals.*

18. Merrill, Sarah A. Bishop, M.S., Ph.D. *Defining Personhood: Distinctive Features Related to the Quality of Clinical Care.* University Microfilms International, Ann Arbor, Michigan, 1987.

19. Section V, Part II.

20. Ibid.

21. For a thorough discussion of "attending," see recent work by Sarah Lucia Hoagland, in *Lesbian Ethics,* Palo Alto, Calif.: The Institute of Lesbian Studies, 1988.

22. I do not mean to conflate the ontological and political sense of "count" here: clearly, the ontological must be primary in a logical sense, and is my major source of wonder here. But because people tend to see what they want or need to see, for political and other humanly-interested reasons, what IS often takes a back seat to WHO is important politically. This tendency represents a natural fall-back to the earlier authoritarian and

aristocratic days of human social and political life, before the modern age of individualism. I am grateful to John Exdell for pointing out to me this fact: that many people, in examining the question of "who counts," will jump immediately to the political sense, (a sense which asks "who gets a share of the resources?" or "whose needs count in our political distributions and uses of power?"). This jump from the ontological to the political results, perhaps, from the often necessary habit of taking a position of advocacy rather than from a more abstract desire to come closer to knowing the truth about the other beings or kinds of existence in the world. Both are good, but ontology is prior.

23. In this passage is found what I call Hume's first and most genuinely believed concept of justice, that of justice as care or particularized sympathy.

24. Winch gave the talk I refer to at Kansas State University in the Spring of 1989. I thank Benjamin Tilghman and the Philosophy Department for inviting Peter Winch to Kansas.

25. [An Enquiry Concerning Human Understanding, Section I, Paragraph 6. The rest of the quotation supports my claims that Hume is interested in human liberation, not in polite and conventional treatment of our topic: " . . . [L]et your science be human, and such as may have a direct reference to action and society . . . All polite letters are nothing but pictures of human life in various attitudes and situations; they inspire us with different sentiments, according to the qualities of the object, which they set before us."

26. There is another reason justifying the claim that only a nonessentialist method provides an adequate moral ontology to ground a feminist moral theory. This reason is that feminism may be what has been called an essentially contested concept [ECC], the essence of which, like that proposed for "democracy" and "the true religion," will and should never be finally settled. Rather, as pragmatist scholar W. B. Gallie has argued, debate which is vigorous and openly defensive or recognizes clearly an opposing definition or practice, only serves to improve such concepts [if they are indeed ECC's], as well as the practices which are guided by them.

27. In such ontology, there is a "test" for personhood, invented by the very people who have vested interests and a power structure which discourages the inclusion of others or encourages them to live in what Sartre called "bad faith," thinking "the test" for their role or objectification is the only and proper tool to assess "what there is to" meaningful existence. David Hume's ontology is not essentialist in this sense.

PART THREE

THEMES OF MODERNITY:
THE CONTINENTAL TRADITION

Women and Rousseau's Democratic Theory: Philosopher Monsters and Authoritarian Equality

Lynda Lange

This essay is a feminist critique of the political philosophy of Jean-Jacques Rousseau, and by extension, that of some other reputedly democratic theorists. My critique proceeds, of necessity, from my own interpretation of Rousseau's political thought, which I present briefly. This is especially necessary in the case of Rousseau, since extant interpretations of him are so diverse—he even shares with Hegel the distinction of having both left and right interpretors politically. In my view, Rousseau found in the ancients, and most especially Plato, a way of thinking that grounded his criticism of modern individualism and rational egoism. I concede that Rousseau is a "democratic" thinker, even though he was not democratic with respect to women. As a democratic thinker, he falls in the geneology of those who espouse what may be called "authoritarian equality".

The analysis also proceeds from a feminist critique of dualism.[1] The critique of dualistic forms of thinking—for example, "the political" versus "the personal", "the public" versus "the private", "reason" versus "emotion", "the universal" versus "the particular", etc., and the claim that they are a specifically male form of thinking, has been a strong theme of feminist theory for the past several years. Without addressing the general feminist claim on this occasion, the argument of this paper is meant to show in detail how one particular political philosopher, Jean-Jacques Rousseau, is both a dualistic thinker and fundamentally male biased.

Rousseau's view of the social relations of the sexes, and the necessity for women to play a feminine role within the family, has been presented and analyzed by a number of feminist authors.[2] While my analysis is in some ways complimentary to that of Okin, Lloyd, and Pateman, it differs from them on other points, and adds new points. Rousseau is one of the few political theorists who attempts what feminist theory attempts, which is to understand the connections between politics and economics on the one hand, and family and sexual life on the other. I argue that in this attempt, Rousseau accords subtle and self-consistent theoretical functions to the male-headed family and the subordination of women within it. In other words, however much we may disagree with him, he is actually self-consistent in his treatment of women, rather than fundamentally inconsistent, as other feminist criticisms have suggested. This self-consistency will turn out to be a more serious indictment of his theory than inconsistency would be, since inconsistency may suggest the possibility of repair.

It is clear that Rousseau believed sexual inequality to be a necessary feature of a good civil society. It is a different point to argue that the structure of his theory really does imply a necessity for the social subordination of women. According to the "democratic" Rousseau, the differences of sex and gender are basic to his thought. It follows that sexual inequality could not simply be excised, and the comprehensive nature of Rousseau's political theory preserved, without so many further changes being needed that the theory might as well be called new theory, rather than revisionist Rousseauean theory. It will be argued that sexual inequality in Rousseau's political thought has its philosophical roots in the same places as the ideas of his which are presently deemed to be the most valuable and unique. This critique is important, not only because of Rousseau's enormous influence on the the shape and course of the Revolution in France (a "revolution" which may have been more politically regressive for women than otherwise[3]), but also because his image of the good woman remains recognizable now, to feminists as something to combat, to others as a plausible image to theorize upon.[4] Unlike Okin, who argues that "he is [. . .] representative of the whole Western tradition regarding women,"[5] I believe that his influence in this area is largely derived from the fact he brilliantly renewed this tradition by re-casting it in specifically modern terms.[6]

Rousseau falls in a tradition of thought concerning human nature and rationality that has historically always been used to defend social hierarchy, in spite of the fact that it also always presents itself as universal. Concepts of uniquely human, transcendent, rationality, have served to divide humans into two shifting groups, the rational versus the non-rational or sub-rational. The philosophic details of the meaning of "transcendent rationality" have varied, but it always exemplifies what Alison Jaggar calls "normative dualism",[7] and it is those deemed rational who are said to be best fitted to govern or control the others. As political theory has in broad outline become more democratic with the passing centuries, the subset of those attributed with the highest type of rationality has grown larger. Most notably, it has come to include all "non-deviant" men, and this is what has counted as "democratic" theory.

A major change of this sort occurred with the work of Rousseau. He turned the tradition of non-instrumental or transcendent rationality to the defense of the equality of all males, by means of an impressive re-conceptualization of it in terms of the social structure and the real good of a nation. The common good is held by Rousseau to be an objective reality, whether or not the majority knows it or appreciates it. This good is most likely to be apprehended by citizens of a certain character and capacity. This in turn requires proper education, and above all equality, in the sense of freedom from dependence on others. For Rousseau, a democratic majority vote does not, in itself, reveal any sort of truth about what should be done. It is merely the most likely means of discovering the general will. This theory enabled Rousseau to go beyond the form of individualist instrumental reason based on rational egoism, while at the same time dispensing, in true modern fashion, with a complicated metaphysical structure, or the authority of the divine will in politics. This explains what to some is the puzzling presence of the elitist "Legislator" in Rousseau's thought. The Legislator is a variant of Plato's "philosopher monarch", one whose personal qualities enable him wisely to see what is for the people's good, whether the people themselves see it or not. It also helps to explain why Rousseau himself considered the exclusion of women from the democratic process self-consistent. He believed that their exclusion from the assembly of male citizens was most conducive to the discovery of the common good. This is because, according to Rousseau, the presence of women tends to generate *amour propre* among males—comparison, vanity, competition, hostility—all, he argues, inimical to the discovery of truth. The transcendent nature of "the general will" as an ideal of reason, paradoxically, does not rule out exclusion from Rousseauean democratic process, even with the proviso of equality, and in spite of his claim to the contrary.

"Le corps moral et collectif" which is created by the social compact, is a rational being, with a will, which by its very nature is not the aggregate of particular desires, but a single will, the will of the people. The ideal point of view of the citizen, per se, is, therefore, that of the general will, and not that of his individual interest in relation to the rest of society. This requires the ability to transcend

one's own particular will and desire. Since willing participation in
the general will is what is meant by liberty, compulsion of an individual to obey the general will, should that be necessary, can be
called, consistently, "forcing him to be free". It is the operation of
the general will that alone can save individuals from the personal
dependence of inequality and enslavement to appetite or desire.

The problem with various concepts of transcendent rationality,
from the point of view of democratic theory, therefore, is not just
with the scope of their application but with the nature of the concepts themselves. From the perspective of feminist theory, Rousseau's concept of rationality is an intellectual fiat, which virtually
entails the social inferiority of women.

Rousseau's is emphatically not a liberal theory. It is a modern
variant on a theme dating back to ancient Greek thought, and perhaps prophetic of the authoritarian democracies of the twentieth
century. This ancient view of uniquely human potential—the ideal
of self-government by knowledge and transcendent reason—is always limited to an elite. There is little question that historically
this view has also been associated with normative dualism.

There is textual evidence that Rousseau was a dualist, and further, that his dualism is directly related to the central features of
his moral and political philosophy. For example, the notion of the
general will acting to force the particular individual to be free, fits
the image of the recalcitrance of the particular will and passions
even in the face of "the light of reason". The valourization of this
struggle is a strong element in this tradition.

According to Rousseau, the characteristics that distinguish humanity from other animals are "perfectibility" (the capacity to
change and progress, to have a history), and the quality of being a
free agent. "Nature commands every animal and the beast obeys",
Rousseau writes in the *Second Discourse,* but "Man feels the same
impetus but he realizes that he is free to acquiesce or resist". The
continuation of this passage displays mind-body dualism clearly:

> It is above all in the consciousness of this freedom that the spiri-
> tuality of his soul is shown. For physics explains in some way the
> mechanism of the senses and the formation of ideas; but in the
> power of willing, or rather of choosing, and in the sentiment of this
> power, are found only purely spiritual acts about which the laws of
> mechanics explain nothing.[8]

Rousseau had no detailed philosophy of mind. As a result, I am
using "dualism" to mean only the general view that the mental and

the physical are different logical catagories, and that the mind is a qualitatively different sort of thing from the body, not governed by its laws, and not confined by its limitations. The body, on this reading, is the category of the "merely" natural, what we may share with animals, whereas reason is transcendent. Ideas such as the Platonic Forms, and the General Will, are purely mental objects. In the history of thought, they are also considered *superior* objects, inasmuch as only human beings who actualize the highest human potential are thought to have them as intentional objects, and these human beings are superior to all other forms of life (or so philosophers have been wont to believe . . .).

There is an alternative view of this. According to Genevieve Lloyd, Rousseau did not espouse a dualism of mind and body, or reason and nature, like that of the Cartesians. In Rousseau, closeness to nature is the mark of what is true in reason, and therefore "Reason is held in check by Nature". In Rousseau, Lloyd claims, (in my view correctly) that "male stands to female in the idealized relation of Reason to Nature".[9] This aspect of Rousseau's philosophy is usually the basis of the strong claim made by Rousseau, and by many a follower since, that this view of the relation of the sexes is not one of dominance or oppression, but one of benign complementarity most conducive to the happiness of both sexes. I argue, however, that this is still dualism, and still one-sided. In Rousseau, reason takes the determining role of reflection and evaluation, and it appears that nature (especially human nature) needs the most careful guidance to *be* what it truly is. Since only those of sublime rationality and virtue can pronounce what nature truly requires (great Legislators and philosophers, for example), *idealized* nature is also a purely mental object. Reason always have, so to speak, the last word. As the dominant husband is held in check by his tender, submissive, wife, according to Rousseau, just as effectively, I say, is reason held in check by nature.[10] The distinction between Rousseau's nuanced philosophy of the relation between reason and nature, and other forms of dualism, are from a feminist point of view, largely a distinction without a difference.

The relation of mind-body dualism to political philosophies of right is often one of direct analogy. This is obviously true of Plato's *Republic,* for example, where the function of the guardian class in the city is very closely analogous to the function of the mind in the individual guardian. I suggest that this is also true of Rousseau's "body politic", in the organic analogy of the state to a living body which he employs. The point of the organic analogy seems chiefly to

establish the identity of interest of all parts of the nation, and demonstrate that "total alienation" to the state of one's person and
goods does not imply sacrifice of authentic self-interest. For example, in *Political Economy,* he writes:

> It is no more credible that the general will would allow any mem-
> ber of the State, whoever he might be, to injure or destroy another,
> than it is that the fingers of a reasoning man would put out his
> own eyes.[11]

The dualism is apparent when he writes not only of a purely
organic unity, but also of the unity of *le corps moral et collectif,*
formed by the fundamental social compact. This might more accurately be called "the person politic", rather than "the body politic",
since it is an abstract moral entity whose existence is purely the result of human artifice and convention. For example, in the *Geneva
Manuscript* in the chapter on sovereignty, Rousseau writes:

> Just as the action of the soul on the body with respect to man's
> constitution is unfathomable in philosophy, so the action of the
> general will on the public force with respect to the constitution of
> the State is unfathomable in politics.[12]

The "moral person" of the State also possesses the essentially
human faculty of free choice. In *On the Social Contract,* Rousseau
writes:

> Every free action has two causes that combine to produce it. One is
> moral, namely the will that determines the act; the other is phys-
> ical, namely the power that executes it. [. . .] The body politic has
> the same motivating causes; force and will are distinguishable
> within it in the same sense, the latter under the name legislative
> power, and the former under the name executive power.[13]

The free acts of the body politic are acts of legislation, in which,
ideally, the input of particular bodily or emotional desires is zero.

It is often helpful in determining the significance of an historically important idea, to ask what it was meant to explain, and/or
what difficulty it was meant to resolve. What is accomplished by
this dualism? First of all, as I have suggested above, it is part of the
attempt to make the transcendence of egoistic self-interest rational,
and not just gratuitous self-sacrifice. Its use in political philosophy

is to escape the individualistic subjectivity of self-interest that generates the necessary opposition of the powers of individuals, and hence creates conflictual individualistic politics. Rousseau's intention is to ground the common good objectively by means of his distinction between the particular or private will, and the general will. The common good, once again, is a mental object available only to those of the highest rationality and virtue. Majoritarian, participatory, politics, are proferred as the most likely means of achieving this understanding, but the truth of the common good in Rousseau is not determined in this way.

These efforts to establish objectivity, the reality of a common good, and hence a non-conflictual common interest, are only necessary, because of the undeniable existence of conflicts of particular or private interest in civil society as it has existed. They are irrelevant, for example, in Rousseau's state of nature, and in the early "golden age" of savagery. A dualistic philosophy is used to explain the ongoing tension within civil society between individual interests or preferences, and the common good, as well as the breakdown of good civil societies. This is a further aspect of a dualistic view of human nature, wherein appetite can never be eliminated, but ought to be controlled and channelled by reason. The acknowledgement of this ongoing tension is evident in Rousseau when he writes that:

> . . . each individual can, as a man, have a private will contrary to or differing from the general will he has as a citizen. His private interest can speak to him quite differently from the common interest.[14]

It is in the paragraph immediately following this where he writes:

> Therefore, in order for the social compact not to be an ineffectual formula, it tacitly includes the following engagement, which alone can give force to the others: that whoever refuses to obey the general will shall be forced to be free.[15]

Thus this philosophy provides not only a standard for the resolution of such conflicts between private interest and the common good as continue to arise, it provides legitimation for the suppression of dissent. Those whose particular wills conflict with the general will may be inadequate in one or more ways. Either they are not sufficiently rational, or they have not learned to control the passions of

their particular will. In the case of women, they have not understood their duties according to nature. (Indeed, how could they
when, in spite of being the human representatives of Nature they
are excluded from discourse *about* Nature?) This provides the state
with at least a *prime facie* justification for coercion in all cases of
individual dissent from the general will.

The dualistic distinction between the general and the particular will which performs so many important functions in Rousseau's
theory is also implicit in the distinction between familial or private
life on the one hand, and citizenship or public life on the other.

Although male adults are members of a collectivity, and pursue
"the general will" and "the common good" as citizens, it is clear, as
we have seen, that they can, and do, have an individual, particular
will as well. In fact, Rousseau believes that abstract generalities
concerning citizenship are useless in the maintenance of a good
state without a developmental foundation in particular affective relationships, and subsequent personal attachment to one's fellow citizens. In Book V of *Emile* (his answer to Book V of Plato's *Republic*),
he argues that the identity of interest as brothers and sisters of Plato's guardians is impossible without their having had any experience as members of a family. According to Rousseau, the family is
essential as a nursery of good citizens, even though the perspective
of the citizen must transcend that of a family member. Thus, in
spite of the fact that private interest and the common good are "mutually exclusive in the natural order of things",[16] controlled and
channelled private interest and affect are actually essential to a
good state.

I think that Plato's elimination of the family in the guardian
class is designed to deal with the selfsame problem of the conflict
between particular interest and objectivity in ruling.[17] Plato's theory of justice, involving the prototypical version of what I have
called "transcendent rationality", demands harmonious governance
by reason. Plato assigns all the functions of particularity to the
classes under the authority of the guardians, including child care
and provision for all of the guardians' practical needs, so as to eliminate the potential sources of conflict within and between the
guardians, who are the bearers of reason. This solution is not available to Rousseau, who has argued most forcefully for the equality of
all adult male citizens. Rousseau has not entirely superceded the
inner logic of Plato's solution, however. I argue that he has taken
Plato's pyramid-shaped hierarchy, and, so to speak, has flattened it
out into a one-tiered hierarchy of men over women.

Since the private interest generated by sociability remains ineliminable in Rousseau, the problem becomes that of establishing an avenue for its legitimate expression—a problem Rousseau shares with theoretical individualism. There are not many candidates for this avenue, and the overwhelming favorite in modern individualistic theory has been private property. Of course, it is misleading to put it that way, for it is more likely the case that the necessity to provide moral justification for the market form of private property was the occassion for the development of the concept of practical reason based on egoistic self-interest, rather than the reverse.

Rousseau, however, does not provide moral justification for unlimited accumulation of private property. In the good civil society, state authority should intervene in the distribution of private property in the interest of maintaining rough economic equality. In Rousseau, economic equality is a structural requirement of the theory of political right. Although he deems private property "a sacred right", its sacredness is derived from its function as the preserver of individual (male) autonomy, and not from the abhorrence of authoritative redistribution of acquired property characteristic of liberal individualist theory. In Rousseau, there is therefore no avenue for citizens for the legitimate expression of strictly individual self-interest except affective relations in the private family and its share of goods. Since its share of goods is carefully metered by the general will and state intervention, there is correspondingly more weight on affective relations.

It may be pointed out at this stage that "a family", in the sense of "a circle of intimates committed to one another", is not of necessity a biological, to say nothing of a patriarchal, unit. It could in principle be a group of people united over time on some other basis, such as preference, legal contract, or other understanding. However, within Rousseau's model of the good civil state, the family must be both biological and patriarchal, in order to fulfill its theoretical functions.

Rousseau's model of a good civil society requires the family as a "natural base", upon which are established conventional (or as Rousseau would be likely to say, "artificial") political ties.[18] However, it is the male citizen specifically who requires this base, for it is *his* attachment to the interest of the state and his fellow citizens that is at issue. The difficulty with this for Rousseau is that the relation of fatherhood is itself more "artificial" than natural.

To begin with, Rousseau himself suggests in the *Second Discourse* that recognition of fatherhood requires a degree of knowledge and foresight he absolutely rules out in the state of nature. Rousseau writes that settling in permanent shelters was a "first revolution" out of the pure state of nature, giving rise to "the sweetest sentiments known to man: conjugal love and paternal love."[19] Since women are assumed to have been rearing children to independence prior to these developments, maternal love was not a development out of this first revolution. Therefore, it must be the case that there is a qualitative difference between these two forms of attachment. Whereas maternal love occurs naturally, and is not uniquely human, paternal love is uniquely human, because it is based on knowledge. The knowledge required is that of authenticated biological paternity. Something is needed to particularize the relation of father to child, and to give some reason for caring for *this* child, rather than some other child, no child, or children in general. The mother, on the other hand, has immediate awareness of her relation to the child, since it emerges from her body. The particularity of the father's relation to the child, therefore, depends on the establishment of a means whereby it can be tied to the particularity of the mother's relation to the child. Failing this, the father-child relation would not only be, but also appear clearly to be, purely conventional. It could not, therefore, be "a natural base" for the development of *amour de la patrie*. The relation would not have its unique quality of being simultaneously a natural and a conventional social bond. The father needs a link to the particularity of the mother-child relation to tie him to any particularity at all. As Rousseau puts it:

> She serves as the link between the children and their father; she alone makes him love them and gives him the confidence to call them his own.[20]

Female monogamy is the only possible means for achieving this. Yet fathers always remain precariously close to being pure artifacts of social relations. Centuries of legal practice have not come down to a better definition of a "father" (i.e., one having a father's rights and duties) than the biologically arbitrary stipulation that "the father" is "the husband of the mother". The legal convention of fatherhood would therefore be meaningless without social practices designed to make it a reality. As Rousseau notes in Book V of *Emile,* "a child would have no father if every man could usurp a father's rights."[21] It is from this requirement that the domestic retirement of women, which Rousseau advocates so strongly, arises. The education of women, which is focussed on the themes of modesty and responsibility, is meant to prepare women for voluntary pursuit of this life. This is consistent with Rousseau's view that a good civil society ultimately depends on correct education, since egoistic individuals will always find ways to circumvent mere force. The "biological/conventional" family, that is, the family which is presented as a natural, biological, unit, but is in a crucial respect really a conventional unit, appears to be very fragile. The fact that it really does hinge on the woman's sexual behavior, may account partly for the passionate, even semi-hysterical, nature of Rousseau's insistence on the woman's responsibility. (The rest of the account is probably best left to psychoanalysis !) He writes in the *Emile:*

> If there is a frightful condition in the world, it is that of an unhappy father who, lacking confidence in his wife, does not dare to yield to the sweetest sentiments of his heart, who wonders, in embracing his child, whether he is embracing another's, the token of his dishonor, the plunderer of his own childrens' property. What does the family become in such a situation, if not a society of secret enemies whom a guilty woman arms against one another in forcing them to feign mutual love.[22]

The moral end of a woman in civil society, within Rousseau's model, is incompatible with that of a citizen. It is to affirm and maintain particular relations, rather than to strive for generality. The dualistic polarity between the particular will and the general will means that any individual who is in theory primarily devoted to particularity, cannot exercise the high form of transcendent rationality needed to participate in the general will. To do so one must be able to govern and deny one's own particularity, and that of others, impartially. But according to Rousseau, to turn away from her particular family in favor of any other concern, is the worst possible immorality for a woman. More importantly for Rousseau's theory, the citizen with the requisite sort of rationality cannot be sustained (even as a mere idea!) without his complement who is devoted to the concrete world of particularity.

A father, of course, also has duties to his family, but as father and as citizen he operates on two distinct sets of principles, and acts as a mediator between the two spheres. In the course of distinguishing between the "natural" association of the patriarchal family, and the human artifice of "public reason," Rousseau writes:

> . . . while nature's voice is the best advice a father can heed to fulfill his duties, for the magistrate it is a false guide, working continuously to separate him from his people, and bringing him sooner or later to his downfall or to that of the State unless he is restrained by the most sublime virtue.[23]

The citizen must be able in cases of conflict to distinguish between the distinct forms of practical reason appropriate to familial and political life, and be willing to sacrifice the former to the latter.

With respect to motherhood, Rousseau gives a dramatic and frightening example in *Emile* of what he believes these choices may be like. He writes:

> A Spartan woman had five sons in the army and was awaiting news of the battle. A Helot arrives; trembling, she asks him for news. "Your five sons were killed." "Base slave, did I ask you that ?" "We won the victory." The mother runs to the temple and gives thanks to the gods. This is the female citizen.[24]

In view of a standard of citizenship such as this, it is understandable that there ought to be someone who is exclusively devoted to the particular members of the family. It is not surprising that Rousseau is a famous champion of the value of natural feeling, in spite of, or more likely, because of, his rarified view of citizenship.

The family as a particular, natural, base for the male citizen, balances his human needs. One could even say, it enables him to have human needs, and therefore to be human, and not the "philosopher monster" of Plato's *Republic*. Within the structure of Rousseau's theory, this positively implies the exclusion of women from public or political life. This exclusion is reinforced by further Rousseauean considerations.

Rousseau maintains that the state must not allow there to be within the general society any "partial associations", because these are in effect little societies whose will becomes "general with reference to its members and particular with reference to the State."[25] This particular will is inimical to the discovery of the general will. The prohibition against partial associations is a corollary of Rousseau's theory of right because the real, as opposed to the apparent, interests of individuals in a nation, are held to be completely harmonious with one another. In relation to such a state, an interest group, for example, or an organized economic class, can only be deemed subversive. Rousseau's politics are totally exclusive of pluralism, which is one reason why he is in the geneology of "authoritarian equality".

If the family were an association of equals, it would be a partial association, and introduce all the conflict between particular and general interest Rousseau is trying to contain. In order to conform to the important prohibition against partial associations, and fulfill its functions as the manageable avenue for the expression of the particular self-interest, needs, and desires of citizens, the particularity of the family must be, from a logical point of view, a manifestation of the particularity of the male citizen as an individual. The family must be, so to speak, in brackets within civil society, in an enclave of privacy represented, in a true sense of the word, by the male head.[26]

Contrary to some other feminist interpretors of Rousseau,[27] I think that Rousseau acknowledges the potential conflict of familial and political life, and also that, in theory at least, he accommodated these tensions most carefully. The conflict in the male citizen between self-interest and citizenship is ameliorated, rather than exacerbated, by the provision of the manageable and legitimate outlet for natural feeling and private interest which the family provides, in the absence of other avenues. What prevents this from being subversive of the State, is precisely the fact that the family is headed and controlled by the male citizen.

Rousseau not only denies the woman responsible participation in public life, he also denies her responsibility for the ordering of family life itself. Even *within* this sphere, she is subject to the will of her husband. This supports my contention that, strictly speaking, the particularity of the family is the particularity of the male citizen, under which the particularity of women and children is bracketted or subsumed.

Two further aspects of Rousseau's political philosophy—the right of private property, and reproductive labour—are interlinked with the subordination of women. (I say "interlinked" because I do not want to tackle the question of what is foundational to what in relation to these questions. It is enough to show that they are linked theoretically.)

The Rousseauean requirement of equality, and hence toleration of a far greater degree of authoritative redistribution of acquired property than is acceptable to the liberal individualist theorists, means that inheritance of private property is not given the moral justification for fulfilling one of its historically important functions. This is the bourgeois function of that of an aid to the accumulation of capital, a process essential to the development of capitalist class division, and, of course, the sort of entrenched inequality Rousseau deplored. Rousseau offers an argument *against* inheritance by the oldest male child, the usual custom in his day. He argues that whereas the father's authority over his children is "natural" because he is stronger and because children have nothing except what they receive from their father, the rule of nature is replaced by that of force if one brother is given economic power through inheritance over brothers of comparable age.[28] Rousseau makes it clear that the inheritance of property should not be automatic, but earned by filial devotion and deference to the father's wishes.[29]

The special value of private property to Rousseau is its role of preserving the autonomy of the citizen in a relation of political equality to other citizens. This essentially petty-bourgeois ideal of economic equality is usually presumed to be quite unfeasible as an *economic* theory. It is also a substantial remainder of theoretical individualism in Rousseau. Nevertheless, it is worth noting that in the theory of the ostensibly egalitarian Rousseau, strictly speaking, women are not subordinated to any essentially bourgeois economic concerns.

However, considering the ideological uses of Rousseau for male domination, it is significant that the autonomy of male heads of families, *as such,* is preserved by the institution of private property, and the male right to bequeath and inherit it, even without the approximate economic equality Rousseau considered so important to a good society. In other words, this philosophy of gender roles functions just as well to justify male dominance in unequal, bourgeois, societies, as it would in the society of equals Rousseau envisioned. Male heads of families remain autonomous in relation to one another, free to act on their rights and duties as husbands and fathers as they see fit, unless they become actually destitute. Although it is difficult to determine what degree of economic inequality is theoretically excluded in Rousseau, the prevention of the economic destitution of (male) citizens, and ensuing incapacity to establish a household, is a clear requirement. The right of citizens to be manly heads of families is more deeply imbedded in the theory than equality !

The citizen clearly needs something more than economic self-sufficiency to be truly autonomous—he needs a wife as well. The mature Emile claims he needs only "a field" (i.e., a farm), and a woman, for authentic happiness. The field without the woman would not merely be less than he needs for his happiness, but considered as a prescription for the best life, it would be a form of nihilism since it does not provide for reproduction.

Emile's need for "a field" presumes social relations and private property. One has no such need in the state of nature. Nor does a man need a woman "of his own" in the state of nature. However, once enmeshed in social relations and property relations, all sexual relations are either a matter of right, or a violation of right, primarily because of the question of inheritance of private property. The petty-bourgeois ideal of autonomy can scarcely escape being an ideal of *family* autonomy within which both real property, and sexual right as a type of property, are established. Given the requirement that the particular interests of women and children be subsumed under those of the male head of the family, an exclusive male right to bequeath and inherit family property follows. This in turn further reinforces the necessity for certainty of paternity.

This brings us to reproduction as a distinct and important question in itself. It may be thought that the question of reproduction, and women's relation to it, has already been dealt with in the arguments designed to show that women are confined to the private sphere, and that biological relations play a fundamental role, and so on. This is indeed the point at which feminist criticism usually ends. However, those theoretical implications are a different matter from the implications for social practice I now wish to deal with, and which are a very important implication of the theory for women.

The recommended confinement of women to the private sphere, with the economic dependence which that entails, creates a social structure for the performance of what I call "reproduction labour". What distinguishes the effects concerning, for example, the subsuming of female particularity under male particularity, from the effect of their being assigned "reproductive labour", is the fact that "reproductive labour", as I shall characterize it, is not defined in relation to, for example, "men" as social constructed, or to the political sphere, or whatever other theoretical entity. "Reproductive labour" is a practical activity which goes on, no matter how it is defined, in the way that the production of food and other material necessities of life goes on, no matter how theory is constructed around it. It is a necessary social activity which is not, in itself, created by the prior existence of sexual inequality, as, for example, the norms of femininity are.

"Reproductive labour" is characterized as the intentionally directed adult activity of providing nurturance and active socialization to young individuals, from birth to the point of personal independence. The purpose of this activity, at a minimum, is to cause the infant to survive to adulthood and be an adequate member of its own culture. "Adequacy" is subject, of course, to class, sex, race, and ethnic variation within a given society. Reproductive labour may be, but need not be, made up of activities which are in themselves gratifying. Like other forms of labour, it may be done for wages, or as part of gaining a subsistence, rather than for the immediate enjoyment of the activity itself. For women, marriage to a man who has access to a livlihood, whether wages, capital, or "a field", is her access to a livlihood, for which she normally undertakes to perform reproductive labour, and general housework as well. In the light of the work of Joan Landes,[30] this is probably especially true of women in the age of bourgeois democracy.

Landes argues that women actually lost ground as a result of the Revolution, since before that women of the upper-classes had been influential in government and what she calls "cultural production". In doing this they had also often publicly abjured their roles as mothers. It appears to be the case that women of the upper-classes in highly class-divided economies often play more influential public roles than women in more egalitarian or democratic economies. An absolutely basic reason for this is that only wealthy women can break the bonds of reproductive labour, (unfortunately by employing women of the lower-classes to do it). With equality of husbands, the wives and daughters of others are not available for hire, so domestic and reproductive labour are returned to all women. This is a practical problem for women, and a form of structural inequality, since these activities generally occupy their time and energy to the exclusion of participation in the public sphere. As has been seen in the case of Rousseau, the public sphere is also structured so as to be incompatible with reproductive labour, and the various normative dualisms provide theoretical legitimation of this hierarchical structure.

In addition, this lifetime expenditure of time and energy on the part of women (i.e., "women's work), is not theorized as labour at all. Rousseau grappled with questions of labour in relation to political right, coming up with conclusions qualitatively different from those of liberal individualism, or a bourgeois economic perspective. In *Political Economy,* for example, he made it one of three major maxims of good government that for citizens work should be always necessary and never superfluous for obtaining a livlihood. He also places great importance on the way in which children are reared. But if we do consider the latter as labour and as life activity, reproductive labour has an absolutely fundamental qualitative difference in this theory from other forms of labour. It does not, and it is never suggested that it might or should, give anyone a right to either citizenship or autonomy. In Rousseau, the social construct of "woman", by contrast with that of "man", is that of a being whose predestined life activity cannot, and should not, provide any access, not only to economic independence, but also to the understanding of general truths and the attainment of what Rousseau calls "moral liberty". Since the main thrust of Rousseau's theory of equality, from which women are excluded, is that its basis is individual autonomy, this alone precludes there being any credibility to his claim of "complementarity" in the different social roles of the sexes.

The sexual division of labour, according to Rousseau, is a state of affairs that is unquestionably pre-political, and from his perspective, arguably even pre-social. In his philosophical anthropology in the *Second Discourse,* the building of permanent shelters was thought to be the immediate cause of this division of labour. Women "grew accustomed to tend the hut and the children, while the men went to seek their common subsistence."[31] That the original basis of "the feminine role" is actually a division of labour is clear in Rousseau from the start. The symbolic, theoretically constructed, role of women discussed in the early part of the paper, of representing particular needs and desires, and above all "nature", is built on this division of labour, not because the activity itself entails any of this, but in the sense that it would be untenable *without* this division of labour. (I believe this is true without excluding the question of sexuality as another aspect of the sexual division of labour which space does not permit me to examine here.)

Rousseau was cognizant of the importance of child rearing to an unusual degree. Indeed, he is famous for it, as a result of his work on education, *Emile,* and other treatments of it. In *Political Economy* he writes:

> The homeland cannot subsist without freedom, nor freedom without virtue, nor virtue without citizens. You will have all these if you train citizens; [. . .] Now training citizens is not accomplished in a day, and to have them as men they must be taught as children.[32]

However, despite the importance of this to Rousseau, and despite even Rousseau's insistence that the contribution of the mother is all important,[33] the performers of reproductive labour (viz. women), are accounted inferior to those who act in the productive and public spheres (viz. men). In the history of theory the qualitative difference between reproductive relations and other sorts of social relations has been defined or rationalized by philosophers through the use of numerous distinctions, all of which signify a difference in value between the two spheres of activity—for example, the distinction between particular vs. general; private vs. public; personal vs. political. Also applied to this question, are other, parallel, sorts of value-laden dualisms—body vs. mind; emotion or appetite vs. reason; feminine vs. masculine; the basely practical vs. the pure; prudential vs. moral; even instrumental reason vs. transcendent reason. This practice is obviously true of Rousseau, who characterizes non-reproductive social relations as the sphere of potential generality, that is, of discourse and judgment about what are considered the loftiest of intentional objects and moral sentiments. Reproductive relations (i.e., the family) are the sphere of the particular, of appetite, sentiment, and private interest. "Reproductive labour" is not really acknowledged to be fully human labour, and the possible recognition of its exploitation is theoretically excluded.

The control of the male head of the family within the private sphere is consistent with the fact that these are not complementary or "different but equal" forms of life, as Rousseau makes a pretence of believing at the beginning of Book V of *Emile*. He is explicit in his claim that women's pre-destined life activity is not a road to "virtue" in the full-blooded sense needed for citizenship. In the *Emile,* he lists the onerous requirements of motherhood, and concludes: "Finally, all this must come not from virtues but from tastes, or else the human species would soon be extinguished."[34] Her "nature" is limited by this, and the rigor of the struggle for "virtue" is not for her. If properly educated, a good woman is happy in her life of service to others.

This mode of reproduction primarily serves the interests of the male head of the family. Where the husband has control of the livelihood, he has considerable control over those whom he supports and this enables him to demand that they perform work for his benefit. He may free himself of work required for his bodily maintenance, such as cooking, washing, and general housework. He may define the conditions of housework and reproductive work. Because of his liability for economic support of the children, as well as the property concerns discussed earlier, one condition of reproductive labour that is always a feature of this arrangement is sexual monogamy on the part of women.

Such a mode of reproduction results in female deprivation of mainstream social values such as active citizenship, economic independence, human excellence and virtue, and moral liberty (to use Rousseau's language). Where a hierarchical dichotomy is maintained between the public and the private, to be confined to what is private is to be denied the potential of full human development.

Given the role that labour plays in the theory of equality, the relegation of "women's work" to the private sphere, and the failure to theorize it as fully human and social labour, entails that women cannot enter either civil society or politics *as women,* but only exceptionally as pseudo-men. This problem persists in the theory of Marx, for example, (who owes something to Rousseau), who theorizes only "productive" labour as the avenue of emancipation. Classical Marxism therefore proposed women's problem to them—exclusion from the "productive" labour force that was said to be the source of uniquely human socialization and history—as its own solution. In order to become truly "political" from the point of view of the *revolutionaries,* they must do the very thing they are oppressively prevented from doing.

According to Iris Young questionable Rousseauean principles are still active in contemporary politics, in the present view that unity is what is wanted in political life. There is a need to make partial associations unnecessary—to "think them away." Yet modernity has consisted in the proliferation of partial associations, and the problem of politics in modernity is how to deal with partial associations within single polities. She suggests that the family must *become* a partial association (and not primarily a manifestation of male possessive individualism).[35]

No matter how democratic a theory may appear concerning economic and political relations, as these have usually been defined, it cannot be considered a democratic theory any longer unless it points to the possibility of sexual equality, and democratic reproductive relations. The personal is indeed political, not only in itself, but also for what it reveals about the meaning of political life.

Notes

This work is financially supported by the Social Sciences and Humanities Research Council of Canada, with a Canada Research Fellowship. It was first prepared for a conference of the Northeast American Society for 18th Century Studies on "The Age of the Democratic Revolution", in Worcester, Massachusetts, October 1989.

1. In my article, "Sexist Dualism", in PRAXIS INTERNATIONAL (January 1990), p. 402, I argue that: "Dualities of this kind, whether sexist, racist, or colonialist, have important features in common which can be systematized in general terms from the point of view of feminist critique. First, they are used by those associated with the superior term to establish

their distinct identity in contrast with "the others", whether female or of another race or nation. Second, they establish norms or ideals for those associated with the superior term, to the exclusion of "the others". A further asymmetry derivative from this second point is that, whereas the superior term is part of a norm for the superior being, the inferior term appears to be descriptive. It ascribes to the allegedly inferior being, or race, or nation, certain empirical characteristics which limit or prevent attaining the superior value. [. . .] Finally, because of the establishment of superior identity and the exclusionary norms of that identity, these dichotomies are used conceptually as a justification of social hierarchy and domination." In her introduction to *Feminist Challenges* (Sydney: Allen and Unwin, 1986), p. 6, Carole Pateman writes of political theory in particular: " . . . feminists have persistently criticized a body of radical thought, liberal and socialist, that has not just happened to exclude women—an omission that could be remedied within the theories as they stand—but which is constructed from within a division between the public (the social, the political, the history) and the private (the personal, the domestic, the familial), which is also a division between the sexes." For an extended treatment of sexist dualism, see Genevieve Lloyd, *The Man of Reason:* "Male" and "Female" in Western Philosophy (Minneapolis: University of Minnesota Press, 1984).

2. See S. M. Okin, *Women in Western Political Thought* (Princeton, N.J.: Princeton University Press, 1979); Carole Pateman, "The Disorder of Women: Women, Love, and the Sense of Justice", *Ethics* 91 (October 1980); Lynda Lange, "Rousseau: Women and the General Will", in *The Sexism of Social and Political Theory,* eds. L. M. G. Clark and L. Lange (Toronto: University of Toronto Press, 1979); and L. Lange, "Rousseau and Modern Feminism", *Social Theory and Practice,* Vol. 7, No. 3 (fall 1981) and in *Feminist Interpretations and Political Theory,* edited by Carole Pateman and Mary Lyndon Shanley (Cambridge: Polity Press, forthcoming 1990); G. Lloyd, "Rousseau on Reason, Nature and Women", *Metaphilosophy,* Vol. 14, Nos. 3 & 4, (July/October 1983).

3. Joan B. Landes, *Women and the Public Sphere in the Age of the French Revolution* (Ithaca and London: Cornell University Press, 1988).

4. See Alan Bloom's Introduction to his translation of *Emile* (New York: Basic Books, 1979). Followers of Leo Strauss find Rousseau particularly useful for anti-feminism. My own view is that Rousseau's philosophy of women is representative of, and seminal to, the uniquely modern view of women's role within family and state.

5. Ibid., Okin, p. 99.

6. In Lange, "Rousseau and Modern Feminism", Ibid., I argue this point at some length.

7. Alison Jaggar, *Feminist Politics and Human Nature* (Totawa, N.J.: Rowman and Allanheld, 1983), especially chapters 3 and 5.

8. Jean-Jacques Rousseau, *The First and Second Discourses,* edited by Roger D. Masters (New York: St. Martin's Press, 1964), p. 114.

9. Ibid., G. Lloyd, p. 321.

10. Ibid., Compare Bloom, p. 25: "Rousseau argues that woman rules man by submitting to his will and knowing how to make him will what she needs to submit to."

11. Jean-Jacques Rousseau, *On the Social Contract with Geneva Manuscript and Political Economy,* edited by Roger D. Masters, translated by Judith R. Masters (New York: St. Martin's Press, 1978), p. 220.

12. Ibid., *Geneva Manuscript,* p. 168.

13. Ibid., *Social Contract,* p. 78.

14. Ibid., *Social Contract,* p. 55.

15. Ibid.

16. Ibid., *Geneva Manuscript,* p. 160.

17. Lynda Lange, "The Function of Equal Education in Plato's *Republic and Laws*", in *The Sexism of Social and Political Theory,* edited by L. M. G. Clark and L. Lange (Toronto: University of Toronto Press, 1979).

18. Ibid. This argument is made in my article, "Rousseau and Modern Feminism".

19. Ibid., *Second Discourse,* pp. 146–7.

20. Ibid., *Emile,* p. 361.

21. Ibid., *Emile,* p. 359.

22. Ibid., *Emile,* p. 361.

23. Ibid., *Political Economy,* p. 211.

24. Ibid., *Emile,* p. 40.

25. *Social Contract,* p. 61.

26. Compare the interpretation of the conservative Bloom, Ibid., p. 24: "Rousseau insisted that the family is the only basis for a healthy society, given the impossibility and undesirability in modernity of Spartan dedication to the community. [. . .] Rousseau further insists that there will be no family if women are not primarily wives and mothers. Second, he argues that there can be no natural, i.e., whole, social man if women are essentially the same as men. Two similar beings, as it were atoms, who united out of mutual need would exploit one another, each using his partner as a means to his own ends, putting himself ahead of him or her."

27. See especially S. M. Okin, Ibid., and Carole Pateman, Ibid.

28. Ibid., *Political Economy,* pp. 209–10, 169–70.

29. Ibid., *Geneva Manuscript,* p. 169.

30. Joan B. Landes, *Women and the Public Sphere in the Age of the French Revolution,* Ibid.

31. Ibid., *Second Discourse,* p. 147.

32. Ibid., *Political Economy,* p. 222.

33. Ibid., *Emile,* p. 37.

34. Ibid., *Emile,* p. 361.

35. Iris Young, commentary on presentation of this paper at the conference of the Northeast American Society for 18th Century Studies on "The Age of the Democratic Revolution", Worcester, Massachusetts, October 1989.

Women in Kantian Ethics: A Failure in Universality

Kristin Waters

I. The Model of Kantian Ethics

Even some vigorous critics of Kantian ethics hold his theory in high esteem, and single it out as a paradigmatic moral theory. Among the attractive features of Kantian ethics are the strict insistence upon universality coupled with the equally strong claim of the inherent worth of each individual as a rational and moral agent. In traditional ethics, universality is a requisite component of moral theory, necessary for discovering the rightness of actions. For Kant, the underlying concept of autonomy is one of individuals as self-legislators bound by a formal concept of persons, who are to be treated as having inherent worth.

I shall argue that Kant's view of women, found in his early writing on aesthetics, is not consistent with his general moral theory. When writing about women, Kant fails to apply his own standard of universality, and as a result, women are not subject to equal treatment under the moral law. In terms of Kantian metaphysics, in the phenomenal world we know of things in a limited way as physical objects, as appearance subject to physical laws. In ethics we are treated to a more complex view of rational beings only. In their "noumenal" aspect, as Kant calls it, things can be known beyond the subjection of physicality as moral agents possessing freedom of the will. Kant's theory can be interpreted as treating men as noumena—things-in-themselves possessing autonomy and capable of moral agency, while women are treated as phenomena—mere appearance subject to physical laws and lacking true reason and morality. Kant, then, is in the tradition of objectifying women, treating women as appearances or inanimate objects rather than as beings with inherent worth. In this way he is in the tradition of great philosophers like Aristotle, who also deny the full measure of reason and morality to women and in doing so leave careful thinking and consistent argumentation behind.

II. Kant on Women and Men—
The Natural Complement Theory

With regard to gender roles and their origins, Kant holds a version of the natural complement theory. Ann Ferguson describes this as the view that "there are traits, capacities and interests which inhere in men and women simply because of their biological differences, and thus define what is normal "masculine" and normal "feminine" behavior."[1] According to Ferguson, and following a long tradition, these differences include hormonally induced physical differences, for instance in strength, which lead to different social roles, such as that of provider for men and nurturer for women. Differences in character also have these natural roots, so the nurturing women is sensitive, caring and emotional, the man is more aggressive, but also more rational. According to the natural complement theory, the ideal love relationship is heterosexual and the complementarity of traits brings man and woman together to form a whole human being. Many supporters of this view claim that men are not superior to women (or vice versa); there is a kind of equality in difference since each performs a necessary function toward creating the whole human being. There is, however, good reason to doubt this claim of equality, especially in a theory like Kant's, and the truth of the claim requires investigation.

Kant is in many ways the ideal natural complement theorist. In *Observations on the Beautiful and Sublime,* he describes the natural masculine and feminine states.[2] Woman is the fair sex:

> "her figure is finer, her features more delicate and gentler, her mien more engaging and more expressive of friendliness, pleasantry and kindness than in the male sex."[3]

The virtue of women, for Kant is a "beautiful" virtue:

> Women will avoid the wicked, not because it is unright, but because it is ugly; and virtuous actions mean to them such as are morally beautiful. Nothing of duty, nothing of compulsion, nothing of obligation![4]

Morality, for women, is an aesthetic and not an ethical act. Kant also states, "Her philosophy is not to reason but to sense," and her moral feeling is governed "not by universal rules," rather women:

> ... do something only because it pleases them, and the art consists in making only that please them which is good.[5]

Women of the right degree of refinement are impelled by a sensation of what is beautiful, not by a cognitive act of moral judgement.
Men, on the other hand, provide a normative model of moral action.
Their virtue is "noble virtue". Still, men may possess some "beautiful" qualities and women some "noble" ones, but these are by the
way of appearance rather than substance:

> ... one expects a person of either sex to bring both [noble and
> beautiful virtue] together, in such a way that all the other merits
> of a woman should unite solely to enhance the character of the
> beautiful, which is the proper reference point; and on the other
> hand, among masculine qualities the sublime clearly stands out as
> the criterion of his kind. All judgements of the two sexes must refer
> to these criteria.[6]

Later in the essay Kant elaborates his comments about nobility
in a woman, saying that it consists in "simplicity" and "innocence,"
and is for the purpose of enhancing beauty, so we find that even the
small part of nobility allowed to women is of a very different nature
than that found in men. Kant generally has a more difficult time
describing male virtues because it is "required of a noble disposition
to decline honorific titles," and he makes the following appeal:

> I hope the reader will spare me the reckoning of the manly quali-
> ties, so far as they are parallel to the feminine, and be content only
> to consider both in comparison with each other.[7]

Still, it is possible to sift out some of the "manly" qualities. For
instance, men have a "deep" rather than beautiful understanding,
which "signifies identity with the sublime." Additionally, Kant explains that effortlessness in all things is a mark of the beautiful
while "strivings and surmounted difficulties arouse admiration and
belong to the sublime."[8]

The primary moral virtue for Kant is truth-telling, but he explains that men must never be completely forthcoming with their
wives: "a man must never tell his wife that he risks a part of his
fortune on behalf of a friend," because it will "fetter her merry
talkativeness."[9] Kant provides a few more clues regarding the virtues of men. We learn that there is no deeper insult for a man than
to be called a fool and for a woman than to be called disgusting. Also
that neatness, which is required of women, when taken to extremes
is trifling for a man. Women are to be attentive to the features

of appearance which contribute to natural and necessary sexual attraction, and men, avoiding the same attention to the accoutrements of sexual attraction, can instead concentrate on "householders' virtues, thrift and such, and to the dowry."[10]

Finally, in a very telling statement, Kant explains that, "the principle object is that the man should become more perfect as a man, and the women as a wife, . . . In matrimonial life the united pair should as it were, constitute a single moral person, which is animated and governed by the understanding of the man and the taste of the wife."[11] These statements show that Kant is very much a natural complement theorist.

III. Analysis—On Moral Judgments and Persons

Kant's remarks about men accord well with his general writing on moral theory while what he says about women is disconsonant with it. The following contrasts between some elements of Kant's ethical theory and his views about women point this out rather clearly.

1. According to Kant's primary formulation of the categorical imperative which states, "act only according to that maxim whereby you can at the same time will that it should become universal law," the rational operation of moral judgment lies in the ability to universalize maxims.[12] As a subjective rule of conduct, a maxim is a rule for personal use, such as "I should tell the truth to my friends." One applies the categorical imperative by extending the maxim to apply in all situations, that is, to the command, "Tell the truth," which applies universally. But for Kant, apparently women can learn about morality only through specific examples, and "not by universal rules." Since, as Kant says, women have little use for principles, the reasoning prescribed by the categorical imperative to universalize maxims will not generally be available to them.

2. For Kant, moral action is always and only that action which is based upon reason, but he holds that the actions of women are based upon sensation, which cannot produce moral action. Given the overwhelming importance of reason for Kant, this observation is especially telling, since moral action is the practice of reason, but women's "philosophy is not to reason but to sense."

3. Moral action is autonomous, which for Kant means strictly, action based upon the laws one gives to oneself, that is, self-

legislated action. Only reason can allow one to see the rightness of a form of action and to extrapolate that form into a "law" or rule which then becomes the basis for voluntary behavior. The moral action of a self-legislating being results from a rational process and is not determined or physically impelled by nature or sensation. Since women make their "decisions" based on beauty, they are, in the Kantian scheme, being impelled by sensation or at best, they are making an aesthetic and not a moral judgment so again they fail as moral agents.

4. Action which "merely accords" with duty but does not issue from a reasoned analysis of what is right is not truly moral action. Thus, a pick pocket snatching a purse may coincidentally pull the victim out of the way of an onrushing truck. The form of the action may have the appearance of being morally correct—saving someone from harm from being crushed in traffic, but an analysis of the intention of the agent reveals that his purpose was quite different. He intended not to save but to steal from the victim. So an action which is superficially "in accordance with duty" is vastly different from one which Kant calls "out of a sense of duty," that is, with the right intention. More simply, a charitable offering given to make the donor feel good is an act done in accordance with, but not out of a sense of duty. If women "do something only because it pleases them," then the motivation is desire or self-interest and the acts cannot be construed as altruistic. Women must be conditioned to behave in ways that appear moral, that is, to make "that which pleases them" congruent with "that which is good." In Kantian terms, the actions of women constitute a perfect example of acts which "merely accord" with duty and so fail as truly moral acts.

5. According to Kant, women see either the beauty or ugliness of certain outcomes and act accordingly. Thus, they operate under a kind of teleology of beauty instead of the required deontology of rightness. The "teleos" or end of feminine action is the beautiful result. But Kant is emphatically opposed to this Millian kind of teleology of morals.

The foregoing observations read like a list of how to fail in Kantian ethics: women don't universalize the maxims of their acts; the actions of women are motivated by sensation, not by reason; women are not autonomous; women don't act out of a sense of duty; and instead their actions are goal-oriented and not motivated by the moral law. Every feature of Kantian ethics, every test one is to apply to evaluate action reveals that, according to Kant's account, women do not by nature or reason act morally and suggests even that true moral action is not available to them. More disturbing still is that Kant is himself untroubled by the fact that his scheme excludes women from the realm of morality; he fails to see the consequences of his own analysis. Notice how exultant Kant is about the lack of moral agency which women possess: "Nothing of duty . . . nothing of obligation!" The lack of agency increases women's charm. Kant has profoundly failed to apply his own theory universally; for him moral agents are men. Women are merely the agents of beauty and style.

Kant applies his ethical theory inconsistently with regard to men and women, and also imposes further limitations on its scope. Clearly, men are his model moral agents, and women, in the form of the eighteenth century aristocratic lady, or in any form, deviate so much from the norm as to be excluded entirely from the moral realm. A related topic also in need of investigation, but beyond the range of the present essay, is the moral class structure which Kant creates along with his gender distinctions. The "lady" can at least imitate morality and provide the appearance of it, but "coarser" women lack the "charm" to be moved by beauty toward the good. The "feminine virtues" through which ladies imitate or complement a masculine morality are less available to the lower classes: innocence, neatness, fineness of figure, as defined by the Kantian ideal. Thus, just as Kant fails to apply his ethical principles universally to include women, it will be possible to extend this criticism to show that another failure in universality applies to the class structure.

The criticisms put forth show that women are not included in the Kantian universe of moral discourse; in an important sense, they are not persons, since their actions are impelled by sensation in the way a rock is impelled by gravity. Women are not, in the Kantian scheme, liberated by reason to be agents of morality. A most effective way to deny a group equality of treatment is to eliminate them from the universe of discourse and this is just what Kant does regarding women and morality.

IV. Conclusion

In his writing about women, Kant explains some things never mentioned in his great works on moral theory, namely, that woman and man combine to form what he calls a whole moral person. They complement each other, each contributing equally to this composite moral agent. Yet Kant never suggests in his other writings that something is lacking in the masculine paradigm which he presents, that reason alone is inadequate for morality, or that it must be accompanied by the aesthetic judgment of woman to be a truely moral act. On the contrary, reasoned judgment is sufficient for morality. Note the asymetry here. Kantian man, with his reason, is capable of being moral by virtue of this capacity. Could the Kantian woman, with her lack of reason, her emotionality and her aesthetic sense be a moral person? Certainly not.

Complementarity, then, does not contain the equality which its defenders hold for it. A man, by himself, is capable of moral judgment. A women without a man to bring reason to the operation cannot be a whole moral person. This is why the concept of a whole moral person appears in his writing about women and not elsewhere. The role of the woman is truely supplementary to the man; she is an accoutrement which brings polish, beauty and charm to the rough edges of the aggressive but noble man. In Kant's version of the natural complement theory women and men are not equal.

Complement theories are many and varied. Kant's is not the only one. Antoinette Brown Blackwell devised a theory of natural complementarity, found in her incisive work, *The Sexes Throughout Nature* (1875), which was in part a response to Darwin's views about female *homo sapiens*.[13] Blackwell exposes a series of faulty and inconsistent arguments leading to Darwin's conclusion that women are physically and intellectually inferior to men. She substitutes an evolutionary view which attributes different but equally valuable biological functions to women and men. Among the different natural features she includes the structure of reproductive organs and rates of circulation. But Blackwell, like Kant, goes beyond what can safely be called "natural" traits when she includes in her list such items as parental love, insight of relations, feeling and moral powers. Traditional theories of complementarity are plagued by the problem of overconstruing the influence of nature and ignoring cultural influence. Additionally, when a natural complement theory holds a "whole person" tenet, as Kant's does, it is from a moral point of view unfairly biased against individuals who are not heterosexually engaged.

A more recent complement theory which avoids the pitfalls of an unsupportable naturalism is that proposed by psychologist Carol Gilligan.[14] Gilligan's empirical studies have discerned a masculine ethic of justice and a feminine ethic of care in the responses of her subjects. But Gilligan reserves judgment on the source of these differences. She proposes a "mature ethic" which combines the masculine and feminine, but she never insists on connecting sex and gender, nor does she attribute anything magical or necessary to the connection between male and female.

Kant appeals to natural differences, and social differences are created by the so-called natural ones. The implication is that these differences are inherent and immutable. Further, and crucial to his theory is the clearly inferior moral role of women. Women are by nature less suited to making genuine moral judgments. This demonstrates a double standard regarding the natural complement theory: men acting alone are moral agents; a women "complements" a man by bringing charm to a relationship. A woman, on the other hand, is not "a whole moral person" without a man to provide the necessary conditions for morality. This double standard is intolerable to a consistent theory of ethics.

Kant's remarks about women are not consistent with his general views about the nature of humanity and morality. His most famous formulation of the categorical imperative holds that one must never treat others as a means only, but always also as end-in-themselves, but on his account, women are rather like animals or pets of men to be protected and not to be treated like rational moral creatures. Likewise, women are to treat men as their surrogate moral agents, since they themselves are incapable of true moral action and can only partake of true morality through the rationality of their husbands. Thus, the so-called complementarity of men and women provides a device for people to treat each other as means and not as ends in the best moral sense.

Furthermore, Kant's theory about women does incalculable harm to them, especially when one recognizes that the great paradigm moral theory, the theory famous for its formalness and universality, the strength of which is its equal treatment for all moral agents, is also a theory which truely excludes women from the moral sphere.

Notes

1. Ann Ferguson, "Androgyny As an Ideal for Human Development," in *Feminism and Philosophy,* ed. Vetterling-Braggin, et al. (Totowa, N.J.: Littlefield, Adams, & Co., 1981), p. 47.

2. Immanuel Kant, *Observations on the Beautiful and Sublime,* trans. John T. Goldthwait (Berkeley: University of California Press, 1960).

3. Ibid., p. 76.

4. Ibid., p. 81.

5. Ibid., p. 81.

6. Ibid., pp. 76–77.

7. Ibid., p. 78.

8. Ibid., p. 78.

9. Ibid., p. 81.

10. Ibid., p. 87.

11. Ibid., p. 95.

12. Immanuel Kant, *Grounding for the Metaphysics of Morals,* trans. by James W. Ellington (Cambridge: Hackett, 1981), p. 37.

13. Antoinette Brown Blackwell, *The Sexes Throughout Nature* (New York: G. P. Putnam's Sons, 1875).

14. Carol Gilligan, *In A Different Voice* (Cambridge: Harvard University Press, 1982).

Rereading the Canon: Kantian Purity and the Suppression of Eros

Robin May Schott

I

Immanuel Kant, writing at the end of the eighteenth century, is still widely considered the thinker who, more than any other, addresses the philosophical concerns of modernity. His attempt to build philosophy on a scientific basis in order to secure for it objective knowledge remains one of the dominant projects of modern philosophy. Kant's identification with the political and humanistic gains of modernity in grounding the dignity of the rational individual is so deeply entrenched in modern Western culture that in challenging Kant, one is accused of supporting the threat of barbarism that has marked the twentieth century. The contradiction between the emotions excited around Kant's philosophy and Kant's overt commitment to a conception of rationality that is purified of all emotion, leads one to question the historical, social, and emotional underpinnings of the Kantian paradigm. What is implied by Kant's insistence that knowledge and reason be pure? What pollution in the sensible, empirical world threatens the project of establishing a foundation for philosophical truth? Does the split between cognition, on the one hand, and feelings and desires on the other hand, capture the essence of knowledge, as Kant claims? Or does this split require the knower to suppress the erotic dimension of existence in order to conform to the conditions of objective knowledge?

These questions are motivated by a conception of philosophy, stemming from Marx and critical theory, as an articulation of relations in the social world. Rather than accepting Kant's claim that true philosophy is unaffected by historical change and social practices, critical social theory argues that philosophy cannot be adequately understood without a theory of history that seeks to understand the processes out of which social groups and the ideas they conceive develop.[1] In order to analyze the problem of society in Kant's philosophy, therefore, one seeks to reveal the social and historical categories which lie at the foundation of his transcendental doctrines. These fundamental categories often indicate more profoundly the nature of historical change than those that are tied more closely to empirical reality. In speaking of the historical transformation of philosophical concepts, Marcuse writes, "It is not so much their content as it is their position and function within philosophical systems which changes. Once this is seen, it becomes clear that these very concepts provide a clearer indication of the historical transformation of philosophy than those whose contents are far closer to facticity."[2] Thus, Kant's analysis of the transcendental conditions of knowledge contains an implicit theory of human relations, which he takes to be universal and necessary. Moreover, Kant's paradigmatic status in the history of philosophy attests to the extent to which he articulates the experience of individuals in modern bourgeois society.[3] Such a critical rereading of the philosophical canon provides an avenue for developing a critical understanding of assumptions that individuals continue to take as natural and necessary in their everyday intellectual and social lives.

Although critical theorists such as Lukàcs, Goldmann, and Marcuse have analyzed the philosophical implications of economic forms of power, one can expand this scope by considering sexual forms of power as well. Philosophers have claimed universal validity for their thought; but they have also systematically excluded women's experience from this domain. Feminists argue that this exclusion sustains the hierarchical valuation of the sexes that exists in the social world. In order to reorient philosophical thought to include women's experience, one can foreground the question, how have sexual forms of domination and control been constituted. This issue remains crucial in women's lives today, as the prevalence of sexual objectification of women, sexual harassment, sexual discrimination, rape, and spouse abuse indicates. In giving a feminist critical reading of Kant, therefore, I seek to uncover its implicit theory of power with regard to both economic and sexual relations, and to explore the connection between these spheres. This approach may appear anomalous, since Kant was committed to the irrelevance of empirical identity to rational thought. Yet precisely Kant's claim to detach thought from concrete identity is suspect. Kant's hostility toward sensuality is correlated with a dismissal of women as sexual beings, who are incapable of rational thought. Since knowledge must be freed of erotic interferences, women, as sensual creatures, must be excluded from philosophy. The contradiction between Kant's claim that his thought is universally valid and his exclusion of women from rationality, calls attention to the significance of his commitment to purity. One can probe how the philosophical hostility to sensuality, which underlies Kant's claim for pure thought, has justified philosophically the hierarchical valuation of the sexes which exists in the modern world.

But in exploring these hypotheses, it became apparent that I myself was so schooled in this philosophical tradition of objectivity that I lacked the tools necessary to critically view Kant's assumptions about knowledge. I had learned all too well the lessons that philosophical thought must be detached from emotion, interest, and personal identity. Although I intended to display the specific commitments involved in the operations that had been accepted as natural and essential components of the philosophical enterprise, I found that the Kantian method of achieving objectivity by establishing universal forms of knowledge itself appeared to me as inescapably necessary.

It became devastatingly apparent that in order to gain perspective on this view of knowledge, it was imperative to delve into the history out of which Kant's thought developed. If philosophy is a reflection of the social world, as Marxist theoreticians claim, it cannot be divested of the history either of its own concepts or of the society in which its ideas developed. To understand these historical connections, it becomes necessary to get down into the mud, as Plato would say, to dirty one's hands with history.[4]

This recognition led to an investigation of the origins of the concept of purity.[5] I sought in the classical period a clue for answering the following questions. From what must the intellect be purified? Why is the body viewed as polluting? How does the philosophical commitment to purity, which enters the philosophical tradition in the classical Greek period, reflect religious and social practices outside of the domain of philosophy? This historical turn provided the first substantive indication of the meaning of purity in philosophy. The emphasis on distancing thought from sensuality grew out of an ascetic practice by which men sought to transcend the vicissitudes of the phenomenal world, to escape the mortal fate implicit in the natural life cycle of human beings. Moreover, the most threatening moments of birth and death were connected, through myth and ritual, with an interpretation of women's sexuality as polluting.

II

These historical insights provide a foundation from which to read Kant. His emphasis on purity in systematic philosophy displays the inheritance of the ascetic hostility toward the body and toward women. Kant's asceticism, inherited in part from his own pietist background, is manifested in both his life and thought. Kant never married, and it is said that although he contemplated marriage once or twice, he lost the opportunity while reflecting on the matter. Kant's lifelong celibacy was one expression of his goal of achieving rational control in his daily life. Kant abhorred any emotional expressiveness, and considered universal respect for freedom of the moral person as the only valid emotion. His sexual abstinence was indicative of his general indifference to the role of pleasure in life. In the *Critique of Judgement,* he wrote that the value of life is "less than nothing" when it is measured according to the sum of pleasure.[6]

Kant's view that feeling and desire are pollutions that must be excluded from knowledge is an expression of this ascetic inheritance. Although in the *Metaphysics of Morals* Kant recognizes a broad notion of sensibility which includes feeling, in the *Critique of Pure Reason* Kant repeatedly emphasizes the irrelevance of feeling, as merely a subjective factor, to cognition. Thus, that aspect of sensible apprehension which contributes to knowledge is only a restricted portion of sensibility, which excludes any feelings of attachment or pleasure, and brackets out as much as possible the influence of bodily existence. For example, Kant identifies the cognitive portion of sensibility with intuition, *Anschauung,* implying that observation is primary for knowledge. Anschauung means to look at or view. By choosing Anschauung as the general term for receptivity, Kant suggests that in perception one's relation to the object is that of a spectator. As a spectator, one can have a distance to objects or events that is not possible if one is directly effected by them. If one observes an event without affect (e.g., empathy or identification), one resists being changed by it, and thus retains control over one's experience. Hence, this cognitive posture remains static and predictable. Moreover, by emphasizing observation as the primary mode of knowledge, Kant indicates that the perceiver also achieves a distanced relation to his or her own body. For example, Kant argues that one is less aware of one's body in looking than in touching, and hence vision becomes the philosophical metaphor for knowing. In *Anthropology from a Pragmatic Point of View,* Kant writes that sight is the "noblest" of the senses, because it "receives its sense organ as being least involved."[7] For Kant, awareness of one's physical involvement actually distorts knowledge. In contrast to sight, touch is the "most limited condition of perception"[8] because it cannot be thoroughly purified of any "admixture of evident sensation." The impurity of touch evidently encompasses the sensations of physical intimacy as well as of physical pain. Here, touch exposes human vulnerability in relations. Since cognition must be impervious to such experiences, Kant allows touch to contribute to knowledge only insofar as it is completely devoid of pleasurable sensation. Thus, touch can contribute to knowledge of the form of an object, but its sensuous qualities (such as the texture of an object or the warmth of a person) are excluded from the noetic dimension of sense experience.

Kant's exclusion of feeling from intuition results in a highly reduced form of both feeling and desire. Emotion and passion share, in Kant's view, certain disagreeable features. In the *Anthropology* Kant writes, "To be subject to emotion and passions is probably always an illness of mind because both emotion and passion exclude the sovereignty of reason."[9] He repeatedly uses the metaphor of illness to describe feelings. Emotion is like a "stroke of apoplexy", like an "intoxicant which one has to sleep off . . . but passion is looked upon as an illness having resulted from swallowing poison."[10] Kant writes, "Passion . . . no man wishes for himself. Who wants to have himself put in chains when he can be free?"[11] In Kant's view, affective responses interfere with cognition, and have neither an intrinsic relation to an external object nor to an individual's own subjective state. Thus, emotion appears as a strictly arbitrary occurrence that can never be considered an appropriate response to a person or event. But emotion is also a means of apprehension. For example, if one is unsettled by an unexpected visitor in distress, this response is a clue both for understanding one's own situation and for having the empathy to understand that of the other. In bracketing out affect from knowledge, Kant identifies with the stoic ideal of apathy: "The principle of apathy, that is, that the prudent man must at no time be in a state of emotion, not even in that of sympathy with the woes of his best friend, is an entirely correct and sublime moral precept of the stoic school because emotion makes one (more or less) blind"[12] Thus Kant explicitly identifies his hostility toward emotion with that which derives from an ascetic philosophical tradition. Although Kant's opposition between feeling and cognition claims to arise from a pure interest in knowledge, it presses instead a disengagement from the world which itself is a form of defense and control.

Like feeling, desire in Kant's analysis is excluded from immediate apprehension. By contrast, for Hegel, desire is part of the process of self-development and the human struggle for recognition. Because desire in Kant's view cannot contribute to the development of self-consciousness, he views sexual desire as a degradation of human nature, which reduces persons to objects. Kant writes, "Sexual love makes of the loved person an Object of appetite; as soon as that appetite has been stilled, the person is cast aside as one casts away a lemon which has been sucked dry . . . that is why we are ashamed of it and why all strict moralists . . . sought to suppress and extirpate it."[13] Since Kant precludes sexual desire from developing relationships of love, the only vehicle for "true human love" is "practical love," which is dictated by the moral law.[14] In practical love we are enjoined to love a person strictly as a moral agent. Practical love allows no distinctions between types of persons—e.g., between a generous person and a manipulative one. Thus, human love in Kantian philosophy is not only desexualized, but there is no place for love of persons with empirical qualities. No wonder Charlotte von Schiller said of Kant that since he was not able to feel love, there was something defective in his nature.[15]

Although in the *Anthropology* Kant distinguishes natural human characteristics from rational determinations, he treats women in particular as defined wholly by natural needs. He notes that nature, concerned to protect the embryo, implants fear and timidity in women's character. Because of these natural characteristics, Kant viewed women as unsuited for scholarly work. To be both a woman and a scholar is so antithetical, in Kant's view, that a scholarly woman, "might as well even have a beard, for perhaps that would express more obviously the mien of profundity for which she strives."[16] In *Observations on the Feeling of the Beautiful and Sublime,* Kant writes that women's philosophy is "not to reason but to sense", and adds, "I hardly believe that the fair sex is capable of principles."[17] Kant echoes these sentiments in the *Anthropology* in mocking scholarly women who "use their books somewhat like a watch, that is, they wear the watch so it can be noticed that they have one, although it is usually broken or does not show the correct time."[18] Thus, Kant ultimately splits apart human attributes and projects them onto different poles of sexual existence. What is manly has been defined by its inclusion in the domain of rationality—the capacity for detached, dispassionate reflection. Womanly attributes, on the other hand, have been defined at the boundaries of this domain. Women appear to embody the emotional, passionate, sexual features of existence which appear to pose a threat to rational thought.

Kant's ascetic commitment manifests itself not only in his desensualization of sensibility, but also in his analysis of objective knowledge in terms of pure concepts of the understanding. Although the notion that the forms of thought are pure reflects the historical attempt of asceticism to filter sensuality out of reason, the specific function of the categories in Kant's system is linked with social developments in eighteenth century German society. In particular, Kant's view of the spontaneity of the human understanding corresponds to the growth of new forms of human activity in the world of work. Consequently, Kantian objectivity is not merely a *theory* of knowledge, but in a broad sense it can be seen as part of a social practice that developed in the emerging system of commodity production and exchange.

Kant's discussion of objective knowledge in the *Critique of Pure Reason* presents a description of human activity that parallels to a remarkable extent the phenomenon of fetishism later described by Marx in *Capital*. Commodity fetishism refers to the phenomenon in which products of human labor appear to individuals not as what they immediately are, as products of labor, but appear instead as independent objects. Although created by human activity, commodities appear to individual producers as themselves rulers over the human world. In *Capital,* Marx characterizes the fetishism of commodities as follows, "There, (with commodities) it is a definite social relation between men that assumes, in their eyes, the fantastic form of a relation between things. In order therefore, to find an analogy, we must have recourse to the mist-enveloped regions of the religious world. In that world, the productions of the human brain appear as independent beings endowed with life, and entering into relation both with one another and the human race."[19] In this situation, human beings become alienated from their own laboring activity, and from the objects that they create, which appear to be governed by laws that are given and immutable.

Kant explicitly disavows the relevance of historical changes to philosophical thought. This judgment is echoed in the philosophical tradition since Kant, which largely accepts his theory of objectivity as describing the essence of knowledge, which is free of any associations with empirical practices. Since philosophy has no history, in Kant's view, it remains unaffected by the particular practices of a society. But in order to have knowledge, the subject must distance himself[20] from a multitude of sensuous, erotic, and emotional concerns. This practice of knowing not only reflects an ascetic discipline, but is expedient for a society based on the production of commodities, with the corresponding abstraction of both persons and things.

Kant has been one of the foremost thinkers in modern philosophy to stress the human contribution to knowledge through the spontaneous activity of human understanding. Nevertheless, his analysis of human activity reflects on the level of cognition the alienation of individuals from their activity in a society built on commodity relations. Although Kant stresses the spontaneous activity of human understanding, the spontaneity of the understanding does not refer to the creative thought process of the empirical knower, but refers to the formal conditions for the possibility of knowledge. The activity of thinking, which determines objects insofar as we can know them, is abstracted from the qualitative, personal characteristics of empirical individuals, and analyzed instead in terms of universal conditions of knowledge. Kant explicitly differentiates this universal condition of consciousness from the empirical consciousness of an individual. Empirical consciousness, in Kant's view, cannot provide the unity by which I can call any representations "mine." Taken alone, empirical consciousness is as "many-colored and diverse a self as I have representations of which I am conscious to myself."[21] Therefore, although human activity is the necessary condition for experience, in Kant's view this activity is not a function of the particular subject, whose feelings and history inform conscious activity. Rather, activity is located in the abstract and universal "I think," which establishes an equivalence between all subjects. My experience in knowing an object is identical with yours. All personal attributes, emotions, desires, and interests, are irrelevant to the formal conditions of knowledge. This abstract equivalence among diverse consciousnesses mirrors the quantitative equivalence of labor in a market economy. Labor becomes reduced to a formal equivalence, measured by a wage, in which all subjective attributes of the worker are eliminated. Like the reified consciousness of the worker, the thinker in Kant's analysis is estranged from his own thought. Moreover, although the subject, through the unity of consciousness, provides the foundation for the unity of the object, this constituting activity is not immediately experienced by the subject. It is only revealed through a transcendental analysis of experience.[22] As the condition of all possible experience, which precedes any particular perception, this constituting activity appears to the subject not as an expression of his subjectivity, but as an objectively given, external force. Thus, although for Kant the subject constitutes the objective world insofar as it can be known, this activity appears only in alienated form.

The abstractness of knowledge is evinced not only in the formal character of apperception but in the categories which are derived from this unity of consciousness. These "pure concepts" are not derived from experience, but exist prior to and independent of any experience. Kant's insistence on the *a priori* character of the concepts implies that the forms of thought, by which one unites the sensuous manifold, are indifferent to the sensible content of experience. Like the formal character of wage labor, which is indifferent to the sensuous nature of the object it produces, the forms of thought apply universally to all sensible impressions. Moreover, the a priori character of the categories implies that they are eternal forms of thought. The pure concepts that are now valid must be valid at all future points. Future thought is confined to repeating the present form of reflection, thereby precluding any change in consciousness. Thus, reason's claim to a priori validity merely freezes the past relations between subjects by defining them as eternally valid. Therefore, the temporal character of entrenched relations, which are reflected in the forms of thought, becomes concealed from view.

Although the categories embody, in Kant's eyes, free human activity, this spontaneity suggests only a very limited form of freedom. The categories provide the unalterable "rules"[23] by which the understanding can know anything at all. The freedom of the understanding is much the same as the freedom of laborers: a freedom to subjugate themselves to the apparently objective, pre-given laws of capital. In Kant's theory of knowledge, any real, spontaneous activity of the subject is annihilated by its subordination to the a priori laws of thought. Through the pure a priori categories, therefore, human reflection acquires a "phantom objectivity."[24] Although the categories are ultimately grounded in the subjective unity of consciousness and apply to the objective world only insofar as it is a world of appearance for us, not as it is in itself, at the same time they appear as an objectively given system to which the individual's thought must conform.

Just as the activity of the knower is abstracted from the concrete needs and desires of the individual, the object which is known through this procedure is similarly abstracted from its concrete sensuous nature. Kant distinguishes between the object as appearance, and the thing-in-itself. In order for the object to enter the system of human knowledge, it must conform to the pure forms of

sensibility and understanding. But in viewing the objects of knowledge as conforming to human concepts, one forsakes knowledge of
objects in themselves. Kant writes, "a priori knowledge of reason . . . has to do only with appearances, and must leave the thing
in itself as indeed real per se, but as not known by us."[25] The object
of knowledge is produced by formal, unchanging rules, which leave
unknown the "true correlate of sensibility."[26] Since Kant's notion of
the thing-in-itself is merely a logical concept, it reaffirms the in-
transigence of the conditions of objective existence, which can never
be transcended.

III

Despite Kant's claim to provide universal and necessary conditions of knowledge, abstracted from any empirical content or historical determination, profoundly embedded in his epistemology is a
specific theory of society. In arguing that only objectified thought is
cognitively legitimate, Kant carries the process of alienation taking
root in the social world into the deep recesses of human subjectivity
and consciousness. In analyzing this relation between Kant's philosophy and social existence, I have followed Marxist thinkers who develop the concept of reification to suggest that patterns of social
domination and alienation are replicated in spheres of life that appear to be either strictly private or wholly abstract. Yet the concept
of reification appears to pose the problem of totalization: if alienation encompasses all spheres of existence, how is change possible?
How can the critic avoid replicating reified consciousness in her
own critique? How can individuals break the grip of reification in
their daily lives, their psyche, and their philosophy? However, this
analysis of alienation does not quash the human dimension of suffering and hope. Resistance is possible through the effort to recover
what is suppressed, but never eradicated. In my own reading of the
Kantian paradigm, in the face of its political legitimation and personal penetration, I sought to explore what it means to read Kant
from inside rather than from outside myself—as a feminist and
critical theorist.

In the attempt to uncover what is suppressed by the paradigm
of objectivity, I sought to examine the significance of purity in
Kant's thought. Kant's commitment to purity reflects an ascetic
heritage which is rooted not only in a response to general features

of bodily existence, but is also a response to specific kinds of bodies—that is, to women's bodies and their perceived role in the life cycle. Thus, the philosophical paradigm of objectivity has not only made normative a split between thinking and emotional, sensual existence, but it has historically justified the exclusion of women from domains of public activity for which women have been viewed as insufficiently rational. Furthermore, the ascetic paradigm of objectivity makes the objectifying social relations between persons and things that are generated in a world ruled by commodity production appear as natural and necessary.

Since I have drawn on both feminist and Marxist frames of reference in this analysis, it is legitimate for the reader to question the nature of this relation. Feminists foreground questions concerning embodiment, sexuality, and emotions, which have historically constituted women's identity both philosophically and materially. Marxist theorists, on the other hand, foreground questions of alienation, class domination, and ideology.[27] In my view, these constellations of factors are linked in the modern form of ascetic objectivity. One is led to ask, has the denial and control of sexuality been a precondition for the flourishing of capitalist relations? To what extent are ascetic demands for hierarchical relations between the sexes implicit in commodity relations? Is it ever possible to liberate oneself from the sexual implications of this heritage while remaining within an economic structure that is ascetic in its roots? These questions shed light on both feminist and Marxist methodologies. Insofar as feminists have been concerned with questions of sexual domination either in isolation from other forms of power or as the fundamental trans-historical dynamic, this methodology has been too narrowly construed. Rather than essentializing sexuality, the task is to examine its historical formations and relations with other forms of power. Similarly, insofar as Marxists have posited the analysis of capital as the fundamental historical dynamic, they have failed to see its connection with both sexual and racial politics. Both methods must be wary of reifying their own categories—of replicating the Kantian paradigm of objectivity whereby certain categories become viewed as essential and necessary, unaffected by the experience of either the critics or the subjects of analysis.[28] Thus, the questions raised above about the relation between asceticism, sexual hierarchy, and capitalism should not be answered in a final manner, which seeks to predict all future forms of thought, but should be guided by the historical demands and experience of those seeking emancipation.

Notes

1. Max Horkheimer, "The Social Function of Philosophy," in *Critical Theory; Selected Essays* (translated by Matthew J. O'Connell, and others, N.Y.: Seabury Press, 1972), p. 263.

2. Herbert Marcuse, "The Concept of Essence," in *Negations* (translated by Jeremy J. Shapiro, Boston: Beacon Press, 1968), p. 43.

3. This analysis draws on Lucien Goldmann's view that great creative works are those that coherently express on an imaginative or conceptual plane the self-understanding of a social class or group. *The Hidden God: A Study of Tragic Vision in the "Pensées" of Pascal and the Tragedies of Racine* (translated by Philip Thody, London: Routledge and Kegan Paul, 1964), p. 17.

4. The attempt to counteract alienation through thematizing it, however, does not thereby eliminate it. I have noted this phenomenon with some dismay as I have attempted to pursue some of the issues developed in my book, *Cognition and Eros; A Critique of the Kantian Paradigm* (Boston: Beacon Press, 1988). In the process of writing this piece I have discovered the extent to which my own thoughts, now in book form, have become objectified, and that the process of circumventing this alienation must begin anew.

5. Because of the limitations of space, I can only indicate some of the questions and hypotheses I develop in Part I of my book, which set the stage for my discussion of Kant.

6. Ernst Cassirer, *Kant's Life and Thought* (translated by James Haden, New Haven and London: Yale University Press, 1981), p. 15.

7. Immanuel Kant, *Anthropology from a Pragmatic Point of View* (translated by Victor Lyle Dowdell, Carbondale and Edwardsville: Southern Illinois Press, 1978), par. 19, p. 43.

Evelyn Fox Keller and Christine R. Grontowski, in their essay, "The Mind's Eye," note that the eyes can also be a keen source of erotic pleasure, as in meeting the eyes of another in a moment of communication (in Harding and Hintikka, eds., *Discovering Reality; Feminist Perspectives on Epistemology, Metaphysics, Methodology, and Philosophy of Science*, Dordrecht: D. Reidel Publishing Co., 1983, p. 220.) The early Greeks acknowledged this quality when they considered the eyes as the entryway of eros. Thus, the desensualization associated with vision is not entailed by the nature of this sense itself, but rather is a feature of the particular philosophical treatment of vision.

8. Kant, *Anthropology,* par. 21, p. 45.

9. Ibid., par. 73, p. 155.

10. Ibid., par. 74, p. 157.

11. Idem.

12. Ibid., par. 75, p. 158.

13. Immanuel Kant, *Lectures on Ethics* (translated by Louis Infield, N.Y.: Harper and Row, 1963), pp. 163–4.

14. Quoted in Cassirer, *Kant's Life and Thought*, p. 18.

15. Ibid., p. 413.

16. Kant, *Observations on the Feeling of the Beautiful and Sublime* (translated by John T. Goldthwait, Berkeley: University of California Press, 1960), Sec. 3, p. 78.

17. Idem.

18. *Anthropology*, p. 221.

19. Karl Marx, *Capital*, Volume 1 (translated by Samuel Moore and Edward Aveling, N.Y.: International Publishers, 1967), p. 72.

20. I use the masculine pronoun here to signify the non-neuter character of Kant's thought.

21. Kant, *Critique of Pure Reason* (translated by Norman Kemp Smith, London: Macmillan & co., 1958), B133.

22. Lucien Goldmann, *The Hidden God*, p. 188.

23. Kant, *Critique of Pure Reason*, B145.

24. Lukàcs phrase, "Reification and the Consciousness of the Proletariat," in *History and Class Consciousness* (translated by Rodney Livingstone, Cambridge, Mass.: MIT Press, 1972), in his discussion of reification.

25. Kant, *Critique of Pure Reason*, Bxvii.

26. Ibid. A30/B45.

27. Horkheimer and Adorno, in *Dialectic of Enlightenment*, have sought to explore the connection between these forms of domination.

28. In my view, Horkheimer and Adorno, in the *Dialectic of Enlightenment*, make this mistake in seeking to provide a universal theory of domination.

Kant's Immature Imagination

Jane Kneller

Immanuel Kant, like many well-known philosophers before him, looked at the women of his social plane and proceeded without much soul-searching to make generalizations about them that were then supposed to be insights into the very nature of "womanhood". In the *Anthropology from a Practical Point of View* he makes by now familiar comments about the natural physical weakness and timidity of women, their natural modesty and loquacity, their "precocious shrewdness" in getting their men to treat them gently, and so on.[1] According to Kant, women achieve their natural ends—reproduction of the species and instilling of culture (sociability and decorum)—by reducing men to folly.[2] For him they are creatures of inclination, not understanding,[3] so it is not surprising when he asserts that their physical weakness is accompanied by rational weakness.[4]

Although Kant does allow that women are rational beings,[5] it seems that for him they are not *fully* rational. Kant classes women—and he has in mind the female members of the western European bourgeoisie—with members of both sexes who are not citizens as "unmündig"—unable for whatever reasons to think for themselves and hence not legally fit to speak for themselves.[6] Thus it seems clear that Kant believes female members of his own race and class, along with all members of certain other races and classes, are naturally less *inclined* to reach rational maturity.

In the 1784 essay "What is Enlightenment?" Kant says that the "far greater part of humanity (including the entire fair sex)" fears maturity due to the fact that their "guardians" have seen to it that they find thinking for themselves too dangerous.[7] This seems to suggest that Kant did not see women as naturally more childlike than men, but rather held that rational immaturity is a result of social conditioning: cowardice and laziness are the reasons the far greater part of humanity remain immature. However, the *Anthropology*, lectures published fourteen years later, makes it quite clear that

141

courage is a *masculine* virtue,[8] and that, in general, Kant continued to believe that women's understanding could never "mature suitably" to allow them to manage their own civil affairs.[9]

Moreover, if women are *naturally* more timid due to their role as reproducers of the species, and if indolence and dissipation is associated with high culture[10] and it is women's *natural* calling to further this culture, then it is hard to see how Kant can possibly escape labelling women as perpetual children. Kant's women are "naturally" immature due to their necessary role in the non-rational tasks of childbearing and enculturation. They are more immediately bound to feeling and emotion and the material trappings of gentility, or to use Kant's terminology, they are more closely bound to "sensibility."

As if all of this were not enough to indict Kant forever in the eyes of feminists, it has recently been argued that Kant's sexism runs far deeper than stray remarks in the *Anthropology*. Critics have charged that Kant's views on women fit hand in glove with some of his most basic philosophical assumptions.[11] In a nutshell, the charge is that Kant's theory elevates reason by denigrating sensibility—that Kant goes to extreme, even pathological lengths to segregate the rational from the sensible aspects of human nature. If certain members of the human race are more closely associated with sensibility than others, then Kant has a theory that is through and through discriminatory. In particular, if women are "naturally" associated with inclination rather than understanding, Kant's philosophy is irremediably sexist, for all women can never be quite as rational, never be quite as moral, and hence can never be quite as human as men.

Yet inspite of all this, it is a mistake for feminist philosophers to dismiss Kant's critical philosophy before studying his own attempt to remedy that aspect of it that feminist critics contend systematically bolsters sexism, *viz.*, the deep schism he creates between sensibility and reason. Kant devoted the latter third of the second *Critique* and arguably, the entire third *Critique* as well to finding a systematic bridge between the realm of reason and morality on the one hand and the natural physical world on the other. The extent to which he succeeded, and perhaps more importantly, the failure of this attempt, is of great interest to feminists. Consequently, in what follows, I will (I) discuss the difficulty that the schism between sensibility and reason poses for Kant's moral theory and his proposed solution to this problem, and (II) argue that although Kant's solution represents an unwillingness on his part to meet the problem of an integrated social self directly, that he came close to a direct solution in his aesthetic theory in his account of an imagination capable of "re-forming" the world. Finally I will argue (III) that even here Kant never grants the imagination the maturity necessary to ground human beings' hope to create a just world in the midst of nature.

I. What May Humanity Hope?

Contemporary treatments of Kant's ethics tend, in general, to focus on its formalist side, that is, on its requirement that the sole criterion for determining the rightness of an action is that it be performed in accordance with and out of respect for the moral law in the form of a categorical imperative. This focus on the legalistic aspect of Kant's ethics ignores the fact that Kant recognized that making ethical choices does not occur in a super-sensible vacuum, but in the physical world where the desire for happiness is natural, indeed, necessary for the survival of the species. Kant was well aware that a human being is a "being of needs."[12] Yet his ethical theory requires that human beings abstract from all personal interest and act only out of respect for the moral law. Reason paradoxically requires that one behave as if one were without desires and emotion while at the same time recognizing that one lives in a world where desire and emotion regularly seem to triumph over reason,[13] and where one must pay attention to one's sensibilities in order to survive. Thus, what is ignored in debates where Kant's is held up as the paradigmatic "rights-based" ethic is that Kant affirms that although being worthy of happiness is the "supreme condition" of the highest good, it does not encompass the *whole* of this ideal. The "highest good" requires "virtue and happiness together."[14]

Kant argues that pure practical reason naturally seeks the highest good, just as theoretical reason seeks the unconditioned, final cause of the natural order.[15] Moreover, so far as moral practice is concerned, Kant goes so far as to say at one point that human beings are *obligated* to bring about the highest good: "It is *a priori* (morally) necessary to bring forth the highest good through the freedom of the will."[16] Thus the question "What may I hope?" that follows "What can I know?" and "What ought I to do?" in the triad of questions that frame Kant's philosophy[17] is answered by Kant in a form that is intended to unite the natural, physical world and the "supersensible" moral realm. That is, it is answered in terms of human beings' "right" to hope for a world in which virtue and happiness are commensurate.

It is not surprising that Kant worries about the possibility of reconciling the moral and the natural realms already in the first *Critique*. The idea of a moral world on earth must play a role in Kant's theory if moral action is not to be utterly in vain and hence absurd.[18] That is, the hope for virtue rewarded is not to be confused with a desire for a pay-off for being moral, but rather reflects an ability to believe that effective moral reform is possible. It would be futile to *act* virtuously at all if there were no hope that human agency could effect some change for the better.

Human beings must therefore have some rational hope, however slim, that moral action can change the world in which they live. They must believe that they are capable at least of making progress towards a moral world, so that the imperative to seek it not be based on an illusion. But Kant also believes that nothing in the natural world, including human beings, gives reason to believe such progress is possible.[19] Indeed, given his sharp division of the moral world and the world of physical nature, one would not expect to find such a connection readily. Thus, attempts to bring about moral betterment seem to be fatally tied, in Kant's philosophy, to the wheels of a mechanical physics, and human moral and physical "selves" seem to be irreconcilably at odds with each other.

At this point feminists might hope to find an account of the "immediate power" of human beings to change their own world, but what Kant offers instead is an argument for the right of practical reason to believe in a higher power—God—who will mediate change by acting as a "supplement to our impotence to [realize] the possibility of the highest good."[20] It thus seems as if Kant allows the ethical imperative to create a better world to be entirely co-opted by a religious authority that now promises to do the job *for* us by making things right in a utopian after-life.[21]

Apart from this problem, however, there is another, internal problem for Kant's philosophy.[22] Morality requires that human beings strive to make the world better, but in order to have any reason to do so they must believe in the possibility not simply of a moral world, but in the possibility of their being able to bring it about solely through their *own* efforts. If human beings cannot even imagine that they themselves are fit for the task, then they have no reason to adopt it as their highest goal. Even if the existence of a higher benevolent power that would rework their clumsy efforts at change could somehow be *known,* such knowledge would not give human beings the confidence in *themselves* that is necessary for attempting and continuing to attempt that change.

The situation would be like that of a child who is convinced that her efforts at co-operative, friendly play will regularly fail. She is encouraged to continue to act as if some day her efforts will have an effect on her playmates, but the encouragement itself is based on the further demand that she believe that her father can and will (one day in the future, and in a way that is completely beyond her understanding) intervene by rewarding her and punishing her intransigent playmates. I think one would have to say that such a child has no reason whatsoever to believe in her own ability to engage others in friendly, social play, and no corresponding hope that such a situation can ever be brought about through her own efforts. To demand of her that she continue to try to change her unruly playmates, and that she take her strength for this task from the belief that her *father* will one day set things right would be an arbitrary and perhaps even perverse exercise of power over her. Moreover, it is no less arbitrary or perverse if one were to suppose that the child makes this impossible demand of herself. Yet this is the state of affairs that Kant depicts in his account of human beings' "need" to postulate the existence of God.[23]

Thus, rather than reintegrating the human subject via the moral imperative to create a better society, Kant only succeeds in further pitting reason against the world of sensibility. Despite Kant's call for "daring" and for freedom from our "self-incurred immaturity;"[24] despite his "Rousseauistic revolution"[25] in ethics, there is evident in his philosophy a deep-rooted need for something like autocratic rule. This is true not only in his political and religious works but also in the realm of cognition and morality. Within these realms the empirical self—the flesh and blood self of the sensible world—is never granted autonomy in the sense of productive power. When in Kant's ethical theory we find reason commanding not only that the form of our choice be rational, but that we strive to bring into being a corresponding *material* good, there appears for the first time to be a concern with integrating sensibility and reason, and of treating the human being as an *embodied* moral agent. But the appearance turns out to be an illusion as reason, fumbling for some way to legitimate its own demands, invents for itself a higher authority rather than granting some degree of autonomous productivity to its subject.

II. Imagining the Highest Good

After the *Critique of Practical Reason* Kant began to be concerned more than ever with linking the rational and sensible aspects of the human subject. In his third major work, the *Critique of
Judgment,* he tried to account for aspects of our experience that his
epistemological and moral works leave unexplained. That nature
exhibits regularities not created by the forms of the understanding,
and that nature can be beautiful apart from any universal rule for
judging it to be so are problems for Kant that he attempts to solve
in the third *Critique.* The solution that he ultimately gives, perhaps
not surprisingly, involves the elevation of yet another principle, this
time of "reflective judgment." In this way the faculties of understanding and reason retain their mastery in the natural and the
moral realm and no major concession is made to sensibility.

Nevertheless, in his account of the creative imagination Kant
puts into place the theoretical apparatus for attempting to solve the
problem in a very different way. In the "Critique of Aesthetic Judgment," which comprises the first half of the *Critique of Judgment,*
Kant introduces a notion of imagination that is far more powerful
than his earlier ones, in as much as imagination becomes a faculty
of creating a second nature out of natural materials. In section 17,
Kant says that the painter, for instance, is capable of embodying the
highest degree of human virtue in portraiture that involves "a
union of pure ideas of reason with great imaginative power." This
artistic embodiment of morality requires "great imagination" on
the part of both artist and appreciator.

This section is extremely interesting because Kant here proposes that there may be a type of judging involving a sensible, concrete individual "ideal" of beauty that holds a moral interest. Later
in section 49, where Kant discusses "the faculties of the mind which
constitute genius" it is found that genius involves an "animating
principle" ["*Geist*"] that Kant says "puts the mental powers purpo-
sively into swing." *Geist* is equated with the ability to present aesthetic ideas that are "representations of the imagination that
occasion much thought, without any definite thought, i.e., any *concept,* being capable of being adequate to it." Since it is the imagination that represents aesthetic ideas, and *Geist* is defined as the
faculty of doing so, it is clear that Kant is working out a new role for
the imagination—one that is far more "spirited" and creative than
any so far discussed by him:

> For the imagination ([in its role] as a productive cognitive power) is
> very mighty when it creates, as it were, another nature out of the

material that actual nature gives it . . . We may even [use imagination to] restructure [*umbilden*] experience; and though in doing
so we continue to follow analogical laws, but yet we also follow
principles which reside higher up, namely, in reason . . . In this
process we feel our freedom from the law of association (which at-
taches to the empirical use of the imagination); for although it is
under that law that nature lends us material, yet we can process
that material into something quite different, namely, into something that surpasses nature.[26]

In light of the discussion of the requirement that human beings
strive to bring about a moral world *within* nature, with its presup-
position of a rational hope that such strivings might not be in vain,
it seems to me that this passage takes on great significance. Kant's
notion of *Geist* is that of a "re-forming" imagination. This goes beyond the faculty of mere reproduction of images, and even beyond
production a priori of "schema," as Kant calls them, for "fitting" intuitions to concepts of the understanding. In the *Critique of Judgment,* Kant has in mind rather the possibility of a human capacity
for fitting aesthetic ideas—creations of imagination—to rational
Ideas. An example of such an attempt is already to be found in his
account of the Ideal of beauty where, as was shown, he speaks of the
imaginative power of both artist and receiver to embody moral virtue. It is quite plausible to suppose, then, that "spirited" imagination could do the same for the rational Idea of the highest good.
That is, if art is capable of portraying individual virtue, it must also
be capable of giving sensible form to social virtue. Imaginative presentation of the ideal human society ought in theory to be no less
possible than the imaginative portrayal of a perfectly virtuous individual. The former may be more complex, so that it may be possible to "embody" it only in "glimpses." But that it could be done
seems quite plausible on Kant's account.
    All of this, of course, is not to suggest that spirited, "reforma-
tive" imagination is sufficient for the creation of a better world, but
simply that it could provide the hope necessary to attempt change
without recourse to a self-defeating flight into supersensibility. All
that is necessary in order to make human obligation to bring about
change a reasonable one—one that can be acted upon, is the ability
at least to *imagine* that it is possible.
    In his account of "spirited" imagination Kant seems to have at
his disposal a simple answer to the question of how to justify human
beings' obligation to produce a happy as well as a moral world. Why,
then, does he fail to make use of it?

III. The Immature Imagination

Even when not merely serving the understanding as "a blind but indispensable function of the soul"[27] for the purposes of cognition, imagination is always, for Kant, an immature counterpart to the "higher cognitive faculties." In moral judgments its position is even worse, for here imagination is not even allowed a function analogous to its function of schematizing concepts in cognition. Imagination in moral judgments is in fact explicitly ruled out.[28] As I will argue, even in aesthetic reflective judgment, that is, in judgments of taste and judgments of the sublime, where imagination's role is more prominent, it is still maintained under the wardship of the understanding in general or of reason. For feminists this is quite interesting, since immaturity (*Unmündigkeit*) and childishness are also the hallmarks of femininity for Kant.

In fact, I think it is not going too far to suggest that the fate of women in Kant's philosophy is closely tied to the fate of the imagination. "Women and hypochondriacs," are associated with "inventive" imagination inasmuch as they are less inclined to "curb" it.[29] Moreover, Kant's civilized and civilizing woman bears a remarkable similarity of function to the "civilized" imagination (taste) in so far as the natural aim of both is the cultivation of society and its refinement. At the same time neither refined women nor refined imagination necessarily lead to morality.[30] Both "civilized" women and the "civilized" imagination are important as tools for moral training, but neither are necessary conditions of morality itself for Kant.

Keeping in mind these similarities, I want now to take a closer look at Kant's account of the imagination in judgments of taste and the sublime. Both, for Kant, involve a mediated, reflective pleasure that is the result of imaginative "free play" with the understanding in the case of judgments of taste or, in the case of the sublime, a pleasure that results when the imagination is forced to attempt to schematize the supersensible.

In judgments of taste the imagination does not have to carry out its usual task of fitting concepts and intuitions but is allowed more latitude for "play" with the representations presented in intuition. A pleasurable feeling ensues as the subject becomes conscious of a "mutual subjective harmony of the cognitive powers" of imagination and understanding, a harmony that "belongs to cognition in general" ("zum Erkenntnis gehört").[31] The relationship of imagination to the understanding may be viewed as one of cooperation, as the imagination and understanding engage in "lively play" "animated by mutual agreement."[32] Thus it sounds as if Kant has granted quite a bit of power to the imagination in judgments of taste.

But it is important to recall that the whole experience "belongs to cognition" and that cognition is under the sovereign rule of the pure concepts of the understanding. Imagination is granted free play just so long as it remains 'freely lawful.'[33] Its relationship to the understanding is not that of an equal partner setting its own limits as it sees fit. Imagination in judgments of taste resembles far more a docile schoolchild let out to play, with the understanding in the background nodding approval at her antics, and keeping a watchful eye lest she attempt to leave the school yard.

Imagination does not fare much better in the case of judgments of the sublime. The experience of the sublime, according to Kant, involves some agitation on the part of the imagination as it refers a given representation either to theoretical or practical reason.[34] In judgments of the sublime no concept is applied, but neither is the imagination in "free play" with concepts. Rather it is compelled to attempt a task that it cannot complete, viz., to find a concept for a representation of infinite magnitude or absolute power. Imagination is thereby humiliated, and a feeling of pain ensues in the subject upon realizing the inadequacy of its own imagination to complete the task. It is in this sense, then, that Kant says that natural objects that evoke the feeling of the sublime appear to "do violence to our imagination."[35]

The feeling of the sublime is thus a rather perverse pleasure. It occurs on the one hand when the imagination is forced to try to comprehend something that cannot be apprehended as a whole, producing in the subject a painful feeling of the inadequacy of the imagination.[36] When the subject, who is always both imaginative and rational, recognizes this inadequacy in himself (I believe that it is safe to assume that the subject is a "he" for Kant), he feels a pain that is superceded by pleasure upon realizing that reason is thus triumphant over nature. Thus the pleasure that the subject takes in this imaginative exercise in futility is a questionable one, "a pleasure that is possible only by means of a displeasure."[37]

In general we may say that imagination's relationship to reason in judgments of the sublime is less docile, and at the same time more abused. It is freed from the constraints of the understanding only to be forced into the role of instrument in "exerting dominance [Gewalt] over sensibility."[38] For this reason Kant recognizes that there is a danger of insurrection here that does not exist in the case of judgments of taste. To the extent that the imagination is unbound by reason so that it may strain after the supersensible, there is always the threat of "enthusiasm." But the feeling of sublimity can only arise as a result of reason's ability to crush any such insurrection by reference to a transcendant realm that is *non*-sensible and hence off limits to the rebellious imagination.

IV. The Failure of Kant's Imagination

Kant's account of the role of the imagination in aesthetic judgments thus admits of two alternatives to the role of servant in cognitive judgments. In aesthetic reflective judgment the imagination is set free. But in both cases the freedom is more apparent than real, because in both cases the point is merely to "entertain [*unterhalte*] the mind."[39] Looked at in this way, imagination's role is in a sense *more* subordinate than it is in cognition, where imagination is a necessary albeit inferior helpmate in the serious task of constituting nature. The imagination in Kant's aesthetic theory seems irremediably immature, so that the question remains: Is there any room in the critical philosophy for a spirited, powerful, equal partner to the understanding and reason—for a reformative imagination?

The answer to this question, it seems to me, is extremely important. It is important to Kant because the viability of his ethics depends upon its ability to take root and have meaning in the physical world. Kant himself saw this, but his effort to inject an element of materiality into his account of the highest good led him further away from nature than ever in search of transcendental grounds for hope for a better world.

It is important to feminists for another reason, however. Whether or not feminists care about the fate of Kant's philosophy, they must care deeply about how it helped shape modern society's expectations of and demands upon it's female members. To paraphrase Kant, although this is an age of post-modernism, it is not a post-modern age. Femininity is, in fact, a decidedly modern construct. The dichotomies that abound and that have come to be accepted as definitive of gender in our society—particularity/ universality, materiality/spirituality, intuition/discourse, desire/ reason—all are modern, all are Kantian. The internalization of these distinctions that Kant theorized is, for better or worse, what the "modern woman" has become, a being at odds with herself and with nature. On the other hand this divided nature provides the motive for an imaginative re-creation of herself that is at the same time a reintegration with nature and a renewal of her hope to be able to take part in re-forming the old order into a moral world. Kant could not accomodate this possibility, but I am inclined to think that may be due to the immaturity of his own imagination. Spirited, reformative imaginations could surely do better.

Notes

References to Kant's works are to the standard English translations cited below. Numbers in brackets refer to the volume and page numbers of the original German text in the Prussian Academy edition of Kant's collected writings (Berlin and Leipzig: 1900–), except in the case of the *Critique of Pure Reason,* where all references are to the standard pagination of the A- and B-editions of that work.

1. Immanuel Kant, *Anthropology from a Pragmatic Point of View,* trans. Mary J. Gregor (The Hague: Martinus Nijhoff, 1974), pp. 167 [VII, 303] 169 [306], 79–80 [209]. Kant acknowledged that his remarks about women's nature applied only to women in civil society, yet for him they are all the more true because it is only in civil society that the characteristics proper to 'woman as such' are first allowed to flourish (*Anthro.* p. 167 [303]). Thus Kant adds insult to injury by recognizing the particularity of his account of the frail, empty-headed chatterbox only to affirm it as the highest stage proper to 'woman in general.'

2. Ibid., p. 169 [305–306]].

3. Ibid., p. 172 [309].

4. See, for instance, *Anthro.* p. 171 [307].

5. Ibid., p. 167 [303].

6. Ibid., pp. 79–80 [208–209].

7. "What is Enlightenment?" trans. Lewis White Beck in *Foundations of the Metaphysics of Morals and What is Enlightenment?* (Indianapolis: Bobbs-Merrill, 1959) pp. 85–92, [VIII 35–41].

8. *Anthro.* p. 124 [256–57].

9. Ibid., pp. 89–90 [220].

10. Cf. *e.g., Critique of Judgment (CJ),* trans. Werner S. Pluhar (Indianapolis: Hackett, 1987), 319–20 [432–33], 121–22 [262–63].

11. Two recent critiques of Kant that are both extensive and persuasive are Robin Schott, *Cognition and Eros: a Critique of the Kantian Paradigm* (Boston: Beacon Press, 1988) and Gernot and Harmut Böhme, *Das Andere der Vernunft* (Frankfurt am Main: Suhrkamp, 1983).

12. Immanuel Kant, *Critique of Practical Reason (CPrR)*, trans. by Lewis White Beck (New York: Macmillan, 1988), p. 24 [V, 25].

13. Cf. Kant, *Critique of Pure Reason*, trans. by Norman Kemp Smith (New York: St. Martin's, 1929) A809/B837.

14. *CPrR*, pp. 114–15 [110].

15. Ibid., p. 112 [108].

16. Ibid., p. 117 [113]. See also *CPrR*, p. 129 [125].

17. *Critique of Pure Reason*, A805/B835.

18. *CPrR*, p. 118 [114].

19. Cf. *CPrR*, p. 129 [124], *CPR* A810/B838, and *Critique of Judgment*, p. 318 [430].

20. *CPrR*, p. 124 [119].

21. The situation is perhaps not as bad as this. Yirmiahu Yovel in *Kant and the Philosophy of History*, argues that the postulation of the existence of God for Kant merely *grounds* human being's hope to succeed in their efforts, while the efforts themselves remain strictly a human obligation (Princeton: Princeton Univ. Press, 1980, p. 96). Work in the theology of liberation seems to take this approach to the problem of maintaining hope and avoiding defeatism, arguing further that the attempt to bring about a just world necessarily *leads* to God. (Cf. Gustavo Gutierrez, *A Theology of Liberation* (Maryknoll: Orbis, 1983) chapter 11: "Faith, Utopia, and Political Action," esp. p. 238).

22. For a more detailed discussion of the difficulties for Kant's theory of social and individual improvement, see Paul Stern, "The Problem of History and Temporality in Kantian Ethics" (*Reveiw of Metaphysics*, 39:3, March 1986, pp. 505–545). If Stern is correct, the command to seek the highest good is rendered problematic by the tension in Kants' ethics between the claim, on the one hand, that the disposition to moral virtue is invariant through human history and his insistence, on the other hand, that moral progress is possible over time.

23. Cf. Kant's essay "What is Orientation in Thinking?" where he discusses the postulation of God's existence as a "felt need of reason." (In *Kant's Critique of Practical Reason and Other Writings on Moral Philosophy*, (Chicago: 1949, [VIII, 131–48]).

24. "What is Enlightenment?" *op. cit.*

25. Cf. Lewis White Beck, "What have we learned from Kant?" in *Self and Nature in Kant's Philosophy,* ed. Allen Wood (Ithaca: Cornell Univ. Press, 1984) p. 22.

26. *CJ* p. 182 [314].

27. *CPR,* A78/B103.

28. Cf. *CPrR,* p. 71 [69].

29. Cf. *Anthro,* p. 55 [180–81]: Letting the imagination run riot is a bad habit that "produces a slackening of the mental powers. So the rule of curbing our imagination by going to sleep early so that we can get up early is a very useful rule of a psychological regimen. But women and hypochondriacs (whose trouble usually comes from this very habit) prefer the opposite course."

30. *Anthro,* p. 169 [306] and *CJ,* p. 188 [319].

31. *CJ,* p. 61ff [217ff].

32. Ibid.

33. Ibid. p. 91 [240].

34. *CJ* p. 101 [247]).

35. Ibid., p. 99 [245]. Somewhat later in the account Kant says that it is the *imagination,* attempting to schematize infinitude, that does violence to the *subject.* Since it is reason that forces the attempt in the first place, however, it is at best disingenuous to claim that it is nature and the imagination that cause pain. Nature, along with the imagination, turns out to be "infinitesimal" (*verschwindend*) in comparison with the ideas of reason" (*CJ* pp. 113–14 [256–57]), and it is the feeling of pleasure arising from the realization of reason's superiority that makes the whole experience "sublime" in the first place.

36. Ibid., p. 109 [252].

37. *"Unlust,"* ibid. p. 117 [260].

38. *CJ,* p. 124 [265].

39. Ibid., p. 131 [270].

Hegel's Theoretical Violence

Amy Newman

Hegel is often credited with being the first major philosopher in the Western tradition to recognize that human social relationships are interdependent and to incorporate this aspect of social existence into his overall theoretical system. For this reason, some feminists have seen Hegel's theoretical model as having a certain affinity with a feminist understanding of the nature of social relationships. However, this requires that one overlook the fact that in Hegel's system, human relations are conceived as fundamentally and necessarily inequitable. In this chapter, I shall maintain that Hegel's theoretical model cannot be properly understood in abstraction from his use of it to legitimate relationships of dominance and subordination.

I

Jean Grimshaw criticizes feminist thinking that claims to identify a characteristically male point of view in philosophy. Grimshaw asserts that "whatever theme or opposition is identified as male, it is always possible to find male philosophers who have profoundly disagreed."[1] She thinks that Hegel, for instance, may be seen as a counterexample to the claim of some feminists that male philosophers tend to deny the social character of human relationships. Grimshaw cites Hegel's emphasis on "the interdependence of human consciousness and social relationships" and portrays him as a philosopher who championed the idea that "human beings cannot either recognize or meet their needs in isolation from other people."[2]

However, Grimshaw's use of Hegel to exemplify an approach that is non-characteristically male is misleading. This implies that Hegel—at least in regard to his theories concerning social relationships—somehow managed to transcend his gender. The problem here is that although Hegel's theoretical perspective cannot be shown to be distinctively male, neither can it be adequately understood in dissociation from his maleness, as Grimshaw seems to suggest. Hegel's system assumes the legitimacy of a model of human relationships in which maleness is idealized and femaleness is devalued, and he himself clearly identifies with the dominant "masculine" pole of this model. His acceptance of this model and the way in which he positions himself within it simply would not make sense if he were not male.[3]

That this is the case is strongly implied by the fact that Hegel, in his elaboration of this model, engages in and advocates theoretical violence against women (and others). As I am using the term, theoretical violence refers to the use of rational argument to justify or normalize the domination or elimination of a perceived adversary. It is an instance of what Janice Moulton calls "the adversary method" in philosophy, i.e., the use of aggressive behavior as a model for philosophical activity.[4] However, I shall maintain that in Hegel's philosophy, theoretical violence is not just modeled upon aggressive behavior, but it also involves the deliberate production and refinement of a formal system that portrays aggression as logically necessary.

Theoretical violence may take a variety of different forms—phenomenological, logical, theological, mythological, metapsychological, etc.—and it may constitute defensive, assertive, or purely hostile behavior. An analysis of what constitutes adequate justification for engaging in theoretical violence is beyond the scope of this paper. Suffice to say that while theoretical violence may be justifiable in some contexts (e.g., for purposes of self-defense), I do not consider such characteristics as gender, race, class, age, religion, or nationality, in and of themselves, to constitute good enough reasons for formulating systematic plans for the domination or elimination of a person or group of persons.

I shall attempt to uncover theoretical violence in the Hegelian text by implementing intersubjectivity theory.[5] The intersubjective view attends to the way in which the writer of a text portrays the field of self and other, and specifically, the extent to which she or he demonstrates, in the construction of the text, the capacity to recognize and co-operate with others, as over against a tendency to devalue, dominate, or even eliminate others. Using the intersubjective approach, I shall focus upon Hegel's description of his own experience as a subject in relation to objects, his characterization of interpersonal and social relationships—particularly the relationships between women and men—and the idealized version of interpersonal relationships found in his portrayal of the relationship between humanity and divinity. What this analysis will show is that Hegel engages very forthrightly in theoretical violence directed against women (and others), and without adequate justification.

II

Habermas has suggested that Hegel's purpose in the construction of his system was "to conceptually legitimize the revolutionizing of reality without Revolution itself."[6] Hegel was studying theology at Tübingen when the French Revolution broke out, and he was teaching philosophy at Jena when Napoleon's forces swept through in 1806. It is not insignificant that the text usually considered to be the point of entry into Hegel's entire system—the *Phenomenology of Spirit*—was written during the tumultuous period culminating in the battle of Jena (the battle which resulted in the collapse of Prussia). It is in this text that Hegel initiates his lifelong exploration of the possibility of establishing the rule of reason without the kind of mindless, excessive violence that followed in the wake of the French Revolution.

The weapon that Hegel proposes to use to bring about his revolution is theory. "Philosophy cannot compel by external force, but it can attack what is limited with the latter's own truth . . . [and] make it surrender itself [*Selbstaufgabe*]."[7] Hegel reveals an important aspect of his strategy in this respect in the section of the *Phenomenology* in which he analyzes the "absolute freedom and terror" spawned by the French Revolution.[8] Here he defines terror as the realization that life can be rendered totally meaningless in an instant through an arbitrary and meaningless death, the "coldest and meanest of all deaths." Such death is characteristic of "anarchy striving to establish anarchy," the production of terror for its own sake. But this threat of "matter-of-fact annihilation" can also have a positive effect: it does serve to encourage submission. "These individuals who have felt the fear of death, of their absolute master, . . . submit to negation" and thereby actualize "their substantial reality." Thus, even terror can be turned into an "absolutely opposite experience," because it can make the option of a life lived in conformance with the interests of a rational state seem quite desirable. When harnessed by the state and rationally implemented to further the interests of the collective, even terrorism can be a positive force.

Here we can see Hegel's dialectical method at work. The key mechanism according to which this method operates is the syllogism. In Hegel's system, for example, if at one extreme is a universal concept, such as "life in general," at the other would be "individual sense-consciousness." The relationship between the particular individual and the universal is that of complementary opposites, "reciprocally necessary moments that take shape as a conflict and seeming incompatibility." This necessitates a third or middle term, "rational self-consciousness," by means of which one justifies, to oneself and to others, one's place in the scheme of things. Through the implementation of rational self-consciousness, for example, one can transcend—at least intellectually—any apparent conflict between one's individual existence and the broader context in which one finds oneself: e.g., between the idiosyncrasies of one's personal life and one's social and political milieu or world-historical context. This syllogistic process, which Hegel calls *Aufhebung,* or "sublation," is characterized by a double movement.[9] First, there is a negative movement by means of which elements of one's experience that are taken to be non-essential are identified and set aside, or nullified. The second movement is a conceptual reversal by means of which one then formulates a reasonable explanation for regarding certain aspects of experience as more essential (or perhaps simply more desirable) than others, thereby preserving these elements and elevating them to a position of logical priority.

III

In the *Phenomenology,* Hegel attempts to provide existential justification for his dialectical method through a description of the experience of consciousness. He describes his own consciousness as being fundamentally conflictual in nature, "a relationship of two extremes." For example, he experiences "sensuousness" as "sheer *otherness,*" and he assumes that any rational person would wish to be completely free of such experience, if possible. However, since this is impractical on the individual level (it would require getting rid of the physical body, i.e., death), "we have to be content" with the subordination of bodily awareness to the rational will.[10] Hegel's description of his experience of himself as a subject in relation to objects reflects this same pattern of organization. He maintains that his "self" is "not constituted by the unity of *consciousness* of itself and the object; on the contrary, the object is, for the self, its negative."[11] Sensible objects merely provide something for consciousness to "come up against." Self-consciousness is constituted by the realization that the objects of experience are "other" than the self, the realization that one's self is *not* those other things. This process of negation is what evokes awareness of existing; it is therefore logically necessary for self-consciousness.

Hegel finds further evidence for the universality of his experience of oppositional duality (and thus for the validity of both his syllogistic logic and his dialectical method in general) in the relationship between the sexes.[12] He maintains that there is found in the state of nature a "specific antithesis of the two sexes," that men and women "come into direct contact with each other as real opposites." The male represents "universal self-conscious Spirit" and the female, "unconscious individualized Spirit." Through the process of sublation, these opposites are converted into "one and the same syllogism"—and the conclusion of this syllogism takes shape as a recognition of the logical priority of male self-consciousness.

Hegel describes his own experience of women, which he assumes is a universal male experience, as feeling like a "downward movement" from "actuality down to unreality . . . to the danger and trial of death." It seems to him that the (un)consciousness characteristic of women has an unsettling, subversive effect upon rational, masculine self-consciousness. But he speculates that a woman's encounter with a man has the opposite effect, since it must represent for her an "upward movement" from her "nether world" to "the actuality of the light of day"—a rather awe-inspiring encounter with fully conscious, rational being. For the sake of sexual gratification and procreation (the creation of the family relationship) a man bravely undertakes the disorienting plunge into the woman's world, but he does so with confidence that the dialectical nature of reality will subsequently impel him "out by the Spirit of the Family into the community in which he finds his self-conscious being."

In contrast, the woman's struggle to emerge from her murky underworld is doomed to failure. The lives of women constitute "an implicit, inner essence which is not exposed to the daylight of consciousness." Women are "exempt from an existence in the real world."[13] It is on this basis, for example, that Hegel derided the idea of educating women beyond the elementary level. The purpose of a secondary education is to provide "a bridge leading boys from the family to a vocation in civil society or the state," and since women are by nature incapable of fulfilling such a vocation, the idea of providing them with a secondary education is rationally indefensible.[14]

This "exemption" of women from the "real" world—the professional, civic, and academic worlds—turns them into "internal enemies" of the state, which further justifies and necessitates their suppression. Hegel attributes conspiratorial intent to "womankind in general," which "changes by intrigue the universal end of the government into a private end" and "perverts the universal property of the state into a possession and ornament for the Family."[15] The structural integrity of Hegel's system as a whole in fact requires the nullification of the influence of women: just as perception requires an object to negate, and just as self-consciousness requires an unessential (un)consciousness to rise above, the rationality that is specific to males arises out of and is made possible by the negation of the perverse and delusional world of the female other.[16]

Furthermore, not only does the practice of gender domination in interpersonal relationships make male rational self-consciousness possible, but it also provides a model for both the organization of the family unit and the relationship between the private and public spheres. "The basis of the patriarchal condition is the family relation; which develops the *primary* form of conscious morality, succeeded by that of the State as its *second* phase."[17] That is, the enforcement of gender domination within the family demonstrates the conditions for the possibility of the establishment of the rule of reason in the public sphere without effective resistance or significant loss of life—the "revolution without Revolution." The ideal government negates internal enemies by the same means that the influence of women is negated within the family: by "consuming and absorbing" them into itself and "keeping them dissolved in the fluid continuity of its own nature."[18] Within the state, as within the family, a failure to persuade others through rational argument to submit passively to domination makes it necessary for the stronger to establish dominance over the weaker by physical force.[19] And where both assimilation and domination fail, the state may then be forced to resort to its ultimate power of negation and eliminate dissension by implementing the death penalty: "In this flat, commonplace monosyllable [*Tod*] is contained the wisdom of the government, the abstract intelligence of the universal will, in the fulfilling of itself."[20]

IV

Reflecting on the French Revolution soon after the battle of Jena, Hegel expressed admiration for Napoleon and frustration that "Fatherland, princes, constitution, and such do not seem to be the lever with which to raise up the German people" to pursue a revolution of their own.[21] The revolution Hegel had in mind was one that would transpose the structure of domination from the private to the political sphere, bringing about the unification of the German states under one centralized government. It occurred to him even at this early stage of his career that the most efficient means to this end might be through the establishment of a state religion.

In his lectures on the philosophy of religion (1821–1831), the mature Hegel finally develops this notion explicitly, constructing a theological system that correlates the interests of male rational self-consciousness, German nationalism, and Protestant Christianity.[22] Or to put it another way, he attempts to authenticate the self-understanding of the nationalistic German Protestant male by identifying this self-understanding with the universal purposes of God in history.

Hegel asserts that "religion stands in the closest connection with the political principle," for in the organization of the state, "the divine has broken through into the sphere of actuality."[23] Philosophy plays a key role in this process. Hegel maintains that "the content of philosophy, its need and interest, is wholly in common with that of religion," because "philosophy is itself the service of God, as is religion."[24] Philosophy is in fact "the justification of religion," and not just of religion in general, but "especially of the Christian religion, the true religion."[25] The purpose of philosophical activity for Hegel is to construct a formal system that brings the interests of the state (the worldly realm) into rational conformity with the interests of the Christian faith (the divine realm), effecting "the reconciliation of God with himself."[26]

This concept of reconciliation [*Versöhnung*] is central to Hegel's philosophy of religion, within which it serves as the theological equivalent of the process of sublation. Hegel views the natural state of humanity as being characterized by an antithesis—"the familiar relationship of the syllogism"—between humanity and divinity.[27] Not surprisingly, he thinks that the consciousness characteristic of women illustrates the "hostile principle" that is "evil and futile in its separation from the universal."[28] In fact, any and all human beings "who stand over against the divine process"—i.e., who oppose or reject the process of reconciliation as delineated within German Protestant theology—are "evil" and subject to domination or elimination. "This humanity . . . on its own account (as against God), is evil, it is something alien to God" and "ought only to be dominated."[29]

Hegel clarifies the way in which this "evil" can be overcome, concretely speaking, in his interpretation of the Christian myth of the death of God, which he calls "the focal point of reconciliation."[30] Hegel interprets the death of Jesus Christ not as an act of *self-* sacrifice, nor as a sacrifice for the sake of others, but he redefines the term "to sacrifice" in this context so that it means "to sublate otherness." Christ's death carries humanity "to its furthest point"— to death. The death of Christ demonstrates the manner in which "the human element is stripped away and the divine glory comes into view once more—death is a stripping away of the human, the negative."[31] The establishment of the dominance of absolute spirit, in Hegel's view, requires this dehumanization of the spirit, this willingness to sacrifice humanity itself.

Hegel saw this interpretation of the death of God as the distinctive contribution of German Protestantism to the historical evolution of the Christian faith. He asserts that "the pure inwardness of the German nation was the proper soil for the emancipation of the Spirit," that the German people were "predestined" to be the bearers of this emancipated spirit, and that German Protestantism represents "the absolute culmination of Self-Consciousness."[32] He believed that the emancipatory potential of the Protestant faith is manifest in the attitude of "spiritual self-sufficiency" that these newly chosen people tend to exhibit. This "revolutionary attitude" is an "elevated" perspective, a distinguishing characteristic of which is a total indifference towards "all things hitherto regarded as ethical and right." This "renunciation, surrender, and setting aside" of all moral bonds—this cultivated insensitivity to even the minimal requirements of ethical social relationships—is in Hegel's system an essential prerequisite for "the concentrated manifestation of the truth," i.e., the homogenization of German society under the auspices of Protestant Christianity.[33]

The widespread assumption of this distinctively German Protestant attitude and the accompanying abandonment of all ethical considerations would, in Hegel's view, facilitate the actualization of God's kingdom on earth. This attitudinal stance is uniquely capable of evoking "the fear of the lord"—a phrase that Hegel uses more than once as a euphemism for the fear of death, the "absolute master"—that would inspire widescale voluntary conversion to Protestantism.[34] Terror in the face of death, he thought, would convince even the most stubborn "others" to surrender their separate identities and submit to "reconciliation." Furthermore, this dissociation of religious faith from ethical conduct also has the theoretical advantage of making it possible to justify on (theo)logical grounds the elimination of those portions of humanity that refuse to submit to the will of the German Protestant state. Their eradication can be interpreted as a sacrificial act, symbolized by the death of Christ, and thus as the highest expression of divine love: "It is out of infinite love that God has made himself identical with what is alien to him in order to put it to death. This is the meaning of the death of Christ."[35]

V. Conclusion

While Hegel does express, as Grimshaw has suggested, an awareness of the interdependence of human consciousness and social relationships, it is his understanding of the nature of this "interdependence" that is problematic. An analysis of the Hegelian text using intersubjectivity theory reveals that interdependence for Hegel always consists of an unequal complementarity. He conceives of the structure of domination as inescapable; any attempt to escape it inevitably results in a life-and-death struggle, and this struggle always ends in the stronger either enslaving or eliminating the other.[36] And whenever Hegel wished to produce readily observable evidence for the existential validity of his system, he pointed to the lives of women within nineteenth century German society. The apparent participation of German women in their own subordination implied to him the conditions for the possibility of the universal implementation of his system. It is with this in mind that Hegel moves methodically from the postulation of a fundamental intrapsychic dichotomy, to the claim that there is a "specific antithesis of the sexes," to a rationalization of the exclusion of women from the political arena as natural enemies of the state, to an identification of women with metaphysical evil, to a plan of salvation within which the idealization of death and sacrifice in the myth of the death of God provides the ultimate solution to this problem of evil.

Hegel's dialectical approach allows him to obfuscate, through equivocation and conceptual reversal, the violence and aggression that the process of sublation represents. The negative moment of the dialectic is always portrayed as a transitory but necessary stage in the production of some seemingly desirable after-effect. Thus, the renunciation of ethical relationships "loses its importance when the truth has achieved a secure existence." The subjugation/negation of the evil non-male, non-German, non-Protestant world is but a necessary prelude to the achievement of a rapprochement between humanity and divinity. Even the death of God, "the most frightful of all thoughts," is happily followed by a reversal in which "God rises again to life," demonstrating that suffering and death are necessary for a full and meaningful life.[37] What emerges from all of this is a formal system designed to justify and normalize the methodical suppression of, and when necessary, the systematic annihilation of all modes of difference that cannot (or will not) be assimilated.

Notes

1. See especially the chapter on "The 'Maleness' of Philosophy," in her *Philosophy and Feminist Thinking* (Minneapolis: University of Minnesota Press, 1986), pp. 36–74.

2. Ibid., pp. 68, 169.

3. Although it is certainly not logically impossible for a woman to be a thorough-going Hegelian, the self-defeating nature of such a stance would seem to compromise its rationality. In contrast, for Hegel, allegiance to a system designed to legitimate (and increase) the personal and political power of the German Protestant male would be ego-strengthening, and thus could be seen as a rational stance (as long as rationality is divorced from ethical considerations—as it is in Hegel's system). The internal logic of Hegel's system is perhaps its strongest point.

4. Cf. Moulton's "A Paradigm of Philosophy: The Adversary Method," in *Discovering Reality: Feminist Perspectives on Epistemology, Metaphysics, Methodology, and Philosophy of Science,* eds. Sandra Harding and Merrill B. Hintikka (Dordrecht: Reidel, 1983), pp. 149–164.

5. This concept of intersubjectivity is derived from the social theory of Jürgen Habermas by way of Jessica Benjamin (*The Bonds of Love: Psychoanalysis, Feminism, and the Problem of Domination* [New York: Pantheon, 1988]) and Seyla Benhabib (*Critique, Norm, and Utopia: A Study of the Foundations of Critical Theory* [New York: Columbia University Press, 1986]).

6. Jürgen Habermas, "Hegel's Critique of the French Revolution," in *Theory and Practice,* ed. John Viertal (Boston: Beacon Press, 1973), p. 123.

7. Ibid., p. 130.

8. *Phenomenology of Spirit,* trans. A. V. Miller (New York: Oxford, 1977), pp. 355–363.

9. Ibid., pp. 2, 136–138, 178.

10. Ibid., p. 368.

11. Ibid., pp. 133, 299.

12. Ibid., pp. 276–278.

13. Ibid., p. 274.

14. *Hegel: The Letters,* trans. Clark Butler and Christiane Seiler (Bloomington: Indiana University Press, 1984), pp. 301–302.

15. *Phenomenology,* pp. 287–88.

16. Hegel apparently implemented this system of domination within his own marital relationship. In correspondence with Eberhard and Caroline Paulus, he confines his wife (Marie von Tucher) to the margins of letters composed by him. Von Tucher timidly raises her "little voice" from the "humble little corner" that "he assigns me," deferring to "the length at which my lord and master goes on." Caroline Paulus herself answers this particular letter, ironically congratulating Hegel upon his establishment of himself as the "lord and master of the house" and upon "sweet Marie"'s submission to his "despotic claim." (*Letters,* p. 248.).

17. *The Philosophy of History,* trans. J. Sibree (New York: Dover, 1956), pp. 41–42.

18. *Phenomenology,* pp. 287–288.

19. Ibid., pp. 113–114.

20. Ibid., p. 360.

21. *Letters,* pp. 122–123.

22. The late date of Hegel's first lectures on the philosophy of religion (1821) leads Peter C. Hodgson to see him as taking a belated and rather sudden interest in this field in reaction to the impending publication of a major work by his bitter rival on the theological faculty in Berlin, Friedrich Schleiermacher. ("Editorial Introduction," *Lectures on the Philosophy of Religion* [Berkeley: University of California Press, 1988], pp. 1–2.). However, while the Hegel-Schleiermacher rivalry may well have been determinative for Hegel's decision to go public with his philosophical theology at this particular time, the deep structure of his philosophy of religion is clearly outlined in an early series of essays written between 1793 and 1800 (*Early Theological Writings,* trans. by T. M. Knox [Chicago: University of Chicago Press, 1948]), which may be considered the key to his mature philosophy of religion in much the same way that the *Phenomenology* is often considered the key to his philosophical system as a whole. Not insignificantly, these early writings reveal that at the heart of Hegel's philosophy of religion is a deeply entrenched anti-Judaism.

23. *Philosophy of History,* p. 50; *Philosophy of Religion,* p. 484n.

24. *Philosophy of Religion,* pp. 78–79.

25. Ibid., p. 487.

26. Ibid., p. 489.

27. Ibid., p. 164.

28. *Phenomenology,* p. 288.

29. *Philosophy of Religion,* pp. 466n., 483.

30. Ibid., pp. 467–468.

31. Ibid., pp. 465–466n., 468–469.

32. *Philosophy of History,* pp. 354, 420, 444.

33. *Philosophy of Religion,* pp. 460–461. Cf. also p. 255.

34. Cf. *Phenomenology,* p. 361.

35. *Philosophy of Religion,* p. 466n.

36. Cf. Benjamin, pp. 54ff. *Phenomenology,* pp. 113–114.

37. Ibid., pp. 461, 465n., 469, 483.

Hegel, Antigone, and the Possibility of a Woman's Dialectic

Cynthia Willett

Feminists reproach the Western tradition for neglecting the constituitive role of feeling in philosophical cognition. The traditional philosopher disengages himself from any particular social context and pursues truths that are abstract. Feminists propose that truth originates not in abstract entities but in particular realities and that these realities are informed not only by categories of reason but also by emotion. In general feminists attack dualism, or that mode of thinking that introduces distinctions in order to subordinate or exclude from consideration some parts of experience, and especially those parts that are interpreted as feminine.

Hegel could be an ally of feminists because of this attempt to develop a dialectic that would weave together opposed realms of experience. For example, Hegel denies the truth of abstraction and demonstrates that experience is unintelligible except as an interweaving of universals and particulars. Nonetheless many feminists have been wary of turning to dialectic in order to generate a countertradition to dualism because of the tendency of dialectic, despite its claims, to reinvoke the same abstract and unerotic logic that mars much of traditional reflection.

In this chapter, the role that eros plays in Hegel's dialectic of ethical spirit will be examined. Hegel locates the origin of ethics in classical drama. My interest is in what a dramatic work performs when it appears in what Hegel calls the "phenomenology of spirit," or the education of humanity. As it turns out the structure of classical drama traces a paradigm and an historical origin for Hegel's dialectic. The ironic reversals and discoveries that emplot tragic drama also constitute dialectic. An immediate consequence of this parallel is that, in accordance with Aristotle's definition of tragic drama, dialectic demands the catharsis, or purging, of emotion from educated spirit.

After establishing the analogy between dialectic and cathartic drama, I turn to the exemplary role of Sophocles' *Antigone* in Hegel's *Phenomenology of spirit*. A reinterpretation of the play suggests that passion, and not reason, in fact orients heroic action. My conclusion is that if emotion cannot be purged from classical tragedy, then, by analogy, emotion must also propel dialectic. Dialectic should be reconstructed in terms of a notion of tragedy that originates not in catharsis but in ecstatic desire.

The Dialectic of Tragedy

In the *Aesthetics,* Hegel places drama after epic and lyric as the third and final moment of the highest stage of art.[1] Only drama can bring together subjective and objective poles of aesthetic experience. Drama advances spirit beyond the subjective expression of lyric and the objective narration of epic events to ethical action.[2]

In general, dialectical advance proceeds by "sublation" (*Aufhebung*). Sublation signifies the process that *negates* and *preserves at a higher level* oppositions that beset lower stages of spirit. This positive result of dialectic constitutes what is called the third, or speculative, moment. For example, ethical spirit expunges desire but preserves subjectivity in the form of an intention to act in accordance with ethical law.[3]

While Hegel borrows the classical notion that the import of tragedy is ethical, he complicates Aristotle's attempt to locate tragic error in the *hybris,* or excesses, of a protagonist who oversteps a limit. By Hegel's account, Aristotle's notion of tragedy is not dialectical but one-sided. The one-sided reading assumes that tragedy results when an otherwise noble character acts in a way that is itself devoid of ethical merit.[4] Aristotle lacks a notion of ethical conflict, or ambiguity, which Hegel claims necessitates tragic action.

Hegel argues that tragedy lies in the necessity of the hero to choose to act in accordance with one of two conflicting principles that simultaneously possess universal ethical significance.[5] The one-sidedness that defines the heroic individual gives rise to a collision with another equally heroic individual. Tragedy ends in the incipient reconciliation of the ethical powers that come into conflict. Hegel writes: "an unresolved contradiction is set up; . . . its proper claim is satisfied only when it is annulled (*aufhebt*) as a contradiction. However . . . necessary the tragic collision, the third thing required is the tragic resolution of this conflict."[6] Tragic *pathos,* or suffering, brings each hero to recognize the opposing ethical law as her or his own. The tragic internalization of an *agon,* or conflict, constitutes the ethical vision that concludes a play. As Sophocles' choruses proclaim, tragedy engenders learning through suffering.[7] The result of tragedy, Hegel insists, is positive knowledge.

Hegel's emphasis on tragic reconciliation advances beyond both the one-sided Aristotelian notion of tragic failure as well as the *aporia,* or ironic endings, that render many of Plato's dialogues tragically unresolved. Classical theory assumes that tragedy moves from social harmony to catastrophic reversal. Tragedies were originally written, however, as trilogies. While the *Oresteia* of Aeschylus is the only extant three-part tragedy, only later do tragedians begin to break up trilogies into single plays. The independence of Sophocles' *Antigone* and *Oedipus the King* from his *Oedipus at Colonus* gives the appearance that tragedy ends without reconciliation. In fact, however, the *Oresteia* makes clear what Hegel believes classical tragedy in general intimates: the ethical individual stands at the uneasy crossroads between opposed but equally legitimate principles that solicit reconciliation.

In contrast to tragedy, comedy, according to Hegel, develops the subjective and one-sidedly negative moment of spirit by freeing the individual from ethical law. The comic hero plays the lord of misrule, or perhaps the Cartesian sceptic, who reduces everything, except him- or herself, to absurdity.[8] The effect is to expose action to what is finite and contingent. Hegel limits his consideration of comic drama to ironic satire and, curiously, leaves aside altogether the marriages of romantic comedy.[9] The *Phenomenology,* then, takes up the contingent and the comic but only as what destroy ethics.

The Tragedy of Dialectic

It is surprising that while Hegel gives emphasis to the cathartic moment of tragedy, he does not explicitly refer to what Aristotle distills as two major components of tragedy, ironic reversal (*peripeteia*) and recognition (*anagorisis*).[10] These two moments of tragic drama coincide well with the negative and speculative moments of dialectical sublation. Moreover, tragedy's reversals presuppose an initial condition of stasis as does dialectical negation. Thus, the triadic structure of tragedy parallels that of dialectic.

Hegel's *Phenomenology of Spirit* provides the clearest analogy between tragedy and dialectic. The *Phenomenology* aims to provide an education for "natural consciousness," or the perspective that fails to see a dialectical connection between opposing realms of experience. The plight of natural consciousness resembles that of the hero of tragedy. Knowledge comes only after suffering through the ironic reversal of what first appears to be true. Recognition of the interdependence of one-sided truth-claims constitutes the positive resolution of tragic dialectic.

If the dialectical movement of the *Phenomenology* parallels tragic drama, the recognition of limits that propels natural consciousness beyond one-sided positions reaches resolution only by way of catharsis. Hegel explicitly draws on the power of purification or purgation (Hegel tends to prefer the medical term '*Reinigung*') throughout the *Phenomenology*. It is a pathos of dialectical advance that every reconciliation of opposed principles demands the systematic explusion of what cannot be taken up into pure thought.

Perhaps the most striking example of cathartic sublation appears in the section of the *Phenomenology* that develops ethical spirit, i.e., the education of humanity to ethical decision, by way of Sophocles' *Antigone*.[11] The ethical order culminates in a tentative *Aufhebung* of the clash between human and divine law.

In the play, Antigone refuses to obey the edict of her uncle Creon, king of Thebes, who outlaws the burial of the enemies of the *polis*. These enemies include the brother of Antigone, Polyneices, who has instigated a war on Thebes and whose death has occurred at the hands of the state. The state insists on its right to punish transgressions committed by the rebellious individual against the universal community. Creon's refusal to recognize the rights of burial threatens to reduce Polyneices' life to an empty, or one-sided, affirmation of the power of the state. That is, the individual would lose any principle of independence from the state. An individual that provides nothing more than resources for the state's needs is reduced to a "transitory particular," i.e., an entity that lacks separate identity and therefore can be replaced by any number of other entities. Only the family's right to burial could protect the memory of the individual from the oblivion and inconsequence of natural decay. If Antigone can not perform memorial services in the name of her brother, Hegel argues, then his remains vanish in the philosophical void of a non-human nature.

On the one hand, failing to recognize the state's dependency on the right of individuals, Creon attempts to preserve state power by repressing the individual. On the other hand, Antigone erroneously insists that the demands of the state count for nothing against the divine right of the family to secure memorial services for each individual.

If the ritual of purification involved in funeral services, is to protect the individual from the irrational forces of nature, then those forces must not contaminate the performance of ethical duty. Hegel writes that "the Family . . . is within itself an ethical entity only so far as it is not the natural relationship of its members . . . [B]ecause the ethical principle is intrinsically universal, the ethical connection between the member of the Family is not that of feeling, or the relationship of love."[12]

Moreover, Hegel argues that if the motives for the ethical deed are to be pure—that is, uncontaminated by the irrationality that mars natural desire—the responsibility for the performance of ethical duty must reside in the relation of sister to brother. Hegel's insistence on the unique character of the sibling relation finds its evidence in a part of Sophocles' play that persistently gives rise to difficulties of interpretation. At the first confrontation between Antigone and Creon, Antigone had defended the burial of her brother by proclaiming that the duty to the dead extends universally: "Death longs for the same rites for all."[13] In an apparent inconsistency, Antigone later singles out her brother as uniquely deserving of her services: Never, Antigone declares, "if my husband died, exposed and rotting—I'd never have taken this ordeal upon myself, never defied our people's will . . . A husband dead, there might have been another. A child by another too, if I had lost the first. But . . . no brother could ever spring to light again."[14]

These lines, spoken with the clarity of vision that writers often grant characters near death, threaten Hegel's reading of tragedy as the clash between universals, or two ethical laws. It seems that Antigone's character does not stem from an abstract duty to the family. On the contrary, it has been suggested that she possesses a "peculiar individuality" that manifests itself in a passionate devotion to a brother.[15] Because these lines threaten interpretations that locate Antigone's motives in a pure sense of duty, many critics, including Goethe, have insisted that Sophocles was not their author.[16]

Hegel's interpretation of lines that otherwise appear external to the tragedy demonstrates the power of the dialectic to salvage much from what is first rendered accidental or irrational. Dialectic cancels all oppositions, including that between essence and accident or abstract universal and bare particular. The dialectical resolution, or mediation, of opposites presupposes a demonstration that opposites are reversible. Only then can it be known that the truth of one-sided claims lies in their mediation. For example, while Creon claims the universal interests of the state, his claim immediately converts into the demands of a tyrant, who, in his particularity, lacks ethical import. Similarly, Antigone's devotion to a particular person against the common interests of the state must be shown to convert into a duty to universal law. Given this dialectic reversal, Hegel can show that the relation between siblings incurs an uniquely ethical status.

The bonds between husband and wife or parent and child, Hegel points out, mix an ethical concern for the family with feelings of love or desire.[17] Such feelings can be interpreted in terms of erotic or maternal instincts. Hegel argues that these bonds have an irreducibly external, or accidental, quality to them. Either spouse could be replaced, their bond lasting only as long as their desire. So, too, maternal devotion to a child may be directed towards another child if the first dies. Thus, alluding to the puzzling lines from Sophocles' play, Hegel writes that

> the relationships of mother and wife . . . are those of particular individuals partly in the form of something natural pertaining to desire, partly in the form of something negative which sees in those relationships only something evanescent and also, again, the particular individual is for that very reason a contingent element which can be replaced by another individual.[18]

The dialectic of ethical law requires the catharsis, or purging, of whatever originates in natural desire. The relationship between the brother and sister alone satisfies the requirement that ethical duty to the family is pure of the vagaries or accidental attractions of natural desire. The relationships of mother and wife can never take part in ethical spirit because their highest ethical moment appears as an abstract universal, an empty role, which can be played in relation to any number of substitutes. Presumably, natural desire or instinct is not very selective. The ethical roles of mother and wife, then, admit a degree of sheer contingency, which in turn sullies their ethical character. Consequently, both roles fall out of the dialectic of ethical spirit. If the family bond between siblings excludes any element of desire then this bond alone carries universal ethical import. Hegel is able to conclude that "the loss of the brother is therefore irreparable to the sister and her duty towards him is the highest."[19]

Similarly, the conflict between Antigone and Creon enacts the dialectic of divine and human law only as long as their intentions aspire to universal principles. If their actions were to be shown to stem even partly from desire, the possibility of resolving their differences would break down, and ethical spirit would be choked by impurities. Natural desire or transitory feeling would irremediably disrupt dialectical closure in accordance with a "bad infinite," an endless series of desires that could not be made true by sublation. If Hegel is correct in his assumption that sublation entails a kind of purgation, then the result of an ethics contaminated by desire could only be paralysis and scepticism.

The dialectic proceeds towards an absolute, or infinite, totality (Hegel's "good infinite") by way of a process that occurs in tragedy as pathetic catharsis, or what the preface to Nietzsche's *Genealogy of Morals* recognizes, in a happier vein, as "active forgetting." The systematic act of exclusion guarantees the relative unity possible for each *Aufhebung,* or tentative resolution, occuring in the *Phenomenology.* Every act of recollection necessarily conceals in its shadow the work of absolute forgetting. Yet, the success with which the dialectic educates us, or natural consciousness, to the absolute standpoint may legitimate this forgetfulness.

The legitimacy of dialectical catharsis falls apart, however, if the dialectic in some unacknowledged way draws from what it would exclude. A dialectic of the ethical order can include neither erotic nor maternal instinct. Hegel can justify the consistency of Anitgone's final defense, which particularizes duty to a sibling, with her earlier demand that burial rites are universal, only if the sibling relation is pure of desire. However, reinterpreting the problematic lines in the context of parts of the play ignored by Hegel undermines the purity of Antigone's motives.

For example, Antigone's emotional speech about the irreplacibility of her brother occurs right after she learns that she is to be buried alive. Hegel's attempt to reconcile the two defenses in favor of abstract law is unlikely if it is supposed that the immanence of death has broken down the artificiality of Antigone's earlier appeal to abstract duty. Moreover, just after Antigone expresses her duty to her irreplaceable brother, the chorus accuses her of confusing impassioned public demonstrations of defiance with an acceptable private reverence for the gods.[20] The accusations of the chorus suggest that Antigone's respect for the divine duty is intertwined with strange passion. It is now the pathos of Antigone's one-sided adherence to divine law that provokes such a brazen act of defiance. Earlier, as Antigone is brought before the king to receive her final sentence, the chorus offers an hymm: "Love," the chorus wails, "wrench[es] the minds of the righteous into outrage, serve[s] them to their ruin . . . and Love alone the victor."[21] Antigone's insistence on duty stems from love.

The nature of Antigone's love is complicated further by images of maternal instinct. For example, the sentry describes the scene in which Antigone encounters the unburied body of her brother as "like a bird come back to an empty nest, peering into its bed, and all the babies gone."[22] Moreover, the image of Antigone's tomb as her bridal-bed and the fact that in other versions of the story she is to be buried with her brother suggest that the intensity of Antigone's feelings towards her brother owes something to the erotic instinct, which more typically binds husband and wife.[23] The play locates the mountain-cave where Antigone will be entombed "down some wild, desolate path never trod by men."[24] "Frenzied women . . . fired with . . . sacred rage" follow this path in celebration of the orgiastic rites of Dionysus.[25] Antigone's "worship of death" carries erotic overtones.[26] Dionysius lies behind devotion to law.

Various lines in the play also lead us to suspect that Creon's defense of the city against the "hysteria" of Antigone manifests more rage than pure devotion to law. When Creon decides to free Antigone, recognizing that he erred in punishing her, he confesses that "[i]t's hard giving up the heart's desire."[27] As a result of similar lines critics suggest that there are incestuous elements in the relation between Creon and Antigone.[28] Finally, the chorus compares Creon to King Lycurgus who, out of a rage that was itself mysterious, failed to suppress passions unleashed by mysteries of Dionysus.[29]

The gods celebrated in a play that Hegel reads as the clash between abstract principles are Aphrodite and Dionysus, gods of passion, not purity or reason.[30] The tragedy of Creon, like that of Lycurgus, suggests that any attempt to erradicate passion is itself passionate. The agony of Antigone intimates that the righteous defense of ethical duty originates not in abstract duty but in a subjective passion that determines the performance of duty.

Hegel admits that the tentative resolution in ethical tragedy perpetually collapses. As Sophocles warns us, "once the gods have rocked a house to its foundations the ruin will never cease."[31] Tragedy forewarns of the endless return of discord even as every play promises to bring the cycle of violence to a halt. That is, every work of tragedy knows itself as a failure. According to Hegel, this failure persists because the city-state of Creon continues to suffer from the contingencies introduced by nature. For example, it is a contingent fact that Antigone has two brothers, both of whom seek to control the state. The dialectic must proceed, Hegel urges, until it either eradicates or incorporates every interruption from nature into the service of spirit.

The reinterpretation of *Antigone,* however, suggests a more complicated understanding of the failure of tragedy and tragic dialectic. My claim is that while Hegel demands the purging of desire from ethical intention, duty originates in desire. Although dialectical sublation would seem to require the undialectical exclusion of desire from pure thought, the element of desire figures into the structure of dialectical progression. Inasmuch as Hegel models dialectic on cathartic drams, every attempt at resolution demands purging whatever is inextricably irrational. But the very act of purgation reinstills what it attempts to purge. Creon's attempt to eradicate passion is itself passionate and Creon's failure tells us something about the failure of any attempt to purge. The curse of cathartic tragedy necessarily haunts any philosophy of spirit, or *Geist,* that would borrow its structure. Consequently, every resolution of dialectic perpetuates the discord it promises to harmonize because no final catharsis of desire is possible.

The Possibility of Ecstatic Dialectic

Not all conceptions of tragedy borrow Aristotle's notion of catharsis. For example, Longinus proposed that the most powerful literature is not cathartic but ecstatic, i.e., induces emotional transport.[32] If Sophocles' play epitomizes tragic drama, then tragic catharsis is no more possible than the suppression of Antigone's terrible love for her brother. The cathartic interpretation of tragedy, then, may suffer from the same abstraction and artificiality that characterizes Antigone's early defense of her brother. The emotional bond between Antigone and her brother suggests that while a play may begin by inviting a rational response from both characters and audience, by the end it solicits not the *logos* of human reason but silence before a strange and compelling desire.

Hegel's exemplary play turns against him in some of the ways insisted upon by Nietzsche's *Birth of Tragedy.* Where Hegel sees reason as the force behind tragic actions, Nietzsche finds the less intelligible god of desire, Dionysus. The attempt to rationalize tragic emotions leads Hegelians such as Stephan Houlgate to defend Hegel's claim that the crimes of Creon and Anitgone are equal.[33] Few readers, however, have not felt inclined to favor Antigone. In effect, to postulate their crimes as equal is already to give more credence to Creon's appeal to the universal community than supported by the play. The result is to deny altogether what Houlgate rebukes in Nietzsche, that "the self is essentially natural, instinctual and individual rather than social."[34]

While a reinterpretation of *Antigone* does suggest that instincts lie behind ethical duty, it resists further comparisons with Nietzsche. *Antigone* does not celebrate but mourns the forces of destruction. These forces do not provide, as Houlgate summarizes Nietzsche, a "stimulant to man's own heroic affirmation, as a hurdle over which man may test his individualistic, gymnastic soul."[35] On the contrary, the drama of *Antigone* figures a kind of partial dialectic, that is a dialectic that does not purge but engages characters and audience in an emotional bond. The dialectic of *Antigone* marches towards a wisdom that is ethical, and hence more than fictive or gymnastic, and yet carries with it a crucial role for desire. Acknowedged or not, dialectic can advance only by way of mediations woven by ecstatic engagement in the world. Antigone's tragic force owes nothing to her "bare particularity," i.e., to an asocial isolation or inexplicable idiosyncracy. Nor does this force stem from participation in an utterly non-human cosmic force. Antigone's duty stems from instincts that intertwine the eros of wife, mother, and sister.

In fact, the possibility of catharsis or, analogously, audience disinterest in the plight of the *pharmakos*, or "scapegoat," might serve to distingish comedy from tragedy. In the second paragraph of the *Poetics*, Aristotle observes that tragic characters are somehow more noble than average people while comic characters fall below average. An audience more likely identifies with the suffering of a noble character than with the abuses suffered by an ignoble one. It is interesting that comedy often ends by laughing the scapegoat offstage and by bringing the audience to the perspective of those who remain on stage. Tragedy, on the other hand, invites the audience to share the perspective of the isolated pharmakos. That is, tragedy allows for sympthetic identification with the suffering of the scapegoat whereas comedy breaks off such emotional engagement. The sharing of pathos between audience and pharmakos rather than its catharsis may define an ethical function of tragedy that is apt to be missing in comedy.

Finally, my suggestion that the tragedy of *Antigone* presents an ethics of desire rather than abstract principle intimates an alternative, or shadow, phenomenology of spirit. Such a phenomenology would retain a dialectical and hence mediating structure but would counter Hegel's own implicit tilt towards Creon and what Creon represents with a dialectic that tilts towards Antigone and what Hegel calls her "shadowy intuition." In effect, Hegel finally and necessarily one-sidedly subordinates a kind of knowledge that he associates with divine law and woman to the reason that he associates with human law and man.

Thus, a reinterpretation of *Antigone* supports feminist critiques of Hegel. In particular, I agree with Patricia Jagentowicz Mills, who argues that Hegel's "partial treatment of woman not only limits woman but limits his philosophy so that he cannot claim for his system of knowledge the universality that he seeks."[36] On the other hand, I also wonder if Mills's critique doesn't somewhat oversimplify Hegel's position. Specifically, Mills claims that Hegel never allows Antigone to become a self-conscious individual: "woman neither is nor can be master or slave [i.e., attempt self-consciousness] in Hegel's schema precisely because for Hegel . . . woman does not experience a contradiction between herself and nature that she must negate."[37]

However, ethical spirit presupposes earlier stages of the *Phenomenology*. As an ethical actor Antigone no less than Creon must possess self-consciousness. Self-consciousness is earned in a "battle for recognition," which the *Phenomenology* has dramatized as a dialectic between master and slave. The "master" proves him- or herself over the "slave," and achieves self-consciousness, by demonstrating a will to risk his or her own life. Hegel insists that Antigone, no less than Creon, rise above natural desire and indeed risk her life for principle. Antigone becomes an ethical creature because she adhers not to immediate particularity, as Mills claims, but chooses to act in accordance with an universal law.[38]

While Hegel does grant Antigone the power to negate natural desire, in fact Antigone's ethical action does not purge but intensifies desire. *Antigone* resists Hegel's attempt to bring women and men into a community whose ethics rests on a logos purged of natural desire. Hegel's failure rests not so much on the exclusion of woman from a scene of recognition as the exclusion of woman's maternal and erotic desire from sublated ethics. This exclusion of desire stems from the fact that Hegel figures the pathos of dialectical negation from a cathartic rather than ecstatic conception of tragedy. The point is not to include woman in man's dialectic but to refigure a woman's dialectic.

Such a dialectic relocates woman and natural desire at the heart of ethical and political actions. If the ethical duty of Antigone to her brother intertwines maternal and erotic instincts, then key elements of dialectic require reformulation.

First of all, sublation should involve the intense expression of a binding desire rather than its non-dialectical exclusion and cathartic sublimation in abstract duty.

Secondly, the *Phenomenology*'s attempt to locate the origin of self-consciousness in a battle or recognition may be reinterpreted from woman's perspective. According to Hegel, the will to risk one's life determines the winner in the battle of recognition. This game, however, sounds suspiciously close to rituals that belong to male and not female members of various animal species. While male animals may risk their lives in a symbolic show of force, which determines either rank or territorial possession, female members more typically risk death—or actually die—in order to protect their young. That is, male animals may struggle until one gives some sign of defeat, perhaps an exposed neck, which ends the conflict. The battle normally ends short of death. Thus, male animals do not so much risk death as play at risking death. The maternal instinct to protect the young, however, could end in actual sacrifice of the mother. Similarly, Antigone's willingness to die in the name of the family owes its strength in part to a maternal instinct. The maternal readiness to die does not determine the same notion of a self-conscious individual that develops in the *Phenomenology*.

Hegel idealizes Antigone to the point where she is no longer an impassioned woman but an allegory of ethical duty. I fear that Mills may rescue Antigone from Hegel only in order to re-fashion her in much of the same idealizing, even masculine, terms. For example, Mills defines Antigone's nobility in terms of action that can be justified only by fully conscious reason: "Antigone's tragedy is the result of strength and moral courage—the so-called masculine virtues—not an emotional 'intuition'."[39]

Mills and Hegel fail to appreciate a more shadowy kind of knowledge that can only be partially brought to consciousness or submitted to a rational dialectic. My reading of *Antigone* resists the law, or logos, of a dialectic that proceeds by purges. In its place is not the dark and mute realm of unmediated and undialectical desire, i.e., Mills's "unconscious particularity," or sheer fragmentation and scepticism. Like Hegel's dialectic, Antigone's dialectic interweaves particularity and universality, nature and culture. Antigone's dialectic also structures its plot from classical elements of reversal and recognition. Suffering brings wisdom. However, while Hegel's dialectic subordinates and finally excludes desire in favor of reason, a second interpretation of dialectic does not exclude reason but turns toward desire. Antigone's dialectic mediates the engagement of wife and mother within an ethics that no longer expunges subjective feeling from duty. And if, as the *Phenomenology* insists, the tragic dialectic of *Antigone* presents a first glimpse into the spirit of humanity, then that rather partial bond is held together by a reconciliation that may not be cathartic but ecstatic.

Notes

I would like to thank Irene Harvey, Carl Vaught, Joseph Flay, Robert Frodeman, and Bat-Ami Bar On for their comments on earlier versions of this essay.

An earlier version of this essay appears in *Philosophy and Literature*, spring 1991, under the title of "Hegel, Antigone, and the Possibility of Ecstatic Dialectic."

1. G. W. F. Hegel, *Aesthetics,* tr. T. M. Knox (Oxford: Clarendon Press, 1975) vol 2: p. 1158 ; *Vorlesungen ueber die Aesthetic* (Frankfurt: Suhrkamp, 1978) p. 474.

2. Ibid., p. 1160; p. 476.

3. Ibid., p. 1158; p. 474.

4. At least one Aristotelian, Martha C. Nussbaum, draws much from Hegel in her interpretation of *Antigone.* Most crucially her argument that the play presents an ethical education on the necessity of interweaving conflicting aspects of experience resembles Hegel's dialectical reading of tragedy. Nussbaum tends to obscure this point of resemblance because of her tendency to misinterpret Hegelian mediation as one-sided abstraction. Nussbaum's argument eventually returns to the kind of one-sided reading of classical tragedy that Hegel wants to avoid inasmuch as she concludes that tragic failure results from the vulnerability of practical judgment to back luck rather than from the conflict between two equally valid ethical principles See her *Fragility of Goodness* (New York: Cambridge Univ. Press, 1989) esp. pp. 68 and 387.

5. *Aesthetics,* p. 1217; *Vorlesungen,* p. 548.

6. Ibid., p. 1197; p. 524.

7. Sophocles, *The Three Theban Plays,* tr. Robert Fagles (New York: Penguin Press, 1984): *Antigone,* line 1470 and *Oedipus,* line 1483.

8. *Aesthetics,* p. 1220; *Vorlesungen* p. 552.

9. Cf. Hayden White, *Metahistory: The Historical Imagination in Nineteenth Century Europe* (Baltimore: Johns Hopkins Univ. Press, 1973) p. 92. White argues that dialectic is comedy.

10. Aristotle, *Poetics* 2:11.

11. G. W. F. Hegel, *Phenomenology of Spirit,* tr. A. v. Miller (Oxford: Oxford Univ. Press, 1977) ch. 6 sec. A; *Phaenomenologie des Geistes* (Hamburg: Felix Meiner Verlag, 1952).

12. Ibid. pp. 268–9 and 320.

13. *Antigone,* line 584.

14. Ibid., lines 995–1004.

15. Fagles, p. 46.

16. Ibid.

17. *Phenomology,* p. 273; *Phaenomenologie,* p. 325.

18. Ibid., p. 274; p. 326.

19. Ibid., p. 275; p. 327.

20. *Antigone,* lines 959–963.

21. Ibid., lines 886–890.

22. Ibid., line 471.

23. Ibid., line 978.

24. Ibid., line 870.

25. Ibid., lines 1239ff.

26. Ibid., line 877.

27. Ibid., line 1229.

28. Bennett Simon, " 'With Cunning Delays and Ever-Mounting Excitement' or: What Thickens the Plot in Tragedy and in Psychoanalysis, " *Hebrew University Studies in Literature and the Arts* II (1983): pp. 226–253.

29. *Antigone,* lines 1052–4.

30. Ibid., lines 1240ff.

31. Ibid., lines 658–9.

32. See Northrop Fyre, *Anatomy of Criticism* (Princeton Univ. Press, 1957) p. 67.

33. Stephen Houlgate, *Hegel, Nietzsche, and the Criticism of Metaphysics* (New York: Cambridge Univ. Press, 1986) pp. 200–1.

34. Ibid., p. 218.

35. Ibid., p. 216.

36. Patricia Jagentowicz Mills, *Woman, Nature,* and *Psyche* (New Haven: Yale Univ. Press, 1987) p. xiii.

37. Ibid., p. 11.

38. Ibid., p. 16.

39. Ibid., p. 35.

PART FOUR

CRITICS OF MODERNITY

Marx and the Ideology of Gender: A Paradox of Praxis and Nature

Wendy Lee-Lampshire

While ecofeminist and Marxist-feminist literature appear both vast in themselves and relatively unrelated to each other, some versions of each share in an ecologically motivated utopic vision very much in the spirit of Marx.[1] The key to this utopia lies in the Marxian concept of praxis for it is within this novel concept of creative activity that nature is alleged to be transformed without being exploited. The best hope for articulating a feminist-Marxist as well as an ecofeminist future, then, would seem to depend upon the discovery of a way to articulate praxis in more explicitly feminist terms. The aim of this paper, however, is to show why such an undertaking is destined to failure. For the assumptions which animate praxis in the Marxian conceptual constellation preclude women from participation in the utopic vision. Thus, although the feminist commitment to emancipation seems to find a common ally in Marxism, this sympathy is actually more apparent than real. For concepts like praxis turn out to be rooted in an untenable philosophical dualism between rational activity and natural proclivity, the practical realization of which finds expression in a Victorian ideology which identifies women with the natural while reserving rationality exclusively for men.

I. The Ambivalence of Praxis

I would like to begin with the critical feminist approach to Marxism known as dual systems theory. This approach attempts to clarify the relation between capitalism and patriarchy by showing the analogous themes which animate and perpetuate these systems of domination. Birke, for example, points out that these systems operate as mutually conditioning but nevertheless independent forms of power.[2] Hartmann elaborates this theme further arguing that

185

males are not only the primary beneficiaries of the capitalist system but also, as husbands and fathers, may expect services to be performed within the home regardless of economic status.[3]

A major insight of dual systems theory is that patriarchy precedes and conditions emergent capitalism by legitimating and naturalizing domination. The naturalized power relationships which inform the Victorian family structure ground the capitalist's unique position of authority while simultaneously reinforcing an advantageous division of labor which legitimates 'his' authority both in the workplace and at home.[4] Furthermore, division of labor by gender functions as the most efficient available instrument towards the maintenance of class division by legitimating the power of the capitalist.[5]

The very success of capitalism, however, depends not only upon the way in which labor has been divided and naturalized but upon an accompanying ideology which identifies women with a nature that is both passive and irrational. For in this light the labor of woman may be legitimately construed as a resource, e.g., as something to be exploited but not consulted. Marxian theory, then, would seem to provide a striking alternative to the capitalist labor scenario arguing that nature is not a resource to be legitimately exploited and subdued but the very material out of and with which humans essentially create themselves.[6] It is this self-creativity that Marx refers to as *praxis*.

Upon closer inspection, however, Marx's definition of praxis reveals several paradoxical assumptions and philosophical ambiguities. The context in which the concept of essential human activity appears proves to be illuminating not only by what specific activities it does include but by what is precluded in what Marx himself takes to be the "natural division of labor."[7] In essence, the kind of activity Marx envisions praxis to consist in predisposes it toward the tacit conservation of a specifically sexual division of labor; the same presuppositions which characterize the division of labor in capitalist production characterize praxis as well. From *The German Ideology*:

> On the other hand, man's consciousness of the necessity of associating with the individuals around him is the beginning of the consciousness that he is living in society at all. This beginning is as animal as social life itself at this stage. It is mere herd consciousness, and at this point man is only distinguished from the sheep by the fact that with him the consciousness takes the place of in-

stinct or that his instinct is a conscious one. This sheep or tribal consciousness receives its further development and extension through increased productivity, the increase of needs, and, what is fundamental to both of these, the increase of population. *With these there develops a division of labor which develops spontaneously or 'naturally' by virtue of natural predisposition (e.g., physical strength), needs, accidents, etc.* Division of labor only becomes truly such from the moment when a division of material and mental labor appears.[8]

And slightly further:

With the division of labor, in which all these contradictions are implicit, and which in its turn is based on the natural division of labor within the family and the separation of society into individual families opposed to one another, is given simultaneously the distribution, and indeed the unequal distribution, both quantitative and qualitative, of labor and its products, hence property: *the nucleus, the first form of which lies in the family, where wife and children are slaves of the husband.* This latter slavery in the family, though still very crude, *is the first property,* but even at this early state it corresponds perfectly to the definition of modern economists who call it the power of disposing the labor power of others.[9]

What Marx assumes to be a necessary and, therefore, natural product of emerging social consciousness—the gender division of labor—in the first passage serves, in the second, as the foundation of property and, hence, class. First, Marx assumes that gender provides a criterion of labor division which, because it may be classified as 'natural' is, thus, not truly a division in the sense he will later give to praxis. Yet the predispositions which are subsumed under this original (non-) division, and later realized in the form of the family become, secondly, the basis of property ownership, and, thus the initial catalyst of class antagonism ("the separation of families opposed to one another").[10] In other words, what Marx has ambiguously and implicitly assumed under the heading of "natural predispositions" is later explicitly subsumed by the "division of material and mental labor," the realization of which will ultimately emerge as praxis. Yet the very familial relations which make the division between the 'natural' and the 'rational' possible simultaneously provide emergent capitalism with its foundational institutions, property and class. As we shall see, then, praxis and its antithesis, alienation, ultimately spring from the same ambiguous source, that is, the 'natural' *gendered* division of labor.

The ambiguity of Marx's conception of the division of labor is that he appears to recognize that the nucleus of property is the family structure, "where wife and children are slaves of the husband." Yet, it must be asked, how can a division alleged to occur "spontaneously" or "naturally" by virtue of the necessity attached to an increase of needs and, therefore, population also produce slavery? If slavery is a natural outgrowth of social evolution, how is Marx warranted in construing it as a *distortion* of natural familial relations? At the level of capitalist production, moreover, slavery describes a relationship between capitalist and worker that, for Marx, is inimical to praxis understood as the non-exploitive relation between human creativity and the natural world. There is no provision in praxis for the treatment of human labor as a resource. Yet by invoking 'natural predispositions' in order to substantiate the division of labor, Marx tacitly promotes a division which requires a 'resource' and 'exploiter', a worker and an owner, a wife and a husband.

By reducing familial relations, described as essentially property/slavery oriented, to the specific exchange value of capitalist trade, Marx has implicitly subsumed the patriarchal component of these relations. The gender division now becomes a derivative feature of an economic unit of production. Moreover, the textual ordering of these passages betrays a duality concealed by the term 'property'. For the order giving rise to the 'material and mental' division is pre-figured in the original gender division which has been subsumed. That is, the very division of 'material' and 'mental' requires some pre-established criteria which may be found, in Marx's case, simply be referring to those attributes arrayed under the 'natural' in the same passage. Thus, the ambiguity which attends Marx's conception of the natural also infects his understanding of 'patriarchal' relations. In the *Communist Manifesto* Marx proclaims that:

> The bourgeoisie . . . has put an end to all feudal, patriarchal, idyllic relations. It has pitilessly torn asunder the motley feudal ties that bound man to his 'natural superiors' and has left remaining no other nexus between man and man than callous 'cash payment'.[11]

First, although patriarchal relations acquire a specific ideological form under capitalism, they are not thereby reducible to relations of exchange. Second, gender relationships may well be reducible to some form of slavery viewed in strictly capitalist terms but this does not entail that slavery is endemic to sex.

Such a conflation of the patriarchal with the capitalistic obscures the whole notion of slavery and with it the 'natural'. The proof of this lies in the fact that neither has the bourgeoisie put an end to all patriarchal relations nor are these relations simply matters of enslavement; although gender may be the root model for other forms of domination, it cannot thereby be reduced to exchange value or 'callous cash payment'. Rather it is the subsumption of the patriarchal to the capitalist which propels a 'natural' division of labor toward the first appearance of property, as Marx, albeit ambiguously, points out. For by specifying the original division as 'natural' the conditions for the emergence of private property are 'fixed', the field of labor and acquisition clearly designated. Thus 'male' and 'female' may be said to provide the working model for further dichotomizations such as owner/owned, capitalist/proletariat. More importantly, however, this same model undergirds Marx's notion of praxis and, thus, aligns it in gender terms much closer to a capitalist mode of production than Marx ever envisioned.

II. The Self-Interest of Praxis

Through 'his' praxis activity, according to Marx, 'man' is both the means and the object of 'his' own existence.[12] Through the creative manipulation of nature, then, praxis also signifies the paradigmatically rational in that species life (human community) derives from the possibility of praxis-activity. Conversely, alienation from the object of praxis promotes alienation from species life and, consequently,the pathologizing of family relations. Marx writes:

> While alienated labor alienates (i) nature from man and (ii) man from himself, his own active function, his vital activity, it also alienates the species from man; it turns his species life into a means toward his individual life, and secondly, in its abstraction it makes the latter into the aim of the former which is conceived of in its abstract and alien form. For, firstly, work, vital activity, and productive life itself appear to man only as the means to the satisfaction of a need, the need to preserve his physical existence. But productive life is species life. It is life producing life. The whole character of a species, its generic character, is contained in its manner of vital activity, and free conscious activity is the species characteristic of man. Life itself appears only as a means to life . . . Man makes his vital activity itself into an object of his will and

consciousness . . . Conscious vital activity immediately differentiates man from animal vital activity. It is this and this alone that
makes man a species being . . . Alienated labor reverses the relationship so that just because he is a conscious being, man makes
his vital activity or essence a mere means to his existence.[13]

Alienation, then, is for Marx the antithesis of praxis; it is the re-
sidual byproduct of the expropriation of a paradigmatically *natural*
human activity and, thus, the negation of human life as such.

If one asks, however, *who* is the natural subject of this 'vital human activity', the universal applicability of praxis encounters serious questions. For, recalling the gendered and dualistic ambiguity
which attends Marx's definition of the 'natural', 'vital activity' itself
divides into two different 'natural' modes, two different categories of
'man'. The first 'category' designates Marx's intended subject for
whom certain conditions are required (namely, freedom from the labor of producing 'himself') which insure the full realization of a self
which is to evolve through the creation of objects. The second 'category', then, designates the provider of these necessary conditions.
This provider does not participate in reciprocal self-realization but
is rather utilized toward the praxis activity of the intended subject
(in a way ironically similar to that of the deliberately exploitive capitalist's utilization of a 'resource').[14]

Given the earlier discussion, then, the 'vital activity' that Marx
describes here is obviously that of a man and the provider upon
which he is fundamentally dependent, a woman. Thus, it is the tacit
but necessary objectification of 'woman' that, in opposition to conscious, rational activity, provides the conditions through which
'man' is preserved and created. This objectification, however, is obscured by Marx's ambiguous definition of 'natural' because the
tasks that women perform toward the maintenance of the male subject are neither viewed as creative *nor* alienating; women's labor is
simply viewed as an expression of her nature, e.g., her sex.

However, 'Woman' in this scenario represents a specific kind of
ideological object, namely that whose value is discovered in the use
made of it by the husband. This object is the product of a dualistic
rationality where the primary relationship resides between the actor and *his* object and not in any form of human reciprocity. The
privileging of the relation between 'man' and the material up in
which 'he' acts describes praxis activity as well as that of the bur-
geoning capitalist. Having been divided away from what Marx ambiguously terms 'natural', the creative activity of praxis emerges as
instrumental and self-interested as its property-oriented counter-

part. By having *presupposed* a notion of the 'natural' through the designation of women and children as slaves of the husband, the question for praxis becomes only one of *how* to act, *what* to produce, not what constitutes essential human nature and, thus, not what constitutes self-realization. For although Marx insists that essential human nature is realized only through self-creative, rational activity, this activity depends fundamentally upon the non-praxis labor of others; it depends upon others being unable or uninclined toward self-realization as an expression of their *nature*. These others become simply part of the material conditions necessary for praxis activity to take place.

To attempt to apply praxis as a universal category of human being, then, generates the contradiction that praxis is both a natural and an unnatural activity. For its very exercise requires the negation of praxis as a possibility for the other upon which it depends, a seemingly unnatural act given the importance of species life, unless we take that other to be naturally unable to act rationally. But to opt for this latter course reinforces the dual nature of the 'natural' rendering praxis non-universal.

On this interpretation, praxis emerges not only as non-universal and, therefore, not paradigmatically human, but is further compromised by the anomalous character of other essential human activities. The most fundamental of these is human reproduction. This quintessentially female act of creation is excluded as a candidate for praxis activity by virtue of the gendered ambiguity which accompanies the Marxian definition of 'natural'. As an expression of 'natural predilection', human reproduction is subsumed as unconsciously motivated; it is neither an expresion of praxis activity nor, therefore, a candidate for self-realization. Lynda Birke, for example, remarks in an historical vein:

> Mary O'Brien has suggested that one reason why reproduction is often left out is because there is a "strong historical tendency . . . to see reproduction as 'pure' biological process (which) carries the implication that reproduction is all body without mind, irrational or at least prerational." That which is pure biological process is assumed to be unchangeable, so biological reproduction falls outside the sphere of theories emphasizing the significance of historical change.[15]

Characterized in this way, the relation between a woman and a growing fetus is easily subordinated in significance to that between an actor and a consciously manipulated, external object.[16]

In this light, praxis emerges as specifically androcentric in character, for it is the product of that rationality which 1) identifies women and children as slaves of the husband, 2) implicitly assigns human reproduction to natural predilection, and 3) founds self-realization in the production of objects as opposed to individuals. The assignment of human-reproduction to the realm of the unconscious, then, merely signifies, in prototypical form, the direction praxis activity is destined to take even before its formal conceptual introduction.

Yet praxis rationality is androcentric in another aspect as well. For it is the signature of such a mentality to discover the basis of a concept, in this case praxis, in an opposition to be reconciled (dialectically) rather than in an evolving and *indeterminate* relation such as that involved in human reproduction. Yet, human reproduction is not merely a matter of conscious production either; it is neither some spontaneously occurring natural event nor a fully specified object-making activity. In fact, any close investigation of human reproduction introduces question into the concept of praxis as rational object-making activity. For human reproduction is simply not reducible to dualistic categories like conscious/unconscious, or 'natural'/rational. Rather it is in some sense all of these and, in another, none. This uniquely female labor places in question not only what constitutes the 'natural' but equally what constitutes the 'rational'.

Marx's discussion of alienation is revealing on this point because it clarifies the nature of the subject for whom praxis is intended as self-realization, namely, a subject for whom creative activity is a conscious externalization and, thus, alienation a restriction or curtailment of rational intention. Given the foregoing, this subject could only be male. Marx writes:

> The alienation of the object of labor is only the resume of the alienation, the externalization in the activity of labor itself.

> Thus the worker only feels a stranger. He is at home when he is not working and when he works he is not at home. His labor is therefore not voluntary but compulsory, forced labor . . . How alien it really is is evident from the fact that when there is no physical or other compulsion, labor is avoided like the plague.[17]

Who is Marx speaking of here?

> [M]an only feels himself freely active in his animal functions of eating, drinking, and procreating, at most also in his dwelling and dress, and feels himself animal in his human functions.
>
> Eating, drinking, procreating, etc., are indeed human functions. But in the abstraction that separates them into final and exclusive ends they become animal.[18]

The alienation Marx describes in these passages not only applies strictly to the male worker but emphasizes the essential importance of the relation between worker and object; alienation is self-realization thwarted through the submergence of its creative aspect in industrialized labor. It is in relation to the object of production, divested of its praxis significance, that the worker becomes alienated both from the object, from *him*self and from *his* familial ties. Just as the Marxian concept of praxis revealed itself to be rooted in a notion of the 'natural' which tacitly excludes women from rational, object-making activity, alienation is a concept which applies only to that individual who discovers self-realization in the making of objects as opposed to the cultivation of human relations. Moreau remarks on this theme:

> Work, which is a source of alienation for the working class in general, can paradoxically become a first condition of release for women, whose bodies and labor have been appropriated by men.[19]

Clearly, the androcentric limitations of the Marxian concept of alienation is given emphasis in the case where some women see labor outside the home as a release from what they perceive to be the oppressive conditions of home life. The point is not diminished, however, by the fact that for many women neither 'outside' nor 'inside' labor presents itself as an opportunity for self-realization. For labor as such in the Marxian scenario is not available as an avenue of potential self-realization to a being destined by nature to provide the conditions for the praxis of another. This insight unwittingly receives further support by Marx himself when he writes:

> In the conditions of the proletariat, those of the old society are already virtually swamped. The proletarian is without property, his relation to his wife and children no longer have anything in common with the bourgeois family relations ... [20]

The alienation described here is the result of the expropriation of praxis activity leaving the proletarian propertyless (and, therefore, selfless). The worker's alienation from 'his' family is implicitly

but directly *derivative* upon the expropriation of 'his' labor. Moreover, the worker that perceives 'his' home as an escape from the toils
of the factory may do so only through the ideological reinforcement
of the division between the 'natural' and the 'rational' and, thus, the
exclusion of women from the latter. The conditions from which the
home emerges as an escape for the alienated male worker, then, are
precisely those which preclude women from being adequately characterized as alienated *or* unalienated, at least within a Marxian
schema; for the same reasons that the Marxian concept of praxis
applies only to men, that of alienation applies only to men. Thus to
describe women's labor outside the home as potentially unalienat-
ing or as a release would seem to be beside the point—'she' is not a
candidate for praxis, and, therefore, not a candidate for alienation—at least to the extent that one abides by the strict differen-
tiation between 'natural proclivities' and 'rational creativity'. From
the perspective of male alienation, then, it is ironic that, however
economically different the familial relations of proletariat from the
bourgeois, the status of women's labor provides no criterion for as-
sessing the status of the family because women's labor is, in principle, no measure of self-realization, and, therefore, no measure of
familial accomplishment.

The character of alienation, then, turns out to be as dualistic
(in dividing the 'natural' from the 'rational') as that of its counterpart, namely, praxis. Though clearly illusory, it is this dual character which allows the home to be perceived as an escape for men
while yet a prison for women. Within such a scenario it is no wonder
that the same work that is perceived as a prison for men is perceived by some women as an escape. The dualistic character of
praxis invites interpretation via role reversal. But there is more to
the dialectic of praxis and alienation than merely a reversal of perceptions or roles.

The assignment of women's role in human reproduction to 'natural predilection' indeed reflects a specific and paradoxical kind of
alienation—*natural* alienation. For it is her very constitution *as* female that destines a woman, according to Marx, to be unable to participate in self-realization. The alienation of gender, moreover, is
radically different than that of alienation from an object for it is
both primary and essential. Thus, although excluded in principle
from the potential for self-realization through praxis, women, in effect, represent alienation in its most totalizing form; a self which
cannot be realized is a self which cannot be lost.

Yet because women also occupy the position of providing the material conditions through which praxis activity takes place, the access to self-realization turns out to be as circumscribed practically as it is 'naturally'. In the Marxian scenario, labor is not only defined by sex, rather sex is the self-confirming ground upon which the division of labor is constructed. The fundamental point to be made, however, is that Marx's blindness to the gendered nature of the dichotomy between the natural and the rational functions to support ideal communist as well as ideal capitalist divisions of labor. For both are equally rooted in an ideology which operates as a highly efficient mechanism for the reproduction of labor power. Thus it is to the context in which the division between the rational and the natural is embedded that we must now turn, that is, to the Victorian ideology of 'woman'.

III. Marx and the Victorian Ideology of 'Woman'

The Victorian ideology of 'woman' operates as the 'linch-pin' in the maintenance of class division explicitly, as Marx recognized, in capitalist economies, but also implicitly in Marxian theory. Both through the provision of conditions enabling the male worker to produce and through 'her' own 'natural' alienation via human reproduction, the ideology of 'woman' helps to insure the perpetuation of class itself. Moreover, it is to the Victorian context in which Marx himself lived, that we must turn for a clearer understanding of the presuppositions which animate praxis.

In Victorian ideology, 'woman' is identified with a particular view of nature.[21] Femininity is a construct that, like nature, is equated with the unconscious, the irrational and the affective, and thus requires control.[22] Marx's own investment in Victorian ideology and its influence on praxis receives illumination in the form of correspondence and personal letters of which we shall now examine several examples. Beginning with Marx's response to the *1875 Gotha Program, Part IV*, "Restriction of Female Labor and the Prohibition of Child Labor":

> The standardization of the working day must include the restriction of female labor, insofar as it relates to the duration, intermissions, etc., of the working day; otherwise it could only mean the exclusion of female labor from branches of industry that are

especially unhealthy for the female body or are objectionable morally for the female sex. If that is what is meant, it should so have
been said.[23]

In this passage Marx disagrees with the presentation but not with
the content. Yet, his letters find him even more revealing. From a
letter to Engels, 1858, we learn:

[T]he mood here is extraordinarily dismal. Withal, my wife is quite
right when she says that after all this misery she has had to go
through it will become worse after the revolution when she will
have the dubious pleasure of seeing all the local humbugs again
celebrating triumphs over yonder. *Women are like that.* And the
feminine behavior of the Freiligraths, etc., and other aquaintances
rightly embitter her. She says *a la guerre comme a la guerre.* But
there is not guerre. Everything is bourgeois.[24]

And, lastly, from a postscript to a letter to Ludwig Kugelmann,
1868, Marx quips:

Is your wife also active in the Great German women's emancipation campaign? I believe that German women must begin by driv-
ing their husbands to self-emancipation.[25]

This last quote makes clear Marx's view that the emancipation
of gender must occur concomitantly with the resolution of class
struggle. This view stems from the assumption that sexual oppression is a derivative of the same conditions as class struggle; thus
oppression will dissolve along with the abolition of private property.
Marx's letters, then, lend credible emphasis to our earlier investigation of the notion of praxis. For here too we find discussions of
class and labor intractibly bound up with gender. Although Marx
rightly assumes that the division of labor has its origins in private
ownership, he seems to either forget or take it as a given that
women and children occupy the status of the first property, are
"slaves of the husband." Once again, we are thrown back upon this
fundamental ambiguity in Marxian thought for there is no compelling reason to believe that the resolution of private ownership will
simultaneously resolve gender oppression. Even in Marx's terms,
(however tacitly, as we have seen), the latter is the *prior* condition.

Moreover, Marx's letters reveal a revolutionary catalyst that is
not only implicitly male but explicitly so. 'He' is the standard for the
revolutionary worker. It is 'his' praxis activity that must be driven

toward self-emancipation (do we detect a contradiction here?). According to Marx, the emancipation of women occurs as the result of 'his' revolutionary activity and 'her' unfailing support. Women's role as 'wife to the revolution', then, can be seen as just one more version of the manner in which 'she' is responsible to provide the conditions for praxis activity while yet being unable to participate in such activity. 'Her' freedom, then, consists in the preservation of a relationship which is antithetical to a Marxian conception of self-realization.

In fact, freedom for the revolutionary woman amounts to mere illusion, for the object of her labor is *always* outside of herself. It is 'her' task to reproduce the man so that he can free '*him*self'. The revolution, then, cannot occur without precisely those individuals who are destined by 'natural proclivity' to be unable to benefit from it. Ironically Marx says as much in a letter to Engels when he writes:

> Anybody who knows anything of history also knows that great social changes are impossible without the female ferment. Social progress can be measured accurately by the social status of the beautiful sex (the ugly ones included).[26]

Given that, for Marx, the "social status of the beautiful sex" is at least in part determined by what he takes to be a natural lack, it is no surprise that he is able to complain to Engels in 1869:

> For some time now I have noticed that my wife does not make ends meet with the money I give her weekly, although our expenses have not increased in any way. Since I absolutely do not want to get into debt again, and since the money I gave her last Monday was "all gone" today . . . I asked for an explanation. *Then the folly of women came out* . . . she had concealed about L75, which she had been trying to pay off by and by from her household allowance. I asked, why this? She was afraid to tell me about such a big sum! *Women obviously always need a guardian!*[27]

And in 1874, Marx writes of his daughter, Tussy:

> Tussy feels much better; her appetite grows in geometric proportion, but this is peculiar to these feminine sicknesses where the hysterical plays a role; one has to act as if one does not notice that she again lives on terrestrial nourishment.[28]

While these passages reveal enough of Marx's Victorianism to warrant investigation, the last passage I wish to quote connects specifically with the issue of praxis and revolution. From a letter to his daughter, Jenny Longuet, 1881:

> I congratulate you on the happy delivery; at least I assume that everything is in order, as you took the trouble to write yourself. My "women" expected that the new "earth citizen" would increase the "better half" of the population; personally, I prefer the male sex among children who will be born at this turning point in history. They have before them the most revolutionary period that men have ever experienced. It is bad nowadays to be so "old" as to have to foresee instead of see.[29]

This somewhat melancholic passage requires little in the way of explanation. Yet it is ironic that a man with so much philosophic vision could not see in the birth of a granddaughter the untapped "ferment" soon to reach boiling point in the coming turn of the century. Indeed, Marx's own immersion in the Victorian ideology of 'woman' destines his theoretical writings on the nature of praxis to reduplicate a dualistic vision of the world which, though he rejects it superficially, simply reproduces patterns of oppression. Much more could be said concerning the implications of Marx's Victorianism for other aspects of his political and philosophical theory (for example, the concept of revolution and its relation to the notorious "community of women"). But for now, as feminism continues to search for a way to thematize power, oppression, dichotomy, etc., I would simply like to close by remarking that the popular slogan that Marxism is dead not only ignores the contribution Marxian ideas have made to feminist thought but also ignores the problematic influence that the embrace of Marxism has had over feminist theory.

In conclusion, even if, as I believe, feminism must ultimately discard Marxian categories as inadequate, contradictory and philosophically untenable, there is a wealth to be gained by the thinking through of a philosophy which is the first to be so committed to human emancipation. While the Marxian concept of praxis ultimately fails to reach its intended goal, the ideal of a human/nature relationship which is both productive and non-exploitive is clearly one worth pursuing—indeed one that must be pursued. The critical thinking through of Marx will help give us a better understanding of both the similarities and the differences between 'western' capitalist economies and the rapidly degenerating socialism of the 'east'. And this, hopefully, will provide feminist theorists with one more tool for understanding each other across difficult political and personal divides.

Notes

1. I had originally written large portions of this paper simply to enhance my own understanding of the internal workings of some Marxian concepts. But with the renewed rise of conservative politics in the United States, the all-but-explicit overturning of Roe Vs.Wade, and recent events in Eastern Europe, I now wonder if the whole discussion of reproduction must be re-evaluated and revalued. It is to this end that I hope this paper makes some contribution.

2. Birke, Lynda. *Women, Feminism and Biology: The Feminist Challenge*. New York: Methuen, 1986. p. 51.

3. Hartmann, Heidi. "The Unhappy Marriage of Marxism and Feminism: Towards a More Progressive Union." *Women and Revolution*. Ed. Lydia Sargent. Boston: South End Press, 1981, pp. 9–11.

4. Mackintosh, Maureen. "Gender and Economics: The Sexual Division of Labor and the Subordination of Women." *Of Marriage and the Market: Women's Subordination Internationally and Its Lessons*. Ed. K. Young, C. Wolkowitz, and R. Mc'Cullogh. Boston: Routledge and Kegan Paul, 1984, p. 6–7.

5. Ibid., p. 7.

6. Marx, Karl. *The German Ideology*. Ed. C. J. Arthur. New York: International Publishers, 1981, pp. 42–48.

7. Ibid., p. 51.

8. Ibid., p. 51 (my emphasis).

9. Ibid., pp. 51–52 (my emphasis).

10. Marx, Karl. *The Communist Manifesto*. Ed. F. Engels. 25th ed., New York: International Publishers, 1983, p. 11.

11. Ibid., p. 11.

12. Marx, Karl. *Karl Marx: Selected Writings*. Ed. D. McClellan. Oxford: Oxford University Press, 1977, p. 81.

13. Ibid., pp. 81–82.

14. Birke, Lynda. *Women, Feminism and Biology*, p. 84.

15. Ibid., p. 52.

16. Ibid., p. 124.

17. Marx, Karl. *Karl Marx: Selected Writings,* p. 80.

18. Ibid., pp. 80–81.

19. Moreau, Noelle Bisseret. "Education, Ideology and Class/Sex Identity." *Class and Power.* Ed. Kramarae, Schultz and O'Barr. SAGE Pubilcations, Ltd. 1984, p. 48.

20. Marx, Karl. *The Communist Manifesto,* p. 20.

21. Birke, Lynda. *Women, Feminism and Biology.* p. 46.

22. Poole, Ross. "Morality, Masculinity and the Market." Radical Philosophy 39: 16–23, p. 19.

23. Marx, Karl. On Education, Women and Children: Karl Marx. The Karl Marx Library, Vol. IV. trans. Saul K. Padover. New York: Mc'Graw Hill, 1975, p. 131.

24. Ibid., pp. 137–138 (my emphasis).

25. Ibid., p. 144.

26. Ibid., p. 144.

27. Ibid., p. 146 (my emphasis).

28. Ibid., p. 105.

29. Ibid., p. 152.

Who is Nietzsche's Woman?

Kelly Oliver

Since Derrida's *Spurs*, Nietzsche has been posed as woman. With his *Postponements*, David Farrell Krell pushes Nietzsche further into Derrida's "feminine operation."[1] Krell claims that Derrida and Nietzsche save real women from dogmatic philosophy by writing with the hand of woman: "Writing now with the other hand, as it were, both Nietzsche and Derrida record the plaint of women against 'the foolishness of the dogmatic philosopher'. "[2] This face of contemporary Nietzsche studies, which not only positions Nietzsche as woman, but also allows Nietzsche critics to position themselves and each other as woman, (Derrida's illusory position on the margin, Krell's claim that Derrida too writes with the hand of woman) is immediately suspect to the feminist reader.[3]

It should seem more than a bit strange that Derrida and his many followers find Nietzsche, the renowned misogynist, defending woman against the dogmatic philosopher, performing the "feminine operation," and "writing with the hand of woman." What kind of a woman would write: Women are "cats, birds, or at best cows."[4] A woman is "a riddle solved by pregnancy." When you go to woman "don't forget your whip!"[5] "Good and bad women want a stick."[6]? By making Nietzsche's the voice of woman, don't we merely hear over again that "yes, we women are animals who want to be raped and beaten"?

In light of these misogynist remarks, it is no surprise that Nietzsche maintains that feminism is a disease.[7] Now, however, it is time to turn the tables and use feminist instruments in order to diagnose Nietzsche's frustration with woman. At this juncture in the post-modern obsession with the position of woman, it is time for a feminist rereading of Nietzsche's woman.

I am suspicious of the woman who Derrida and friends claim that Nietzsche imitates/desires. I will argue that Nietzsche's desire can be read as a desire for woman as mother. In his writing he fears woman as anything else. Moreover, Nietzsche does not desire to **be-**

come woman, as Derrida, Krell, and others, suggest. Rather, in his writing he desires to **possess** woman. As he writes it, Nietzsche's desire, then, is not a woman's desire. Rather, it is a man's desire, the desire to possess woman through impregnation. Moreover, the woman whom Nietzsche desires is an ideal, fetishized woman, never actualized, therefore, always frustrating. In his texts, Nietzsche's relation to woman is always agonizing: not only can't he become woman but also he can't have woman. I will argue that the agonizing desire in Nietzsche's texts can be read as the manifestation of an unresolved Oedipal complex.

The Position of his Fathers

In a classic Oedipal struggle, in his writing Nietzsche is torn between identifying with the father (in this case the rationalist fathers of philosophy, or culture in general) while denying the mother, on the one hand, or affirming the mother in order to do away with the father, on the other. Nietzsche wants to overthrow the tradition in philosophy and culture in general, to overthrow the fathers, in order to take their place and replace their impotence with his potency. The images, however, that Nietzsche uses to criticize the truth of philosophy and religion, expose his alliance with those traditions.

Emasculated Truth

Nietzsche suggests that philosophy castrates the intellect: "to eliminate the will altogether, to suspend each and every effect, supposing we were capable of this—what would that mean but to **castrate** the intellect."[8] He calls philosophy "the will to truth as the **impotence** of the will to create."[9] That is, those motivated by the will to truth claim to discover reality because they are too weak to create it. For Nietzsche, detached objective truth is "castrated" because it is "impotent" to create truth. "Supposing truth is a woman," begins *Beyond Good and Evil*, " . . . all philosophers, insofar as they were dogmatists, have been very inexpert about women."[10] Philosophers lust after woman (truth), but they don't have the potency to possess her. Their "**emasculated** leers," says Nietzsche, "wish to be called 'contemplation'."[11] Nietzsche criticizes philosophy's will to truth, but he does so in the name of masculine anxiety: the anxiety about impotence.

Nietzsche wages the same attack against religion. He criticizes the Christian treatment of sexual excitation, the consequence of which, he says is:

> not only the loss of an organ but the **emasculation** of a man's character—And the same applies to the moralist's madness and demands, instead of the restraining of the passions, their extripation. Its conclusion is always: only the **castrated** man is a good man.[12]

Nietzsche can wage the same attack against philosophy as religion because Socratic culture, like Christian culture, is motivated by the ascetic ideal. Nietzsche criticizes the ascetic ideal for its denial of the body. However, his anxiety about castration and impotence displays Nietzsche's own fear of the body. But, Nietzsche's is a bodily anxiety. He is afraid of the impotent body. He is afraid that the body is not powerful; that it cannot perform; that it is sick; that it will die.[13] Fear of the limitations of the impotent male body suggest a fear of the limitations of the body in general. Nietzsche wants a bodily philosophy, a revaluation of the incarnate values of the earth. Yet, he too fears the limits, the finitude, of the body.

Because Nietzsche fears the body, he identifies with the tradition which denies the body. His metaphors of castration, impotence, and emasculation are evidence of his tendency to usurp, rather than undermine, the paternal position. He desires creativity and procreation/reproduction which are free from the limitations of objective truth. He desires maternal creativity, however, in order to prove his potency, his manliness.

Manly Truth

Although the passages where Nietzsche attacks traditional science, reason, and truth, far outweigh the passages where he praises them, there are places where Nietzsche explicitly valorizes the traditional truth for its manliness.[14] For example, Nietzsche claims that:

> truths that are *hard* won, certain, enduring, and therefore still of consequence for all further knowledge are higher, to keep to them is *manly*, and shows bravery, simplicity, restraint . . . Eventually, not only the individual, but all mankind will be elevated to this *manliness*, when men finally grow accustomed to the greater esteem for durable, lasting knowledge.[15]

Here Nietzsche identifies with the eternal **manly** truth and
looks forward to the day when all of mankind is manly. In the *Gay
Science,* Nietzsche welcomes signs of a more "manly, warlike age."[16]
In *Twilight* "How to Philosophize with a Hammer," Nietzsche orders
us to become "hard!". Zarathustra tells others, or is told, to become
"hard," to become "manly."[17] Zarathustra says that all creators are
"**hard**."[18] The third essay of *On the Genealogy of Morals,* "What is
the meaning of Ascetic Ideals," begins with a quotation from Zarathustra: "Unconcerned, mocking violent—thus wisdom wants *us;*
she is a woman and always loves only a warrior."[19] Dionysus, the god
of male fertility, is the warrior loved by woman.

Nietzsche envies this warrior. He envies the conqueror, an image of the manly hero.[20] He admires Napoleon and Caesar.[21] The
Dionysian type is a Caesar with the heart of Christ. Nietzsche sings
praises to these heros, those who can overcome. For Nietzsche, it is
the tradition which must be overcome (*überwindung*). Even the self
must be overcome (*selbsüberwindung*). Nietzsche's Dionysian type,
the *Übermensch,* is the master of self-overcoming. The *Übermensch*
is a conqueror who overcomes self and all pain. Unlike his philosophical fathers, Nietzsche's *Übermensch c* can embrace both pain
and pleasure. Traditional philosophers try to justify the pain by
making it part of pleasure. Nietzsche criticizes his philosophical fathers, dialecticians, because they cannot embrace both pain and
pleasure. Rather, they make difference and pain into moments of a
higher reality. Nietzsche sees "dialectical dryness" as a "tyrant in
opposition to a 'tyrant' (instinct)."[22] Dialectics seek to overcome contradiction; they "no longer distinguishe[s]."[23] Everything is leveled;
everything becomes the same in the dialectic. The negative elements are always recuperated by the dialectic; difference is always
covered over. Nietzsche calls for creative difference, "no" as a creative, potent, deed.[24]

Nietzsche suggests that dialecticians cannot affirm difference
and pain. Like priests, they can only redeem or justify pain and difference, the mess of the body, through some higher purpose. The
Übermensch, on the other hand, takes pleasure in pain. The
Übermensch is man enough for it. Moreover, the *Übermensch* can go
one step further and **affirm the affirmation** of pain and difference. For Nietzsche there is something higher than the reconciliation of the teleological dialectic. There is multiple affirmation: "For
that will which is the will to power must will something higher than
any reconciliation."[25] The *Übermensch* is the direct reflection of this
will to power and can affirm difference **and** the affirmation of dif-

ference. Dionysus jubilantly proclaims "eternal affirmation of being, eternally I am your affirmation."[26]

The Position of the Mother

Strangely enough, in addition to being the conqueror, Nietzsche's Dionysian type **is** the "eternally pregnant mother." She affirms herself continually through procreation. Nietzsche repeatedly uses metaphors of biological reproduction—"womb of being," "mother eternally pregnant," "procreative life"—to describe the Dionysian force, the will to power.[27] For example, the mystical vision of Dionysus—that eternal life flows indestructibly beneath the surface of phenomena—is figured as the "**maternal womb** of being."[28] Just as that Dionysian prophet, Zarathustra, cries out that the "unexhausted **procreative** will of life is the will to power,"[29] so "a voice that rings authentic" cries out, through Dionysian art and its tragic symbolism, "be like me, the **original mother,** who constantly creating, finds satisfaction in the turbulent flux of appearances."[30]

In addition to the figures of the maternal in Nietzsche's writing, there is also the suggestion that woman exists in order to be pregnant. "Everything about Woman," says Nietzsche's Zarathustra, is a "riddle" solved by "pregnancy."[31] You can "cure" a woman by giving her a child.[32] Feminine love, claims Nietzsche, is "maternal love."[33] Nietzsche cannot face a feminine love that is not maternal, a love that is not dependent on man, a love that does not create a child. Thus, the only characteristic that Nietzsche desires in woman is her womb. Our consuming desire, says Nietzsche, is due to the loss of the "mythic womb."[34] Woman, then, for Nietzsche, is nothing other than this mythic womb. Moreover, the "womb of being," the origin of all force, is a **myth,** an origin that does not exist. Thus, woman is a myth. She is layer after layer of masks with no face behind them:

> MASKS, There are women who have no inner life wherever one looks for it, being nothing but masks.[35]

She is a *papier maché* balloon, an empty womb, (until man impregnates her). At this point Nietzsche exposes his frustrated desire for the eternally fecund woman, whom he admits does not exist. The womb of being, as it turns out, is a "mythic womb," an empty womb. There is no woman; she is only masks. Nietzsche wants to use this fetishized "woman"—his ideal of woman as eternal phallic mother—as a means to give birth. He wants, in a sense, to "artificially inseminate" this lost "mythic womb" with a potency that his predecessors lacked. He longs for the womb where he can prove his virility to his emasculated fathers.

Birth

To whom/what does this eternal mother give birth? How is the eternally pregnant mother a symbol for the will to power? Nietzsche's will to power is like a pregnant mother because it is the generative and differentiating principle of life. It is what generates and differentiates forces: "The will to power . . . defines limits, determines degrees, variations of power."[36] It is an "eternally self-creating, self-destroying play of forces."[37] Nietzsche stresses the indiscriminancy with which the will to power both creates and destroys. Through self-creating and self-destroying, the will to power gives form to chaos.[38] It is this creating/destroying life force that he likens to a womb.

While the image of a creative womb is familiar, what does the womb destroy? Through birth the womb destroys the unity with the original mother. Birth is a process of individuation. Through birth, the child is separated from the mother and it becomes an individual. Like the mother/child fusion prior to birth, in its most primordial form, the will to power is undifferentiated. Only in its most derived forms is it individuated. Individuation according to Nietzsche always covers over the chaos and arbitrariness of what was before individuation. Through birth, unity is what is destroyed and individuation is what is created. The Dionysian womb of being gives birth to the Apollonian individual:

> I see Apollo as the transfiguring genius of the *principium individuationis* through which alone the redemption in illusion is truly to be obtained; while by the mystical triumphant cry of Dionysus the spell of individuation is broken, and the way lies open to the *Mothers of Being,* to the inner most heart of things.[39]

This individuation, however, like childbirth, is always painful. Therefore, Nietzsche invokes Silenus' wisdom: it is best not to be born at all.[41] And in order to enjoy the child, one must forget the more repellant and painful aspects of pregnancy.[42]

In addition to the bizarre effects on the body in a literal pregnancy, in Nietzsche's metaphorical pregnancy, we have a bizarre unassimilated unity between the creator and the created. It is this chaos, that both creates and destroys, that constitutes the horror of the womb.[43] It is the horror which must be forgotten. Ultimately, it is the womb itself, this creative/destructive force, which must be forgotten in order to enjoy the child, or more precisely, so that the child can enjoy. The child (Nietzsche?) cannot bear to imagine its unity with its mother. The undifferentiated fusion is horrifying. The indeterminate identity between mother and child is too much to bear, especially for the male child. How can this child be a man if it was once part of a woman? In order for the child to be autonomous, it must forget that it was once part of its mother, expelled from her womb.[44]

Nietzsche argues, in a note, that procreation is a reactive process. It is the inability, "impotence," to deal with excess.[45] This excess can only be tolerated if it is broken off; if it is separated into another individual; if it is born and the process through which it is born is forgotten. In fact, Nietzsche suggests that this is how truth is born. Truth is born out of chaos that we forget was once chaos. According to Nietzsche, it is Apollonian individuation which cures the eye hurt from staring at this chaos, the womb of being.[46] Only individuation can make this creative/destructive life bearable. Yet, for Nietzsche, it is only the weak who need to make life bearable. His Dionysian *Übermensch,* on the other hand, is a strong new type who can bear the excesses of pregnancy without individuation. He can take his pregnancy like a man! The *Übermensch* has no need for truth or individuation. These are for the weak who cannot bear life's excess, for those who cannot affirm pain and difference. The *Übermensch* is truly the **eternally pregnant;** the one who does not need to give birth; the creator without creations; the artist without works of art; life become creative.

My analysis of Nietzsche's pregnancy metaphors, however, cannot bear the excess of those metaphors. In Nietzsche there is always a pregnancy that cannot be assimilated; there is another side of Nietzsche's pregnancy, both creative and destructive, both life affirming and an illness. It is nausea . . . morning sickness?

Nausea

Nietzsche identifies a nausea in man. Man, in his nihilism, is sick. His longing for another world, a higher purpose, is the result of a nausea with life: "Christianity was from the beginning, essentially and fundamentally, life's nausea and disgust with life, merely concealed behind, masked by, dressed up as, faith in 'another'

or 'better' life."[47] Nausea at life and the mess of the body, its finitude, leads to Christian redemption. Christian redemption, and any
other type of redemption that denies the finite life of the body, overcomes the nausea at life.

Nietzsche, however, identifies another nausea: His own nausea;
Zarathustra's nausea: "The great disgust with man—this choked
me and had crawled into my throat."[48] "Not my hunger but my nausea
gnawed hungrily at my life."[49] Christian redemption itself makes
them sick. Their's is the "great nausea" at man's nausea.[50] Their
nausea is overcome through another 'redemption', Dionysian redemption, a redemption of the earth, the *Übermensch's* redemption:

> he must yet come to us, the redeeming man of great love and con-
> tempt, the creative spirit whose compelling strength will not let
> him rest in any aloofness or any beyond . . . This man of the future,
> who will redeem us not only from the hitherto reigning ideal but
> also from that which was bound to grow out of it, the great nausea,
> the will to nothingness, nihilism.[51]

Out of nausea grows something beyond nausea: Out of man's
nausea at life grows the life beyond, Christian redemption. Out of
the nausea at man's nausea grows the beyond man, the *Übermensch,* Dionysian redemption. "[C]lose beside this sickness stands
signs of an untested force and powerfulness of soul. The same reasons that produce the increasing smallness of man drive the stronger and rarer individuals up to greatness."[52] Nausea produces both
smallness—Christian redemption—and greatness—Dionysian redemption. Nausea is a pregnancy that gives birth to something beyond it. Nietzsche describes this pregnancy as an illness out of
which something grows. "Bad conscience," he says is "an illness . . .
but as pregnancy is an illness."[53] Nietzsche suggests that man is
"pregnant with the future"[54] The nausea of pregnancy is necessary
in order to get beyond sickness, in order to give birth to health. This
is the purpose of Zarathustra's nausea. He hopes to sire the new
healthy Dionysian type.[55]

Immaculate Conception

Nietzsche hopes that his own nausea can be productive. He
imagines an eternally productive pregnancy, yet his texts manifest
a fear of contact with women or sexual desire. Like the ascetic

priest, he wants conception without the mess and desire of the body. For Nietzsche, pregnancy implies chastity; he cannot seem to imagine pregnancy as the result of bodily lust. He claims that it is natural for philosophers and artists to be chaste since their creativity is a type of pregnancy.[56] Some how pregnancy, potency, and chastity belong together in the artist:

> Making music is another way of making children; chastity is merely the economy of the artist—and in any event, even with the artists fruitfulness ceases when potency ceases.[57]

Yet, the artist is stronger in his pregnancy than the "hysterical" woman is in hers. He's man enough, she's not. The artist, says Nietzsche, cannot be expected to "become a woman—that he should receive."[58] The artist's potency is not passive. Also, the artist, unlike "hysterical females," should be able to bear the excess that would be harmful to weaker sorts.[59] This excess is associated with chastity and the ability to sublimate sexual desire.[60]

While, on the one hand, in his writings Nietzsche desires the body and wants to liberate the passions from the oppressive philosophical tradition, on the other hand, he fears his own desire for the female body. In addition, he fears woman's desire and its articulation. "Even now female voices are heard which—holy Aristophanes!" exclaims Nietzsche, "are frightening: they threaten with medical explicitness that woman wants from man, first and last. It is not in the worst taste when woman sets about becoming scientific in that way?"[61] Like the ascetic priest, Nietzsche sublimates his sexual desire because it is dirty ("sinful"). Like the ascetic priest, the only purpose of feminine potency that Nietzsche will endorse is procreation: Only procreation is innocent; desire without procreation is sheer lechery.[62] Nietzsche's disgust with philosophy results from what he conceives of as its purely lecherous lust for life.[63]

What philosophers (including Nietzsche) desire and yet fear, says Nietzsche, is the "eternally feminine."[64] It is the lover, the representative of feminine sexual power, and his desire for her, that Nietzsche's texts deny out of fear. The woman embraced in Nietzsche's writings is the mother. Yet, he fears even the sexual nature of his desire for the mother, an incestuous desire. It is the sensuality, sexuality, of his desire that is denied. This sensuality is forbidden by the paternal tradition, especially when it originates in incestuous fantasies, that demand the death of the paternal tradition.

Death

Nietzsche's desire is to kill his philosophical and cultural fathers, whom he claims are impotent, and impregnate the "womb of being." Nietzsche does not want to be woman. Rather he wants to be man enough, "hard enough," to impregnate that which his fathers could not. He wants to take over their potency. Yet this desire brings with it the fear of punishment—the fear of castration.[65]

In *The Birth of Tragedy,* Nietzsche even mentions his fascination with Oedipus:

> With the riddle-solving and mother-marrying Oedipus in mind, we must immediately interpret this to mean that where prophetic and magical powers have broken the spell of present and future, the rigid law of individuation, and the real magic of nature, some enormously unnatural event—such as incest—must have occurred earlier as a cause. How else could one compel nature to surrender her secrets if not by triumphantly resisting her, that is, by means of something unnatural? It is this insight that I find expressed in that horrible triad of Oedipus' destinies: the same man who solves the riddle of nature—that Sphinx of two species—must also break the most sacred natural orders by murdering his father and marrying his mother. Indeed, the myth seems to whisper to us that wisdom, particularly Dionysian wisdom, is an unnatural abomination.[66]

The Oedipal desire for woman as mother demands the death of the father. Thus, Nietzsche fears punishment for his murderous desire. In addition, the "son," the *Übermensch,* whom he hopes to sire as a result of his incestuous desire, demands **his** death as the father—the *Übermensch* is beyond all philosophers, including Nietzsche. On the other hand, Nietzsche fears castration and impotence. Perhaps he isn't man enough to impregnate the "womb of being." Perhaps, like his fathers, he is impotent. Nietzsche's writings exhibit this complex of fear and desire, the Oedipal desire, full of patricidal fantasies and fear of death.

For example, patricidal fantasies and the fear of death show up in *Zarathustra* and unpublished notes written around the same time. In Nietzsche's notes for an unwritten tragedy about Empedocles, Corinna, the mother of tragedy, dies and Empedocles restores her through the heat that remained around the middle of her body.[67] For Nietzsche, Corinna is the mother of tragedy and a symbol of rebirth. It is through the heat in the middle of her body, the womb, that she is revived. She lives only through the activation and reactivation of her womb. Corinna needs Empedocles to give her life through her womb. Empedocles' restoration, however, is not sexual. He does not desire Corinna except for her life-giving womb. Dionysus, on the other hand, is infatuated with Corinna, yet he runs away.[68] So too, in his writings Nietzsche runs away from his erotic desires, his incestuous desires, unless they are transferred into desires for procreation.

"Empedocles feels like a murderer, deserving of unending punishment; he hopes for a rebirth of penitential death."[69] He feels like a murderer although he's (literally) killed no one. Could his guilt be for his incestuous desire? His desire for Corinna, the mother of tragedy? The desire which demands the death of the father? Patricide becomes more apparent in *Zarathustra*. Zarathustra also proclaims that the creator is the mother.[70] Once again this creation/procreation is innocent of sexual desire: "if there is innocence in my knowledge, it is because the will to beget is in it."[71] Zarathustra wants a child, but he wants it without sexual contact. He wants it innocently.

Zarathustra is figured as both pregnant and desiring to impregnate. For his children's sake Zarathustra must perfect himself. This great love of oneself, this excess, is a "sign of pregnancy."[72] Zarathustra is pregnant with the teaching of both the *Übermensch* and the eternal return.[73] Zarathustra also desires to impregnate. He wants heirs, children. Those who want heirs, however, says Zarathustra, are those who suffer, those who do not want themselves. Those who are joyous, on the contrary, do not want children.[74] The joyous are strong enough for their excess. They do not need to give birth to something other than themselves. For "all joy wants eternity—wants deep, wants deep eternity;"[75] it wants itself eternally. Or, perhaps it wants the eternal mother? Zarathustra wants eternity:

> . . . in its dark bosom prepared for lightning and the redemptive flash, pregnant with lightning bolts that says Yes and laughs Yes, soothsaying lightning bolts—blessed is he who is thus pregnant! . . . Oh, how should I not lust after eternity and after the nuptial ring of rings, the ring of recurrence?
> Never yet have I found the woman from whom I wanted children, unless it be this woman whom I love: for I love you, O eternity: for I love you, O eternity: *For I love you, O eternity!*[76]

Zarathustra, the "advocate of the circle," wants the nuptial ring of rings, marriage with eternity. He wants to sire children with

eternity. We wants to impregnate the eternal womb of being in order to sire the *Übermensch*, the redemptive flash. Repeatedly, Zarathustra foretells the coming, the fathering, of the *Übermensch*.

> But you could well create the overman. Perhaps not you your-
> selves, my brothers. But into fathers and forefathers of the over-
> man you could recreate yourselves: and let this be your best
> creation.[77]

This is Zarathustra's purpose. He must perfect himself for the
sake of his children. He must create himself into the father of the
Übermensch. He must become hard enough to impregnate eternity.
In addition, he must die for the sake of his children. He must "lose
himself to his children . . . become his children's prey."[78] Zarathustra teaches death at the right time:

> My death I praise to you, the free death which comes to me be-
> cause I want it. And when shall I want it? He who has a goal and
> an heir will want death at the right time for his goal and heir.[79]

Zarathustra must die for the sake of his heir, his goal, the
Übermensch. Zarathustra longs for this death. He longs to return to
the earth "that I may find rest in her who gave birth to me."[80] He
longs to return to mother earth, but only after he has sired the
Übermensch by her. Perhaps, Zarathustra wants to climb back into
the womb in order to become the *Übermensch*, in order to sire himself? For, the *Übermensch* "is the meaning of the earth."[81] The child
is the meaning of the eternal womb of being. Even nature is a riddle
solved by pregnancy; even her meaning, the meaning of mother
earth, is the child she gestates in the eternal womb of being.

He Comes too Soon

Thus, Nietzsche's is a classic Oedipal tale, patricidal and incestuous. He is jealous of his philosophical fathers. He challenges their
potency in hopes of displacing/replacing them. He requires the death
of the father, including himself, for the sake of the son, the *Übermensch*. The son takes the place of the father in relation to the
mother, for his own sake, in order to sire himself. On another level,
Nietzsche and his Zarathustra, as sons themselves, want to have
the mother for the sake of the son, the *Übermensch*. The mother's is

a (phallic) power that is given and controlled by the father/son. She exists for the sake of the son, who is provided as a result of the father's potency. She is the womb in which, and through which, the struggle between father and son take place.

The struggle within the womb is the will to power. It is the life struggle, a struggle for power. The tension and expansion within the womb causes nausea, morning sickness. But, this nausea is necessary and productive. It always leads beyond itself. It is always also the overcoming of nausea, in the way that pregnancy and birth are the overcoming of morning sickness. Yet, in Nietzsche's story, a pregnancy, if it is strong, gives birth to another pregnancy. Out of the strong womb, no individual is ever born. The strong womb is eternally pregnant. It can continue to expand with its excesses. It has no need to expel excess or difference. In Nietzsche's story, every birth is premature.

Nietzsche's own birth is premature. He calls himself a man of the future, a posthumous man. He comes for the sake of another "man" of the future, the beyond-man, the *Übermensch*, who will come for the sake of excess energy. Nietzsche himself, however, is not beyond-man. He is not beyond-man, **woman,** enough to come for the sake of the excess energy left out of his desire: sexual energy, sexual pleasure, bodily lust, especially woman's desire, woman's lust. Rather, Nietzsche is the madman of the *Gay Science*[82] who comes too early . . . to experience anything of woman's desire.

Notes

1. Jacques Derrida, *Spurs/Eperons,* The University of Chicago Press: Chicago, 1979, 57. This essay was written in 1988. Since then many of my views on these issues have developed significantly.

2. David Farrell Krell, *Postponements,* Indiana University Press: Bloomington, 1986, 10; see also p. 85.

3. For an analysis of Derrida's *Spurs,* see Gayatri Spivak's "Displacement and the Discourse of Woman," in Mark Krupnick edited *Displacement: Derrida and After* (1983), and my "Woman as Truth in Nietzsche's Writing," *Social Theory and Practice,* vol. 10, summer 1984. For a detailed criticism of Krell's *Postponements,* see my "Nietzsche's Woman: The Poststructuralist Attempt to Do Away With Women," *Radical Philosophy,* spring 1988. See also my *Womanizing Nietzsche,* Routledge Publishers, New York, 1994.

4. Nietzsche, *Thus Spake Zarathustra,* in *The Portable Nietzsche,* trans., Walter Kaufmann, Vintage Books: New York, 1972, Book I, "On the Friend."

5. Ibid., "On Little Old and Young Women"; Cf., for example, *Gay Science,* trans., Walter Kaufmann, Random House: New York, 1974, II § 63–77; *Human all too Human,* trans, Marion Faber, University of Nebraska Press: Lincoln, "Wanderer and his Shadow," § 17, "Woman and Child," § 383–437, "Miscellaneous Maxims and Opinions," § 272–283, 286, 292.

6. Nietzsche, *Beyond Good and Evil,* trans., Walter Kaufmann, Vintage Books: New York, 1966, § 147.

7. Nietzsche, *On the Genealogy of Morals,* trans., Walter Kaufmann, Vintage Books: New York, 1969, III § 19, 27; *Ecce Homo,* trans., Walter Kaufmann, Vintage Books: New York, 1969, p. 267.

8. Ibid., *Genealogy,* Book II, § 12, p. 119.

9. *The Will to Power,* trans. Walter Kaufmann, Vintage Books: New York, 1986, §585; Ibid., § 7.

10. *The Birth of Tragedy,* trans., Walter Kaufmann, Vintage Books: New York, 1966, p. 2.

11. *Op. cit., Zarathustra,* p. 235.

12. *Op. cit., Will,* § 343, p. 207.

13. Thanks to Elizabeth Geer who pointed out that Nietzsche's anxiety about impotence can be read as an anxiety about the body and its finitude. Luce Irigaray presents a fascinating analysis of Nietzsche's fear and denial of the body in *Marine Lover of Friedrich Nietzsche,* Columbia University Press: New York, 1980. For an analysis of *Marine Lover* see my *Womanizing Nietzsche,* Routledge Publishers: New York, 1994. See also my "The Plaint of Ariadne" in Keith Ansell-Pearson edited *Nietzsche and Feminism* Althone Press: London, 1993. I had not read *Marine Lover* in 1988 when I wrote this essay.

14. See, for example, *Dawn,* § 427, 550; *Human all too Human,* § 3, 244, 252, 257; *The Will to Power,* § 469.

15. *Op cit., Human,* p. 15.

16. § 283.

17. *Op. cit., Zarathustra,* pp. 202, 326. Krell quotes an unpublished note in which Zarathustra tells the cat maidens: "weep no more Pallid Dudu! **Be a man,** Suleika!" *op. cit.,* 64; see also pp. 24, 27, 58, 77.

18. *Op. cit., Genealogy,* pp. 202, 326.

19. *Op. cit., Genealogy,* p. 97. In his preface, Nietzsche maintains that the rest of the third essay is an exegesis of this aphorism. (1969, 23). In the third essay of *On the Genealogy of Morals,* Nietzsche attacks the sickness, seriousness, and impotence of the ascetic ideal. The ascetic ideal is not the mocking warrior loved by wisdom. The ascetic ideal is impotent. It is not manly. It is not hard enough to love a woman. Opposed to the serious, sickly, impotent ascetic ideal is the playful, healthy, potent Dionysus. For an analysis of the relationship of the aphorism to the third essay see my "The Ethics of Reading *On the Genealogy of Morals" International Studies in Philosophy,* Summer 1993.

20. For passages in which Nietzsche praises war and conquering, see *Human all too Human,* §477; *The Will to Power,* §53, 125, 975; *Beyond Good and Evil,* § 200. Also, in *On the Genealogy of Morals,* Nietzsche argues in favor of the master morality.

21. See, for example, *The Will to Power,* § 27, 41, 104, 128, 129, 380, 422, 544, 665, 740, 829, 877, 975, 1017, 1026, 380, 684, 751, 776; *Beyond Good and Evil,* § 199, 209, 232, 244, 245, 256; *Human all too Human,* § 164.

22. Ibid., *Will,* § 432, 236.

23. Ibid., 437, 241.

24. *Op. cit., Genealogy,* Book II, §10.

25. *Op. cit., Zarathustra,* II "On Redemption."

26. Dionysian Dithyrams, "Glory and Eternity"; Colli & Montinari Abt. 6, Bd. 3, pp. 400–403.

27. For a criticism of Nietzsche's use of biological metaphors of reproduction in order to describe the Dionysian force, see my "Woman as Truth in Nietzsche's Writings" (1984), and my dissertation *Woman's Voice, Man's Language: A Reading of Gender and Langugage in Nietzsche,* Northwestern University, 1987.

28. *Op. cit., Birth,* § 16.

29. *Op. cit., Gay Science,* p. 226.

30. *Op. cit., Birth,* § 16.

31. *Op. cit., Gay Science,* § 178; op. cit., *Genealogy,* III § 8.

32. *Op. cit., Ecce Homo,* p. 267.

33. *Op. cit., Human,* p. 197, 203.

34. *Op. cit., Birth,* § 28.

35. *Op. cit., Human,* p. 198.

36. *Op. cit., Will,* p. 643.

37. Ibid., § 1067.

38. Ibid., p. 842.

39. *Op. cit., Birth,* pp. 99–100. Second emphasis is mine.

40. Ibid., § 3.

41. *Op. cit., Zarathustra,* II "Blessed Isles," p. 99.

42. *Op. cit., Genealogy,* p. 101.

43. *Op. cit., Birth,* §9.

44. This male phobia that takes the mother's pregnant body as its 'object' is what Julia Kristeva calls the abject. I have presented this interpretation of her notion of the abject in *Reading Kristeva: Unraveling the Double-bind,* Indiana University Press: Bloomington, 1993. Also, I apply the notion of abjection to Nietzsche in my "Nietzsche's Abjection," in Peter Burgard edited *Nietzsche and the Feminine,* University of Virginia Press: Charlottesville 1994.

45. *Op. cit., Will,* § 654, 657.

46. *Op. cit., Birth,* §9.

47. Ibid., p. 23.

48. *Op. cit., Zarathustra,* p. 331.

49. Ibid., p. 208.

50. *Op. cit., Genealogy,* p. 125.

51. Ibid., II § 24.

52. *Op. cit., Will,* § 108.

53. *Op. cit., Genealogy,* p. 88.

54. Ibid., p. 86.

55. I will deal with Zarathustra's desire in the last section of this essay.

56. *Op. cit., Genealogy,* III § 8.

57. *Op. cit., Will* § 800.

58. Ibid., § 811.

59. Ibid., § 812.

60. *Op. cit., Genealogy,* III § 8; op. cit., Will, § 811.

61. *Op. cit., Will,* p. 163.

62. *Op. cit., Gay Science,* p. 235.

63. Ibid., p. 235.

64. *The Case of Wagner,* "A Musician's Problem," trans., Walter Kaufmann, Vintage Books: New York, 1966, § 3. See also, *Beyond Good and Evil,* author's preface.

65. Freud suggests that the Oedipal complex is resolved by both identifying with the father and fearing the father. According to Freud, it is castration by the father that the boy fears as punishment for his incestuous desire.

66. *Op. cit., Birth,* § 9.

67. *Op. cit.,* Krell, pp. 45–6, 86.

68. Ibid., pp. 50, 86.

69. Ibid., p. 49.

70. *Op. cit., Zarathustra,* p. 199.

71. Ibid., p. 199.

72. Ibid., p. 273.

73. Ibid., pp. 339–40.

74. Ibid., p. 434.

75. Ibid., p. 340.

76. Ibid., p. 340.

77. Ibid., p. 198.

78. Ibid., p. 273.

79. Ibid., p. 184.

80. Ibid., p. 186.

81. Ibid., p. 125.

82. *Op. cit., Gay Science,* § 125.

Nietzschean Debris: Truth as Circe

Margaret Nash

"Truth as Circe. *Error has turned animals into men; might truth be capable of turning man into an animal again?*"

Nietzsche, Human All Too Human (519)

I

What is it to know a self? Who is the subject that knows and seeks knowledge of itself? Are these questions still questions that admit of an answer in a postmodern climate in which *the* subject has been erased by multiplication, a climate in which the subject, like Nietzsche's God, is dead or at least in the process of dying? In killing or erasing God we unsettle a redemptive, purposive order. Humanism too is dying as we dethrone the universal 'man' ensconced between the humus and the ism of a tradition marked by a hope attached to method. Nietzsche's thought spurs on this project of deposition. This deposition holds out another hope, however. It is the hope of utilizing the humus, this decayed, rotting, nourishing matter, for ends other than silencing, static universalizations.

Can feminists find a foothold here? Does relinquishing universalizations entail relinquishing knowledge claims or is it rather that the idea of self-knowledge is transformed once we refuse to pose it or to frame it as if the object is transparent and limited? The pursuit after such knowledge, far from being purely cognitive, requires struggle, tears, laughter, deceit and endless repetition that is never quite a repetition. These phenomena muddy attempts to pin down a referent and hence transgress the boundaries of traditional epistemology. The knower is both implicated in what is known and called into question as an inquiring subject who really seeks to know. In sundering a straight forward opposition between knower and known, inner and outer, we sunder the fiction of a unified self.

Nietzsche opens up a space for understanding the multiple, fluid identity of the subject, an identity held together by opposition

219

and surrender. Such an understanding of the subject affirms the otherness and difference at the heart of all identities. In addition to the affirmation of multiplicity, Nietzsche's focus on the value of play is important for feminist practices. Genuine play reminds us that meaning is largely a carnal matter, a matter that resists fixity and that feeds greedily on image after image. The yearning and the hunger for meaning to which Nietzsche gives expression both provoke and challenge readers of his texts to create and enact meaning. It is my contention that Nietzsche's challenge creates the opportunity for the detritus of the philosophical tradition to find some humus and the nourishment residing therein.

Nietzsche's influence on and appeal for contemporary thought lie in his break with tradition, his critique of metaphysics and ethics, and his diagnosis of the decay and nihilism at the root of modern life. Much of his appeal may rest on the image of him as an exciting iconoclast, a demystifier engaged in shattering illusions. The illusions and false idols that Nietzsche purports to shatter are all connected with beliefs in rationality, truth, progress and the methods held to be conducive to attaining these ends. In calling into question many of the staples of traditional philosophical enquiry and discourse and in unmasking pretensions to truth, Nietzsche unsettles attempts to anchor philosophical reflection in certainty. His anti-foundationalism, perspectivism and opposition to systematic philosophy pre-figure postmodernist skepticism regarding ahistorical, totalizing theories. Nietzsche seeks out and opts to voice the discontinuities and ruptures which resist accommodation within a unified perspective or dialectical synthesis. In doing so he lets contradictions stand and calls attention to the violence entailed by silence and/or the erasure of difference. Nietzsche's philosophical style embodies his peculiar desire to impact and move the reader. He does not produce neat arguments; he shoots pointed arrows in unexpected directions; his language is deliberately metaphorical and provocative.

It is the provocative side of Nietzsche which I wish to emphasize. Feminists engaged in writing and voicing what has been repressed by our culture may see in Nietzsche's attention to language and style an avenue to a biting critique. Incisive strategies are not all that Nietzsche offers, however. His stylistic and thematic focus on play and the value of the disunity of the subject who plays are an important subversive corrective to the philosophical tradition. Play, multiplicity, the body, and sensuous reality have propped up metaphysical discourse without adequate recognition for centuries, just as women have served and supported a world which devalues and erases their contributions. In what follows I will first explore Nietzsche's critique of philosophy in light of these themes and will then turn to some feminist uses of these themes and strategies.

II

In *Twilight of the Idols: or, How One Philosophizes with a Hammer* Nietzsche critiques metaphysics and shatters illusions that offer solace in the name of rationality. According to him values have a material grounding and inform all quests for knowledge. Writing out of a space which decries the choking character of a morality that denies this material basis and so reveals an antipathy to the body, sensuousness, passion and the very roots of life, Nietzsche understands the subject as actively engaged in interpreting the meaning of her experience. Nietzsche criticizes Cartesian epistemology and anticipates many of the critical insights which Freud systematized in psychoanalytic theory. He focuses on the gaps in what are supposed to be rational processes and on the unconscious and unintentional dimensions of experience. Consciousness is relative to other psychic processes; it is not veracious. Hence the location of knowledge cannot rest with consciousness. The ego or "I" is a projection, a fictive entity created out of bodily needs and processes. For Nietzsche, the unconscious (the it) is by far the more significant locus of knowledge. As he states in *Beyond Good and Evil,* "a thought comes when 'it' wishes to and not when 'I' wish, so that it is a falsification of the facts of the case to say that the subject 'I' is the condition of the predicate 'think'."[1] The 'it' controls the process of thinking; texts are not produced by unified authors, though authors may serve as the means by which texts are written. Neither are authors in full control of nor the guarantors of the meaning of the text. Meanings like selves are multiple, rich and varied. Language is always excessive; it says too much.

For Nietzsche, a multiplicity of selves underlies the complicated structure of the 'I'. His shift from consciousness to the unconscious is a shift from a surface phenomenon to an infinitely cacophonous repository, a shift that requires that we read authorial intentions as signs or symptoms that conceal as much as they reveal. Though fluidity, multiplicity and disunity characterize the Nietzschean subject, it is important to note that this subject is an embodied one; Nietzsche is not an idealist.

The body says I, performs I, is I; but the body is not one; it is composed of and exudes multiple drives, desires and needs. In *Thus Spoke Zarathustra* Nietzsche critiques the despisers of the body—in other words, the moralists, metaphysicians and priests who fear and repress the body. This denial of the sensuous character of all thought shuts off access to the experience of participating in the materialization of knowledge. Nietzsche esteems reasoning or thinking which acknowledges its embodied origins. Traditional epistemology restricts bodily contact to the eyes, privileging sight both as metaphor for knowledge and as the percept most conducive to it. But are not hearing, touch, taste and smell rich modes of sensing and knowing and is not their denial symptomatic? Carnal phobia, perhaps. "Body am I entirely and nothing else" states Nietzsche; "and soul is only a word for something about the body."[2]

The carnality at the heart of Nietzschean meaning is also reflected in his aphoristic style and attention to the effects of language. Non-figurative, literalized language is dead language which carries few surprises and exerts little pull on us. In contrast, a figurative, sensuous style can explode conceptual schemes and so open up new ways of approaching the world of our concern. Such a style artfully constructs and plays with the material words—their sounds, their shapes and the images they evoke. For Nietzsche, "anything truly productive is offensive."[3] and to offend in this context is to break through complacency, indeed, it is to anger and to violate the old order. Such an attack on the tradition is most productive when aimed at the sensual level where meaning is lived and felt and not merely grasped cognitively. Nietzsche aims to offend moral and aesthetic sensibilities; revulsion his its value in grounding our feelings.

Nietzsche attends to other bodily phenomena; these include laughter and crying, dancing and singing. Activities such as these point to an unbounded experience of self, since they break down or at least put into question the usual lines we draw or assume between inner and outer. Laughter and crying can be convulsive and disruptive by involving the leaking and spilling of fluids and expenditure of energy for no apparent end. In dancing we give ourselves over to a rhythm and surrender a defined sense of self. These phenomena, as Nietzsche recognized, are also dangerous. They rupture bodily integrity; they are weapons which can be used to tear down and humiliate. How often is humor used to degrade and express hostility? How much are tears interpreted as a sign of weakness and defeat? And yet Nietzsche affirms the dangerous, uncontrollable aspects of these phenomena, phenomena which reveal conflict and passion and mock the border between reason and unreason, happiness and sadness, inside and outside. Nietzsche advocates that we risk devolution, that we embrace these ecstatic experiences and use them to our advantage. As Nietzsche's Zarathustra proclaims:

> I would believe only in a god who could dance. And when I saw my devil I found him serious, thorough, profound and solemn: it was the spirit of gravity—through him all things fall.
> Not by wrath does one kill but by laughter. Come let us kill the spirit of gravity![4]

The spirit of gravity props up a sense of purposefulness which tends to repress the marginal and to devalue surrender. The experience of losing one's self and of suspending a functional goal orientation involves a self-forgetfulness which is both a mode of being present and the positive possibility of being wholly with and/or subject to something else. Of course not all experiences of this sort are playful. However the willingness to suspend an instrumental, goal-directed orientation and to relinquish a rigidly defined sense of self is requisite to the affirmative, free play that Nietzsche advocates. Self-forgetfulness on the part of the player allows her to interact in a reciprocal, as opposed to a manipulative, way with the environment. Such a reciprocal interaction binds us in a give and take fashion to our present experience and to the present moment, but it does so only insofar as we actively maintain our engagement.

Another value of adopting a playful perspective lies in not taking norms and conventions seriously and in not taking one's self seriously. I am using 'serious' here to mean a goal directed attitude dominated by the weight of a practical future. In relinquishing a serious attitude, we are free to search for meaning in places other than in the past or the future. The now is potentially more playful. Of course the quest for meaning may not and need not be playful, but for Nietzsche it certainly seemed to be. Playful interactions serve as transvaluing sources. By acting 'as if' or by inserting fiction into what gets played out as reality, we both affirm the constitution of the real and mock nihilism. In adopting a playful perspective we locate ourselves in a place where the grave quest for meaning holds no attraction. In a sense, it does not matter. The surrender and/or suspension at stake in giving up the matter of the practical future means that we are free for involvement in the present. Such involvement is not without its perils. Nietzsche's open-ended notion of affirmative free play involves risk, but if we have a multiplicity of selves, then placing our self at risk never involves all of us. We cannot even formulate what all of us would mean. In play, we place parts of our multiplicity at risk in the sense that what gets played out cannot or probably does not affect all of the aspects of our selves to the same degree.

In suspending a goal orientation toward the world of our concern and in ceasing to believe in the old idols, new properties of the world or new possibilities for interpreting it are open to us, and hence new perspectives and values may suggest themselves. What is at stake in play is a privileged viewpoint. The liberating quality of the play attitude opens up the restricted view of rationality that a serious or goal directed attitude closes off. Play involves a nonserious use of reason; it is not the suspension of reason. Such a nonserious use of reason means that playful activity may not answer any specific quest for knowledge or meaning though it may clarify what is involved in the quest by reminding us that we are caught up in a play of questions and answers; a playful attitude is one that embraces such a predicament.

III

Now, one might ask, what can feminists garner from the shambles of Nietzsche's hammer? The thrilling and at the same time potentially dangerous appeal of Nietzsche's texts resides in their lability, their adaptability, suggestiveness, and openness to multiple interpretation. This lability means that Nietzsche's "wicked thoughts"[5] can lacerate as well as nourish. This at least double possibility, conjunctive as well as disjunctive, is not unique to Nietzsche's language, though he, unlike many, attends to the figurative doubleness of all signs—their materiality and the meanings to which their shapes, sounds and images give rise. In so doing, he plays the double entendres at the root of all signification and composes aphoristic pieces meant to be heard yet not to be slavishly repeated. Nietzsche, the lone, nomadic warrior, is not free of blind spots but these will not concern us here. Be examining rather than sweeping away the debris from his hammer, we, like Nietzsche, may be able to love and appropriate the waste products that threaten to invade tidy systems. As feminists unearth the non-neutral 'man' at the heart of humanism, the rotting humus is there for the taking. Nietzsche's fertile themes can be and are being used to create, dramatize and write anew the experience of those who have been relegated to the margins. The themes which I have stressed—multiplicity, play and the body—are the most relevant to feminist practice. Though a mere focus on these themes is not itself feminist, I will highlight two different feminist uses of these themes in an attempt to illustrate that the shattered tradition in its post-mortem state is rich enough to allow for many re-writes.

Feminists are not a unified group. The recognition and appreciation of differences have consequences for understanding divisions within and between women and within and between men and women. To accept multiplicity is to accept split, divided, and, so, conflicted subjects as well as various kinds of subjects with different racial, ethnic, gender, class, and religious backgrounds and with different constitutions and erotic preferences. The differences between people and the multiple modes of knowing to which we have access have led some feminists to celebrate differences and epistemological pluralism, even at the cost of disunity and a cacophony of voices. Such disunity is to be expected and is important if we are to really interact with and learn from each other.

Maria Lugones, in her article, "Playfulness, 'World'-Travelling, and Loving Perception," develops a notion of playfulness which depicts an experience of integrity and the possibility of connecting with and being with others in a way that does not dominate or erase them. For Lugones, we are a plurality of selves, we inhabit many different 'worlds' and we may be different people in different 'worlds'. A 'world' may refer to a location, construction, or experience that we materially and psychically inhabit.

> "One can 'travel' between these 'worlds' and one can inhabit more than one of these 'worlds' at the very same time. I think that most of us who are outside the mainstream of, for example, the U.S. dominant construction or organization of life are 'world-travellers' as a matter of necessity and of survival. It seems to me that inhabiting more than one 'world' at the same time and 'travelling' between 'worlds' is part and parcel of our experience and our situation."[6]

Lugones terms "the shift from being one person to being a different person"[7] 'travel'. Such a shift need not be conscious and it is not a matter of role-playing; who I am in one world need not be consistent with who I am in another world, a world which may construct me, as well as I it, differently. 'World-travelling' which can create solidarity between women who inhabit different and disparate worlds involves a particular kind of playful openness. Lugones criticizes agonistic, competitive, rule-governed conceptions of play which privilege competence and emphasize winning. Such a conception of play applied to 'world'- travelling ends in conquest, which in turn erases difference by destroying it or assimilating it to what is familiar to the winner. The playful attitude developed by Lugones involves:

> openness to surprise, openness to being a fool, openness to self-construction or reconstruction and to construction or reconstruction of the 'worlds' we inhabit playfully. Negatively, playfulness is characterized by uncertainty, a lack of self-importance, absence of rules or a not taking rules as sacred, a not worrying about competence and a lack of abandonment to a particular construction of oneself, others and one's relation to them.[8]

This kind of play is loving in that it allows for differences to surface; in embracing plurality it is akin to Nietzschean, Dionysian, creative abandonment which involves being open to surrender. Playful 'world'-travel as Lugones notes, is not a safe way to enter some 'worlds', (particularly the dominant white woman's world, if one is a woman of color) but it can be a liberating way in which we can enter some worlds and so a way of understanding what it is to inhabit a 'world' we do not know. In identifying with others in a 'world' that is not ours, we can experience their 'world,' others and ourselves through their eyes, their bodies, and their positions. Such an experiential move may also help to put us in touch with the others in us. The free play that Lugones seems to value is important not only for opening up the possibility of being with and learning from others, but also for realizing a practice, that avoids arrogance and dogmatism. In play the undecidability of meaning is left standing. One might play with or go with the consequences of one interpretation to see where it leads, but one recognizes that the plurality in the play of all images, concepts, and signs may call for resistance to a single integrating synthesis. Such a call is neither escapist nor programmatic. Playful 'world'-travel is a way to feelingly understand and explore our own and other peoples' lives without trying to reconcile their differences. Sometimes differences must be seen, heard, felt, tasted, smelled, allowed to grow or wither away; in their starkness and multiplicity we may then find ways to love, change, and/or live with them.

Knowledge comes through bodily engagement. French thinkers such as Hélène Cixous and Luce Irigaray have especially emphasized this engagement. They have artfully given expression to possible interpretations of being an embodied being, especially a female. Their writing has been termed 'writing through the body'. They deliberately wish to call into question women's erasure and indeed the erasure of all difference that threatens the univocal interpretations imposed on bodily experience. The body, and specifically a female body that writes out of its marginalized, repressed location, is the source of generative, challenging meaning. While playing with language, whether through mime, poetry, parody, or myth, they subvert old categories and ways of understanding sex, gender, and power. In writing through the body, they write from the assumption of a polymorphous, bisexual sensuality. Writing of this and out of this complexity and doing so by refusing to stay within the bounds of dominant discursive forms explodes patriarchal assumptions and discourses.

Both Cixous and Irigaray write from and hence create the possibility of a different imaginary,[9] a different economy, and so a different reality. They envision female eroticism (jouissance) as multiple, plural and outside a scopic or specular economy in which women have been conceptualized by and have served as a support for male fantasies.[10] Touch, taste, smell and voice inform this new economy of excess which subverts and exposes the hidden hierarchies of a rationality grounded in a juridical conception of power that emphasizes appropriation and accumulation as if these actions cover the range of power configurations. The affirmation of a non-linear, non-goal directed economy displaces notions of desire and value based on "equitable" exchange. These feminist writers appropriate and use for their own ends philosophical speculations and traditional mythical portrayals of women. In so doing, they re-write and re-authorize their own past and their own future in a repetition that is never quite a repetition. Their writing is political, transgressive, irreverent, and playful. Such writing might make Nietzsche smile, if not sing and dance.

But it doesn't really matter how Nietzsche would receive it. What matters: Can we eat it? Will it nourish us?

Knowledge, particularly self-knowledge, is an uncanny sort of thing. As Freud's essay "The Uncanny", makes clear: "The uncanny proceeds from something familiar which has been repressed."[11] Self-knowledge is the outcome of an interactive process based on uncovering and concealing the frighteningly familiar. In returning again and again to the deceit at the root of all self-knowledge we perhaps get hold of both the limits and the elasticity of the knowledge process. Error consists in taking *our* limits for the end. Our deceit is modifiable. To write our bodies and to voice our experiences may transfigure our lives. Yet despite the seductive side of this enterprise, such writing in no way guarantees the character of this transfiguration. To surrender universalizations, to multiply truths, to face our others,—this too is risky; but is certainty that reduces ambiguity really so comforting? At the risk of heavy-handed seduction, I will close with the opening to a Nietzschean preface: "Supposing truth is a woman—what then?"[12]

Notes

1. Nietzsche, Friedrich, *Beyond Good and Evil*. Trans. Walter Kaufmann. New York: Vintage Books, 1966, p. 24.

2. Nietzsche, Friedrich. *Thus Spoke Zarathustra* in *The Portable Nietzsche,* Trans. Walter Kaufmann, N.Y.: Viking, 1982, p. 146.

3. Nietzsche, Friedrich. "David Strauss, the Confessor and the Writer", *Untimely Meditations*. Trans. R. J. Hollingdale. Cambridge: Cambridge University Press, 1983, p. 49.

4. Nietzsche, Friedrich. *Thus Spoke Zarathustra* in *The Portable Nietzsche*. Trans. Walter Kaufmann. N.Y.: Viking, 1982. Part I, "On Reading and Writing", p. 153.

5. At the end of *Beyond Good and Evil,* Nietzsche refers to his "written and painted thoughts"—thoughts that lose their color, bite, and sting as they wither in the open air, thoughts that make him sneeze and laugh—as his "beloved, wicked thoughts". p. 237.

6. Lugones, Maria. "Playfulness, 'World'-Travelling, and Loving Perception," *Hypatia,* vol. 2, no. 2 (Summer 1987), pp. 10–11.

7. Ibid., p. 11.

8. Ibid., p. 17.

9. 'Imaginary' as used here refers both to the unconscious structuring of experience, and to an alternative interpretative rendering of the meaning of experiences.

10. A scopic or specular economy privileges sight/looking as the mode of knowledge and as the underwriter of value. Scoptophilia (Freud's term for love of looking) informs this closed economy (or system) which is marked by its mirroring function. What is other, alien or strange gets reduced to the

same. Philosophical discourse has yet to 'see' or understand women since women have always been conceptualized/specularized as a reflection/projection of men. Luce Irigaray (*This Sex Which Is Not One* and *Speculum of the Other Woman,* Ithaca: Cornell University Press, 1985) develops and explores the multiple meanings and implications of a specular economy. She disrupts this specular closed economy by showing its underpinnings and by imagining a different one.

11. Freud, Sigmund. *The Standard Edition of the Complete Psychological Works of Sigmund Freud.* trans. Strachey. London: Hogarth Press, 1955, Vol. 17, p. 247.

12. Nietzsche, Friedrich. *Beyond Good and Evil, op. cit.,* p. 2.

Nietzsche's Psychology of Gender Difference

Ofelia Schutte

Different perspectives of feeling.—What does our chatter about the Greeks amount to? What do we understand of their art, the soul of which is—passion for naked *male* beauty! It was only from that viewpoint that they were sensible of female beauty. Thus their perspective on female beauty was quite different from ours. And similarly with their love of women: they reverenced differently, they despised differently.

(Daybreak, § 170)[1]

Nietzsche's philosophy, like the Greek passion for beauty of which he speaks here, is male oriented. Thus it would make much more sense to speak of what he thinks of man (in the gender specific sense of the term) than what, by contrast or default, he thinks of woman. While his conception of man admits of plurality and difference, his conception of woman tends to be reductionistic. In this essay I shall explore some key aspects of Nietzsche's view of the gender difference, that is, the categories he uses to differentiate between men and women. I suggest that the specific structure of his psychological perspective on gender lies at the foundation of his narrow views on women.

Departing from this analysis of the gender difference I will consider two other questions of special concern to feminists. First, what is Nietzsche's position regarding equal rights for women in society? In particular, how are his views on women's role in society influenced by his view of femininity? A second question of interest in this essay is Nietzsche's position on women's writing. It is thought sometimes that because Nietzsche was a rather unorthodox writer who called into question important dogmas in the Western tradition, he would also be supportive of women writers who question the "tradition" of sexism. Since he wrote *from* his own experience, outwards, to a society differing from his views, my question is, did he also consider women ought to have an opportunity to do something

231

similar? Or did he think only men should write? If he placed restrictions on women's writing, what does this tell us about his views on the gender difference—a view which permits men who are "free spirits" to question even the most sacred beliefs, but which does not permit the exercise of the same rights and privileges for women?

I intend to show that with respect to these questions Nietzsche's position was neither feminist nor neutral. It was, in fact, for the most part, strongly and explicitly anti-feminist. To these questions, therefore, I will also add another one: is there any way to interpret Nietzsche's position as anything other than anti-feminist, particularly as we move from a modern to a postmodern perspective? Today Nietzsche is considered one of the initiators or precursors of a postmodern perspective, a theoretical position which in some of its most radical expressions denounces or rejects the presuppositions of a logocentric/phallocentric discourse. Is it possible through some unusual turn in our interpretation of Nietzsche to consider him, the most anti-feminist of philosophers, as precisely the opposite of himself in this regard? If this were the case, I want to ask, what are some of the variables that would allow us to reverse our interpretation?

I

Nietzsche's comments on the gender difference often appear in the context of various observations he makes about culture and/or psychology. His limited conception of the nature of femininity, the social role of women, and the relations between the sexes also tends to be defended in psychologistic or culturally-oriented terms. The principal standard he uses to define women's role in society is, paradoxically (since he is not a utilitarian), utility to a "higher" culture. His arguments, which are rarely moderate, except in the period of *Human, All too Human,* convey the idea of a multi-tiered society in which a relatively small, exceptionally qualified, all-male ruling class exerts its powerful will on subordinate groups.

Nietzsche turned to the Greeks for his model of what he explicitly referred to as "a male culture" (*eine Kultur der Männer*):

> *A male culture.* Greek culture of the Classical era is a male culture. As for women, Pericles, in his funeral oration, says everything with the words: "They are best when men speak about them as little as possible."

> The erotic relationship of men to youths was, on a level which we cannot grasp, the necessary, sole prerequisite of all male education . . . The more important this relationship was considered, the lower sank interaction with women: the perspective of procreation and lust—nothing further came into consideration . . . If one considers further that woman herself was excluded from all kinds of competitions and spectacles, then the sole higher entertainment remaining to her was religious worship.
>
> To be sure, when Electra and Antigone were portrayed in tragedies, the Greeks *tolerated* it in art, although they did not like it in life . . .
>
> Women had no task other than to produce beautiful, powerful bodies, in which the character of the father lived on as intact as possible . . . [I]n Greek mothers, the Greek genius returned again and again to nature.[2]

As we shall see, some of these views, at first attributed to the Greeks, were later voiced as his own.

According to Nietzsche's view of the gender difference, woman's "proper" place is in the family, as a mother and wife. In *Human All, too Human,* he discusses this role in the chapter entitled "Woman and Child." In the context of the family, Nietzsche speaks in favor of an improved status for modern women in contrast to that of their counterparts in antiquity. In modern times, he concedes, a spiritual friendship between a man and a woman is encouraged or at least permissible in marriage. *"Friendship and marriage.* The best friend will probably get the best wife, because a good marriage is based on a talent for friendship."[3] This aphorism dates from a period in Nietzsche's life when he was least intolerant toward women's improved standing in Western culture. I say least intolerant because the juxtaposition of the terms "friend" and "wife" shows that he still does not posit a relation of equality between men and women, nor does he imagine independent, active friendships among women.

But in *Human, All too Human,* Nietzsche draws the line sharply against the view that women can be "free spirits." Instead, he argues that women must follow traditional social norms. Men who are free spirits must therefore keep an unbridgeable distance between themselves and women. The "free spirit" must be like Socrates, who asked his male friends, prior to his death, to send away the women who were visibly expressing their sadness about his situation.[4] A second argument used by Nietzsche to keep women tied down as much as possible to the home is his suggestion that, if women are trained for public life, this will mean the degeneration of philosophy and politics, at least for a period "of transition" lasting several centuries.[5] Since philosophy and politics represent (since the times of the Greeks) some of the highest activities that the human being can accomplish in society, Nietzsche's belief that women's entry into these activities would lower their value expresses his gender-related view that women are inferior to men. In other words, Nietzsche thinks that women are less capable of acting freely than men. The general structure of his views leads to the following conclusion: the gender difference cuts human beings into two kinds: *men,* who fall on the side of *freedom,* and *women,* who fall on the side of *unfreedom.*

This reasoning leads him to a third point. Custom and tradition, which are on the side of unfreedom, will also be the place to which women's lives are attached. By contrast, he argues that some men, a select few, are born to stand *outside* custom, which is also to stand *apart* from women, both physically and emotionally. To this type of man, which he believed he himself embodied, he gave the name of "free spirit." Thus he states: "A man is called a free spirit if he thinks otherwise than would be expected, based on his origin, environment, class, and position, or based on prevailing contemporary views. He is the exception: bound spirits are the rule."[6] The principal characteristic of the free spirit is that he has released himself from tradition. "It is not part of the nature of the free spirit that his views are more correct, but rather that he has released himself from tradition . . . "[7] This means, among other things, that the man who does not penetrate women physically, the man who does not follow the heterosexual normative tradition of marriage and family life, is a free spirit. But women, in the view articulated by Nietzsche here, represent *tradition itself.* Women are not only *bound* by the normative, heterosexual customs from which the "free spirit" is able to escape. They represent the very action, pull, and attraction of the binding force itself. Women are magnets of unfreedom from which men (who are free spirits) should try to keep as distant as possible. What about women who would refuse either to represent these chains or to be tied down by them? As Nietzsche has argued in the same work, such a move would be most difficult. Women cannot be released from tradition without appearing ludicrous in their own, and by implication, everyone else's eyes.[8]

I have deliberately chosen the above mentioned passages from Nietzsche's middle period (sometimes referred to as his "positivist" period) to illustrate the fact that even in his less strident years, he maintains what can be characterized fundamentally as an anti-feminist position both on the gender difference and on the issue of social and political equality. His argument is simple. He uses the notion of gender difference to limit women's role and vocation to very specific functions in life, at the same time that he defends these restrictions in the name of a higher culture. His anti-feminist perspective grows bolder in his later works. Learned references to Pericles's funeral oration are no longer needed. In *Beyond Good and Evil*, for example, his beliefs are put forward simply as the view of a plural masculine subject, "We men." "We men wish," he says, "that woman should not go on compromising herself through enlightenment."[9] Women should not speak out in matters of church or politics, he argues, placing himself in the role of the friendly advisor of (outspoken) women. "I think it is a real friend of women," states Nietzsche, "who counsels them today: *mulier taceat de muliere* [women, be silent about women]."[10]

This indictment against women having a voice in public affairs is closely linked to another aphorism touching on the subject of women's writing. Here, in a sentence marked by an excess of both words and feelings, Nietzsche attempts to discredit the voices of women who speak out on behalf of equality.

> To lose the sense for the ground on which one is most certain of victory; to neglect practice with one's proper weapons; to let oneself go before men, perhaps 'to the point of writing a book,' when formerly one disciplined oneself to subtle and cunning humility; to work with virtuous audacity against men's faith in a basically different ideal that he takes to be *concealed* in woman, something Eternally-and-Necessarily-Feminine—to talk men emphatically and loquaciously out of their notion that woman must be maintained, taken care of, protected, and indulged like a more delicate, strangely wild, and often pleasant domestic animal; the awkward and indignant search for everything slavelike and serflike that has characterized woman's position in society so far, and still does (as if slavery were a counter-argument and not instead a condition of every higher culture, every enhancement of culture)—what is the meaning of all this if not a crumbling of feminine instincts, a defeminization?[11]

Nietzsche's argument shows an obsession with feminine normativity, even to the point (let us throw the expression back at him) of endorsing a society built on slavery. The *split* in the gender difference with women lying on the side of unfreedom is apparent, again, in this passage. Women's protest—especially their intelligent protest, expressed in the form of books, articles, and public denunciations—against their having to live a life of unfreedom is called "a crumbling of feminine instincts, a defeminization."

The above references from Nietzsche's middle and later works, as well as many more passages which cannot be included in this brief essay, lead to the following conclusion about the structure of his thinking about the gender difference. In Nietzsche's realm of free spirits, women are banned while men lead a difficult, ambiguous existence (trying to stay away from women as much as possible, yet also having to show they can dominate women, on pain of losing their coveted "masculine" identity, which is equated with power and freedom). A "double standard" of thoughts and feelings therefore separates women from men in Nietzsche's normative psychology of the gender difference. For example, he holds it is proper for man to be an atheist, whereas it is proper for woman only to be a believer. Despite his own proclamation of the death of God, he states: "Here and there they even want to turn women into freethinkers and scribblers ['scribblers' is a devaluation in relation to 'writers,' an activity properly belonging to men]—as if a woman without piety would not seem utterly obnoxious and ridiculous to a profound and godless man."[12] Or, although it is proper, indeed, necessary, for the free spirit to avoid sexual contact with women as well as emotional involvement through marriage or family life, he considers it entirely inappropriate for woman to enjoy anything but "her first and last profession—to give birth to strong children."[13]

In *Beyond Good and Evil,* Nietzsche claimed that psychology (in contrast to philosophy) would soon become the path to understanding the fundamental problems of the human being.[14] Having studied his psychology of gender we must conclude that the type of "psychology" he defends, however, is significantly flawed. With respect to the gender difference, it places women in the position of *reflecting* traditional values rather than challenging them, or creating new values. What, if anything, can a contemporary feminist perspective do to unravel this apparent contradiction between Nietzsche the "free spirit," advocate of the most radical undermining of traditional values, and Nietzsche the moralist, who does not cease to put forward an ultraconservative view of gender roles? Are gender roles—which function as a part of our culture—so sacred to him that not even the author of the statement "God is dead" can demolish them?

II

In contrast to Nietzsche, whose view of culture is explicitly male-oriented, feminists want to work for a culture where women will have a major role in shaping sociocultural values, a culture where they will not be adversely discriminated by men. In feminist theory today, there is a strong critique of what is known as "essentialism." This means feminists are distrustful of statements of the sort, "The essence of woman is X," or "The essence of man is Y," or "The essence of truth is Z." Such statements have a way of leading to oversimplification and/or dogmatism. For the same reason, we hesitate to say, "The essence of feminism is . . . ," lest we rush too fast to a conclusion and leave out something important, which will later be used by our opponents to divide us against each other. Still, we must not be so complacent as to call anyone who claims to speak on behalf of women a "feminist." The feminist movement includes a variety of epistemological and political perspectives. But its views have a specific orientation, in particular, stopping violence against women, promoting equal rights for women in the economic and sociopolitical spheres, and defending women's capacity to make decisions concerning what pertains to their own bodies and their choice of lifestyles.

It might appear that Nietzsche, who made it a point to be a strong critic of "herd values" as well as the proponent of a certain epistemological perspectivism, would side, in the last analysis, with those who defy the practices of the majority, particularly conservative majorities. Yet his anti-egalitarian, elitist political views and his ultraconservative views on gender create, at worst, an explicit opposition to women's rights, and, at best, an ambiguity or impasse in his position. For example, even when he criticizes the social conventions of his time, he asserts the value of personal solitude rather than join with others, his contemporaries, who oppose violence and exploitation. The return to the healthy body and the affirmation of life of which he speaks so eloquently are seriously hampered by his limited and alienated view of the gender difference, among other things.[15]

It was pointed out above that Nietzsche's conception of the gender difference involves a double standard of value in terms of the psychological "lots" assigned to men and women. The example of man's capacity to be an atheist in contrast to woman's assignation to the role of a believer is a case in point. Absurd as it may seem, the dogmatic essentialism guiding Nietzsche's views on woman's gender identity can take over his freedom-loving views which, in a separate context, allow him to question even the most powerful and sacred values. His normative view of gender therefore obstructs the work of his radical, critical spirit, which is willing to defy absolute values. Nietzsche's psyche is divided just along this line, with the dogmatic, authoritarian side gaining ground over the freedom-loving side, especially after the writing of *The Gay Science* and *Zarathustra*. In the end, he is only be able to escape his psychic division and pain through a tragic fall into insanity.

The insane, non-conformist Nietzsche has been attracting a lot of attention lately. Today's postmodernist generation does not see the symbolism of his insanity as a sign of despair, but as one of hope or defiance. Among those drawn to the riddle of Nietzsche's insanity, a significant number have come to distrust the portrait of Nietzsche as an anti-feminist. Portraying someone as an anti-feminist, they charge, is part of the old "essentialist" attitude of trying to pin down a problem to an easy answer and rushing into oversimplifications. Some of these critics even consider Nietzsche an advocate of a more enlightened feminism than that of the modern era—a feminism that defies "logic" and "equality" in the sense of refusing to adjust to conformist and universal standards of value and conduct. A new intellectual movement developed, primarily in France. It was influenced directly or indirectly by Jacques Derrida's reading of Nietzsche and by the psychoanalytic perspective of Jacques Lacan.[16]

Postmodernist readers of Nietzsche have tried to use psychological rather than philosophical tools of analysis—as Nietzsche himself recommended—to try to come to a better understanding of his thought. Applying these psychological categories, they try to distinguish between two kinds of "economics" regulating the conscious and unconscious lives of individuals. One of these is an economy of "lack," which they also call an economy of "castration." The economy of lack says: either "X" is one thing or its opposite, but it can't be both. For example, either something is true or it is false. The economy of lack is drawn to reasoning employing opposites which exclude each other. For example, with regard to gender, it will allow for something to be either "masculine" or "feminine," but not both.

In contrast to the economy of lack or "castration," postmodern readers suggest the hypothesis of an economy of excess or overflow. Much of this analysis is already found in Nietzsche, incidentally, who antedated these Freudian and post-Freudian hypotheses.[17] It is not easy to define the economy of excess because its own rules place it beyond definition. Instead of using logic to conceptualize it, the postmodernists appeal to jokes, slips of the tongue, double entendres, metaphor, irony, dreams, or anything that seems to contain more than one meaning in a single expression or image. According to the economy of excess or overflow, no one is ever caught in a corner, because reality is not defined by straight lines.

Feminist postmodernists like Hélène Cixous and Luce Irigaray claim that sexism, at least as we have known it, either comes from or is manifested primarily in and through an economy of lack. This starts very early in life. "Is it a boy or a girl?" The answers cut across the psyche, restricting the feminine side, which in our inherited culture is the side of unfreedom. Feminist post-Lacanian critics argue that since the initial setting of the gender difference is one in which girls are devalued or delimited in relation to boys, the very process of limiting anything becomes associated in our unconscious mind with the restriction of the female image or the feminine self in all of us. The close relation between masculinism and the imposing of limits upon the reality of the other runs through the work of Luce Irigaray.

Under this theoretical approach, the line dividing feminism from anti-feminism shifts to a different conceptual as well as psychological ground. The strict use of logic (which limits the meaning of statements) appears to fall on the side of male dominance, whereas the use of literary devices such as ambiguity, excess, metaphor, irony, and various figures of speech are taken as the signs of a new, avant-garde feminism. This new, postmodern feminism believes itself to be redeemed from the errors of modernity, where, as in Descartes's theory, the edifice of reason was intentionally built on the straightest and most secure foundations. The new approach stresses paying attention to the cracks and gaps in the foundation. These gaps are thought to reveal the privileged places through which the (repressed) unconscious spills over and "speaks" its contradictory and baffling language. The advocates of this approach to meaning—a theory that also privileges psychoanalysis and literature over philosophy—find a friendly voice and inspiration in Nietzsche, who in his time was a genius of irony, metaphor, and the love of excess, even to the point of madness.

III

Is a reinterpretation of Nietzsche which places him on the side of a postmodern feminist renaissance justified? Can postmodernism's critique of logocentric discourse place Nietzsche on the side of feminism, rather than against it? To illustrate the point that neither postmodernism, nor the use of certain literary styles of writing are guarantees, in themselves, of the presence of a feminist perspective, I will distinguish between Hélène Cixous's and Luce Irigaray's notion of gender and Nietzsche's, noting why the former perspective is feminist and the latter is not.

The position towards woman taken by Cixous and Irigaray illustrates this important point. Why is this the case? From a post-Lacanian perspective, they reject the normative concept of gender difference upheld by Nietzsche. In particular, they reject all views which define the formation of feminine subjectivity as mediated both by a concept of lack (absence of a penis) and by the notion of boundary (exclusive difference of masculine from feminine and conversely). Their writings attempt to subvert an imaginary order where women's gender identity is something fixed, rather than something fluid. They also subvert the view that femininity is something limited and incomplete. Such a view of the feminine results from a phallocentric economy of lack. This phallocentric economy combines the either/or economy of lack explained above with the privileging of the male-designator (or phallus), which functions as the positive end (or "mark") of value. By reversing this psychic mechanism and suggesting another in which the image of the feminine appears as something boundless, Cixous and Irigaray attempt to free the notion of the feminine from the restrictions imposed on it by a phallocentric order.

One important activity emerging from this new imaginary order is a type of writing linked directly to desire as experienced in/by women's bodies, and by the type of rapture characteristic of women's orgasm, which these writers call *jouissance*. Writing, desire, and pleasure—born in the transgression of normative phallocentric boundaries—are some of the themes exploding from the unconscious of the postmodern feminists. Women's writing, or writing the body's *jouissance*, is seen as a process through which new life is continually created.

Cixous, in particular, subverts the phallocentric order of castration by stressing the bisexual nature of creativity. In imagining this type of creativity she expresses an alliance with the mad Nietzsche. Thus she writes:

> Admitting the component of the other sex makes them [exceptional poetic beings] at once much richer, plural, strong, and to the extent

of this mobility, very fragile. We invent only on this condition: thinkers, artists, creators of new values, 'philosophers' of the mad Nietzschean sort, inventors and destroyers of concepts . . . This does not mean that in order to create you must be homosexual. But there is no *invention* possible, whether it be philosophical or poetic, without the presence in the inventing subject of an abundance of the other, of the diverse . . . But there is no invention of other I's, no poetry, no fiction without a certain homosexuality (interplay therefore of bisexuality) making in me a crystallized work of my ultrasubjectivities. I is this matter, personal, exuberant, lively masculine, feminine, or other in which I delights me and distresses me.[18]

Cixous suggests that the writer must nourish the many selves, feminine and masculine, inside of her/him. This plurality of selves is part of the creative energy manifested in one's writing.

Irigaray also expresses a special affinity with Nietzsche. Both her writing style and her view of gender are extraordinarily close to Nietzsche in spirit despite their contrasting feminist/anti-feminist perspectives. If we recall, for example, Nietzsche's idea that women should reflect custom and tradition, we will see Irigaray meeting him at least part of the way on this point. In *Speculum of the Other Woman,* she writes in such a way as to "reflect" the philosophical tradition through a mirror that is curved.[19] While Nietzsche expected a woman to hold up a straight mirror to tradition and match her role in society accordingly, Irigaray holds up a curved mirror in which the many absurdities (as well as the violence) of the tradition's view of women stand out in exaggerated, distorted, ridiculous, mocking forms. Thus, her style is Nietzschean in that she does not exploit the logic of "either/or" reasoning in order to condemn women's oppression. She relies primarily on presentational devices, namely, letting the patriarchal mind reveal itself to the reader through the series of privileged images reflected on her mirror. Her prose carries a type of blending of the Dionysian (intoxication) and Apollonian (imagistic) elements appearing in Nietzsche's *The Birth of Tragedy.* But her Dionysian laughter is aimed at the masculinist logos, while the disfigured/distorted images which she displays before us—for example, of the history of philosophy from Plato to Hegel—can no longer be subsumed, as in the case of Nietzsche, by contemplating the beautifully serene image of the male god, Apollo.

In contrast to Cixous and Irigaray, who reject an economy of castration in order to replace it with a boundless image of woman's desire and *jouissance* in a new feminine imaginary, Nietzsche employs the metaphor of fullness to refer to the ideal masculine, to the will to power of the (male) creator of values. One could point to a subversion of an economy of castration in Nietzsche's works, but such a subversion is not linked to a feminist transformation of the imaginary and symbolic orders. In *The Birth of Tragedy*, for example, Nietzsche chooses two masculine deities, Apollo and Dionysus, to express his critique of the Socratic or logocentric order of Western culture. This idea of choosing masculine symbols for his project of reviving a "decadent" and "effeminate" culture remains a pattern with Nietzsche's writing from his earliest to his most mature works. While some of Nietzsche's readers may speculate on whether the Dionysian elements he emphasized so strongly do not constitute a veiled reference to feminine power, the fact remains that no goddess is invoked by Nietzsche in his rallying cry for a rebirth of Western culture.[20]

In his major work, *Thus Spoke Zarathustra,* an important passage depicting the symbolic reversal of the order of castration also takes place wholly apart from women. In this passage, Zarathustra has a vision of a shepherd into whose mouth a snake has crawled and whose only way of redemption is to bite off the head of the serpent. The images used are those of a shepherd and a "superhuman" figure into which the shepherd is transfigured following the reversal of his state of impotence. As with his earlier Apollonian/ Dionysian transformations, the transfiguration taking place here *excludes* women, while it takes place in a space far removed from women's space. Thus, in terms of the psychology of gender found in his work, Nietzsche leaves his readers with two predominant options: either contact with women, mediated by the normative concept of gender, as shown above, or distance from women, a psychological state in which the creator of values, strengthened by his solitude, overcomes his all-too-human condition and attains occasional moments of superhuman spiritual power.

At the height of its ecstasy in *Zarathustra,* the latter of these voices in its solitude rejects all actual women, opting instead for the "woman," Eternity. "Never yet have I found the woman from whom I wanted children, unless it be this woman that I love: for I love you, O Eternity!"[21] This important refrain combines the normative concept of gender in which women are linked to procreation (exclusively) while men are associated with a higher kind of creation, together with Nietzsche's lifelong insistence that the free spirit and creator of values must be distant from women in order to create.

IV

To conclude, I would sustain that Nietzsche's psychology of gender fluctuates between a normative model of heterosexual relations in which women are systematically repressed in relation to men and a model of rebellion and excess in which normativity appears to be transgressed. Both models, however, are part of the same coin in that they constitute a celebration of the masculine, either in a position of dominance over the feminine or in a position of independence from the latter, in such a way that the first view is merely escaped, but not discarded. A third option may have dislocated the preeminence of the other two. Such an option, I believe, is symbolized in Nietzsche's short-lived relationship with Lou Salomé and their common friend Paul Rée. Lou was a rebel against the normative gender type whose image appears recurringly in Nietzsche's writings. But their friendship did not work out.[22] His late writings show, if anything, an excessive outpour of normative attitudes with respect to gender, with an emphasis on male domination as a prerequisite for high culture. In this sense, Hélène Cixous is intuitively on the right track when she sides with the mad Nietzsche. In his case, madness appears to have been the ultimate position of rebellion against his tragically doomed masculine imaginary, which broke apart, as legend has it, when he saw a horse whipped viciously in the streets of Turin.

From a theoretical standpoint, a further point is warranted. While postmodern feminism cannot persuade at least this reader that Nietzsche was on the side of women's release from constricting traditional norms, its profound psychological challenge to phallocentrism has allowed us to uncover significant aspects of Nietzsche's anti-feminist stand besides his opposition to women's rights in a democratic society. In particular, I have hoped to show that the psychological and ideological structure identified here as a normative view of gender and gender relations both informs Nietzsche's anti-feminist position and helps to disseminate it, even to the point of overtaking his defiant protest against fixed and absolute values.

The same normative concept of gender is widespread in our society, affecting individuals of many political and epistemological persuasions. The postmodern psychological approach to the construction of a feminist theory shows that the feminist focus on sociopolitical reform is still only part, even if a major part, of the feminist struggle. For the important goal of a real feminist transformation of culture and society, feminist theory must unite the movement for equal rights in society with the struggle against the normative image of gender which seeks to regulate and control the free expression of sexuality, desire, and imagination.

Notes

1. Friedrich Nietzsche, *Daybreak,* trans. R. J. Hollingdale and Michael Tanner (Cambridge: University Press, 1982), p. 170.

2. Friedrich Nietzsche, *Human, All too Human.* trans. Marion Farber with Stephen Lehmann (Lincoln: University of Nebraska Press, 1984), § 259, pp. 156–157.

3. Ibid., § 378, p. 195.

4. Ibid., § 437, p. 209.

5. Ibid., § 425, p. 205.

6. Ibid., § 225, p. 139.

7. Ibid., p. 140.

8. Ibid., § 425, p. 205.

9. Friedrich Nietzsche, *Beyond Good and Evil,* trans. Walter Kaufmann (New York: Vintage Books, 1966), p. 164.

10. Ibid.

11. Ibid., § 239, pp. 168–169.

12. Ibid., p. 169.

13. Ibid.

14. Ibid., § 23, p. 32.

15. See Ofelia Schutte, *Beyond Nihilism: Nietzsche without Masks* (Chicago: University of Chicago Press, 1984).

16. See Jacques Derrida, *Spurs: Nietzsche's Styles,* trans. Barbara Harlow (Chicago: University of Chicago Press, 1979) and Jacques Lacan, *Écrits: A Selection,* trans. Alan Sheridan (New York: W. W. Norton and Company, 1977).

17. Cf. Friedrich Nietzsche, *The Gay Science,* trans. Walter Kaufmann (New York: Vintage Books, 1974), § 370, pp. 328–329.

18. Hélène Cixous, "Sorties," in *New French Feminisms,* ed. Elaine Marks and Isabelle de Courtivron (New York: Schocken Books, 1981), p. 97.

19. See Luce Irigaray, *Speculum of the Other Woman,* trans. Gillian Gill (Ithaca, New York: Cornell University Press, 1985).

20. For recently published sympathetic perspectives on Nietzsche's use of feminine imagery see Sarah Kofmann, "Baubô: Theological Perversion and Fetishism," in *Nietzsche's New Seas* (Chicago: University of Chicago Press, 1988), pp. 175–202, and David Farreli Krell, *Postponements: Women, Sensuality and Death in Nietzsche* (Bloomington: Indiana University Press, 1986). For a radical feminist questioning of the masculine figures of Apollo and Dionysus, see Luce Irigaray, *Marine Lover of Friedrich Nietzsche,* trans. Gillian G. Gill (New York: Columbia University Press, 1991), pp. 123–63.

21. Friedrich Nietzsche, *Thus Spoke Zarathustra,* trans. Walter Kaufmann (New York: Viking Press, 1966), III, pp. 228–231. The refrain is repeated seven times.

22. Rudolph Binion, *Frau Lou: Nietzsche's Wayward Disciple* (Princeton: Princeton University Press, 1968), pp. 81–111.

Interaction in a World of Chance: John Dewey's Theory of Inquiry

Lisa M. Heldke

Introduction

The epistemological program of John Dewey stands as a challenge to Cartesian-inspired conceptions of the nature of inquiry, a challenge that is both significant and suggestive for feminist epistemology.[1] Some of the projects to which feminist epistemologists have turned our attention include: replacing the subject/object model of inquiry with a non-hierarchical, non-dualistic model; reintegrating theory and practice by developing a theory of inquiry that emerges from an understanding of concrete practical activity; and reconceptualizing the world in which inquiry takes place as a changing-yet-stable one, a world more accurately portrayed by approximations and "flexible rules" than by fixed and immutable laws.[2] Dewey's philosophy also takes up many of these projects, and develops a position with which feminists may have substantial affinities.

In particular, Dewey's position acknowledges the fact that the real world in which we "find ourselves" is a world of chance as well as certainty, change as well as stability; and he attempts to portray inquiry in that world as a communal activity. Such an acknowledgment distances him from the Cartesian model of inquiry, with its faith in the notion of a fixed, immutable Reality to which our inquiry aspires, and its emphasis on the separation and power imbalance between the knowing Subject and the known Object. Furthermore, Dewey's recognition of the intimate relationship between the theoretical and the practical, and his consequent attention to practical activity, represent a significant advance upon the Cartesian model of inquiry, in which the theoretical is exalted at the expense of the practical.

Dewey's project does not mark anything like a complete liberation from Modern epistemology.[3] For one thing, although Dewey's

epistemology stresses the interrelation between theory and practice, and the importance of practical activity, the only "practical" activity to which his epistemology devotes substantial attention is
science. Feminists will recognize at least two problems with such a
view. First, it is not at all clear that, in the sciences, the theoretical
and the practical intertwine in the way Dewey suggests they do.
And second, Dewey neglects to acknowledge the existence of at least
one entire domain of human activity in which the relation between
theoretical and practical is obvious, compelling, and arguably more
integral than it is in the sciences—namely, "women's work" of
homemaking, childbearing and childrearing, etc.

A more formidable but related problem emerges from Dewey's
descriptions of the scientific method—which he considers to be the
form of inquiry that has most fully come to grips with the reality of
change and the significance of the practical, and has most successfully shaped its inquiry methods to address this reality. In these discussions, Dewey heaps praise—which feminists may well consider
unjustified—upon a method that he describes as emphasizing manipulation and control. In praising a form of inquiry in part *because
of* its ability to control and manipulate, Dewey seems not fully to
have appreciated the significance of his own emphasis on the communal nature of inquiry. In describing his position, I shall attempt
to show that, to this extent, Dewey remains caught in a hierarchical
subject/object model of inquiry.

In what follows, is an account of Dewey's epistemological program. This chapter begins with a discussion of his ontological commitments, and proceeds to an exploration of the practice-oriented,
communal conception of inquiry that emerges from those commitments. My account of Dewey is a sympathetic one, for, as already
indicated, I think there is much to be found in Dewey's conception of
reality, and of the inquiry that takes place in that reality, that is of
value for feminists.

This account is also a critical one, for I think there are elements
of Dewey's conception of inquiry that are deeply problematic. My
critical remarks will focus on two of the issues introduced above;
namely, Dewey's virtually exclusive use of science as his model
of the activity most clearly exemplifying the interdependence between chance and certainty; and his praise for science as a form of
inquiry that enables humans successfully to manipulate and control nature.

Though both of these criticisms focus on Dewey's use of or attention to science, it must be noted that my criticism is of Dewey's

conception of science and inquiry, and of his analysis of what constitutes a useful notion of inquiry. It is not my intention to determine what "science" is or is not; the legitimacy of my critique of Dewey's epistemology does not depend on my providing a "true" account of the "nature" of science. I aim to show that, whether or not Dewey's description of science refers to any actual scientific activities, his description and praise of what he calls science are misguided, represent only a partial rehabilitation of the epistemological tradition he inherited, and entail some grave practical consequences for those who would engage in the form of inquiry he admires.

Dewey's Ontology

Dewey's epistemology is most clearly understood if one sees how it emerges from his rejection of the traditional ontological hierarchy between certainty and chance, permanence and change.[4] When we consider the evidence of our experience, Dewey suggests, we see that we live in a world that's best understood as an inextricable compound of stability and chance. To define stability without chance, to conceive of the latter as derivative of or dependent upon the former, flies in the face of our experience; we are misguided if, "when we pull out a plum we treat it as evidence of the *real* order of cause and effect in the world."[5] Chance is an active element of the world; and the existence of doubt, uncertainty, error, ignorance mark its presence: "The world must actually be such as to generate ignorance and inquiry; doubt and hypothesis; trial and temporal conclusions . . . "[6]

This denial of an unchanging, independently-real world has two prongs. The first prong is Dewey's contention that positing a fixed reality makes of reality " . . . what we wish existence to be, after we have analyzed its defects and decided upon what would remove them . . . "[7] In one's desire for stability, one creates an ontology that replaces the world in which one lives with a world that is more secure. If, instead, one accepts the all-pervasive ambiguity and ambivalence of one's experience of the world as "genuine", as illustrative of the way we-and-the-world are, one realizes that at least one of the debates that goes on between realists and anti-realists is founded on a dichotomy that is not exhaustive.[8]

Realism might be described as the view that there exists a real, unchanging world, independent of human interaction, and that the

aim of inquiry is to "get at" this pure world by systematically eliminating any elements which distort our vision. The realist view may
most easily be understood by the following model: think of a sealed
room—"reality"—which is observed through a one-way window by a
group of investigators. The aim of the investigators is to eliminate
any distortion that might be caused by imperfections in the glass,
and any irregularities that might result from their own prejudices,
predispositions, or passions, in order to make accurate, "value-free"
observations of the goings-on in the room. Realism argues that it is
possible to "see the world clearly" and describe it with "objective"
accuracy.

Anti-realism, on the other hand, might be described as the view
that there exists no real, independent world, but only the worlds
which humans create. The myth of the sealed room and the observation window is just that—a myth. Rather than regarding inquirers as observers standing behind a glass wall, this view might
portray them as artists with sketch pads and modelling clay, "making up" worlds. For the anti-realist, all inquiry is value-laden, all
facts are theory-laden. Dispassionate, value-free observation is
impossible.

The realism/anti-realism dispute is often characterized as if
these two positions were mutually exclusive and exhaustive; as if either there is a real, independent world to which one may have clear
access, or there are only the worlds which one creates. Dewey suggests that the dichotomy is not exhaustive, but that there is another
possibility; namely, that there exists a real world of instability in
which one is a player, and many are co-creators. Dewey's alternative
unseals the room, and places the inquirer alongside their objects of
inquiry, allowing—indeed necessitating—two-way communication
and influence to take place.

The second prong of Dewey's denial of an unchanging, independent reality is his contention that it's senseless to speak of a world
"out there", separate from us. Dewey *is* a realist, if all that is meant
by the term is that he believes there is a physical world that we can
observe and investigate. But he is not a realist, if that terms refers
to someone who posits an independent and prior existence for the
physical world. Dewey maintains that we are part of the world, that
we observe and organize the world from within it. One is an inquirer *in* and *of* the world, not an external observer of it.

Such an ontological position obviously holds much promise for
creating non-dualistic, non-hierarchical epistemologies. It represents an important step toward undermining a Modern epistemology that views inquiry as a process of revealing the fixed nature of

an inflexible, independent world. In doing so, it anticipates in interesting ways some of the projects currently being undertaken by feminist philosophers of science and ecofeminists.[9]

Dewey's reform of the tradition he inherited is, however, only partial. Although he places humans in the world of experience, he still assigns to us the task of controlling the rest of the world. His ontology may have eliminated the problem of how human subjects can ever know anything external to ourselves—by showing that things aren't external in a Cartesian sense—but, he has maintained the view that human inquirers are the controllers of the rest of the world.

Dewey's Epistemology

[A] Dewey's assertion of the genuineness of chance-and-certainty shapes his theory of inquiry, a theory that emphasizes knowing, the activity, over knowledge, the state. Knowing is the task of building stability in a not-altogether-stable world. It is a process of coming to live with and utilize instability. Its aim is not the construction of a body of fixed knowledge-for-contemplation, but the development of a flexible body of ways to prosper in a world of chance.

Knowledge, the static body of "data" that is the property of some knower, is useful and interesting when it allows the knower to "go on," to ask the next question, to solve the next problem, to relieve some anxiety, to throw over the whole project and assume a different tack. Inquiry proceeds in an atmosphere in which objects of knowledge retain their provisional character.[10] Knowledge works in the service of knowing.

Dewey is often criticized for his conception of knowing, precisely because of its radical de-emphasis of knowledge. Arthur Murphy, for instance, claims there is no such thing as knowledge for Dewey, that one is forever moving toward a goal that never materializes. Murphy implies that such a theory of knowing is empty. What's the point of inquiring if it's never going to get one to the *end* of inquiry, lead one to the spot where one can say "I know"?[11]

Dewey does indeed cast knowledge off the privileged pedestal it has occupied in most epistemological systems. But in response to Murphy's criticism, he would say, in the first place, that one always is in the process of modifying, reassessing, discarding and assimilating claims, notions, hypotheses. That is simply a fact about human experience. Knowledge, for us, serves as a temporary firm spot, a launching pad from which to undertake further inquiry. That is how one actually employs it in one's ordinary life. To behave otherwise is to believe in "plum-pulling."

Furthermore, Dewey would emphasize the fact that he does not deny the existence of knowledge altogether; his criticism is of the notion of permanent knowledge as an end in itself. He does not question the value of contemplation of essences, but only the all-importance of this activity.

Related to his emphasis upon knowing as an activity is Dewey's assertion that knowing is ultimately practical. He disavows the traditional hierarchical distinction between theory and practice, a distinction which links theory, a "purely mental" activity, with knowledge (the armchair-and-smoking-jacket "thinker"). On this traditional view, theory is regarded as epistemologically superior to practice, which is merely *practical,* aiming as it does at coping with the uncertainty inherent in everyday life. The range of the practical is limited to the everyday world:

> Instead of being extended to cover all forms of action by means of which all the values of life are extended and rendered more se- cure . . . the meaning of "practical" is limited to matters of ease, comfort, riches, bodily security and police order, possibly health, etc., . . . In consequence, these subjects . . . are no concern of "higher" interest which feel that no matter what happens to infe- rior goods in the vicissitudes of natural existence, the highest val- ues are immutable characters of the ultimately real.[12]

Dewey erases both the dichotomy and the hierarchy, expanding the scope of practice and ascribing to it an epistemological status befitting its role.

The example of science, Dewey claims, with its dependence upon the experimental method, renders the rigid distinction be- tween theory and practice arbitrary. The physical sciences, he sug- gests, treat theory and practice not as two diametrically opposed modes of approaching the world, but as essentially-related modes of inquiry that depend upon each other for the development and con- firmation of their own findings. If " . . . it can be shown that the actual procedures by which the most authentic and dependable knowledge [i.e., scientific knowledge] is attained have completely surrendered the separation of knowing and doing . . . the chief for- tress of the classic philosophical tradition crumbles into dust."[13]

The difference between theory and practice is one of degree, not kind; a distinction between " . . . two modes of practice. One is the pushing, slam-bang, act-first-and-think-afterwards mode, to which events may yield as they give way to any strong force. The other mode is wary, observant, sensitive to slight hints and intimations."[14]

I think that it is not being unreasonably generous in my interpretation of Dewey's view to say that the scientific method to which he refers may (intentionally?) bear very little resemblance to methods actually practiced in the physical sciences. The physical sciences do not strike me as paradigm examples of disciplines that have eliminated the hierarchy and separation between theory and practice. As John Herman Randall has pointed out, "Dewey's experimentalism is not primarily based on the method of the laboratory. It is at once the experimentalism of practical common sense, and the coming to self-awareness of the best and most critical techniques and concepts of the social sciences."[15]

William Gavin notes in this regard that, "Dewey advocates that the form of [the experimental method], as opposed to any specific content, serve as a model."[16] According to Gavin, characteristics of such a method include its future-orientedness, its interpenetrating use of thought and action, its communal nature, and its ability for self-correction. While some sciences have at times adopted this method, it is clearly not science alone that can do so. In evaluating Dewey's admiration for the experimental method, then, these things must be taken into account: he speaks not specifically and not only of the methods of physics or chemistry, but of experimentalism broadly conceived; and he argues for the superiority of the *method,* not the *subject matter* of experimental science. Presumably any subject matter could—and should—be treated experimentally in this general sense.

However, even if one accepts this broad definition of the scientific method, and agrees that it need not be taken to refer to actual scientific practice, one cannot ignore the fact that Dewey's praise for the actual physical sciences is frequent and zealous. To Dewey, writing early in the twentieth century, it seems very clear that science is the form of inquiry that achieves the most successful practical-and-theoretical interaction with the world. Its claim to this achievement is neither exclusive nor guaranteed. Its privileged status, according to Dewey, stems purely from the fact that scientists are the most successful users of the experimental method, and not from anything inherent in science's subject matter. Science emerged from craftwork—from practical, hands-on activity—and its has grown into a set of disciplines that bear an intimate relationship to the technologies they support.[17] Throughout its development, science has been an activity whose roots are in concrete practice. This emphasis on practice is an integral element of science, and it is an element that is in part responsible for the success science has achieved.

Feminists can recognize the value of Dewey's claim about the need for philosophical recognition of the importance of the practical, and for understanding the intimate interrelation between the theoretical and the practical. However, we have good reason to be skeptical of the claim that science—or the experimental method—provides us with the "best", "most successful" example of that connection. Attention to the lives and labor of women reveals activities in which the theoretical and the practical are "successfully" merged, activities in which theory and practice are necessarily linked. But these are activities which Dewey only barely explores.[18] Feminists' attention to "women's work" enables us to create an understanding of the relation between the theoretical and the practical, between abstract and concrete, that does not depend on the shaky example of the sciences for its insight. Indeed, it might be argued that many tasks traditionally assigned to or performed by women portray the intimate connection between mental and manual, abstract and concrete, more clearly than any other human activities.[19] Of course these activities are also not traditionally regarded as "epistemologically relevant".

One feminist theorist who studies women's labor in these terms is Dorothy Smith. Smith explores the sexual division of labor by looking at the way it has divided up conceptual and concrete activities. She writes that women who work in managerial environments

> . . . do things which give concrete form to the conceptual activities. They do the clerical work, giving material form to the words or thoughts of the boss. They do the routine computer work, the interviewing for the survey, the nursing, the secretarial work. At almost every point women mediate for men the relation between the conceptual mode of action and the actual concrete forms on which it depends. Women's work is interposed between the abstracted modes and the local and particular actualities in which they are necessarily anchored. Also, women's work conceals from men acting in the abstract mode just this anchorage.[20]

Such concrete "mediation work", while frequently menial, also affords its workers the possibility of a more accurate view of the world, and a more realistic place from which to engage in inquiry, than that afforded the "abstract worker."

Similarly, Nancy Hartsock suggests that

[t]he unity of mental and manual labor and the directly sensuous nature of women's work leads to a more profound unity of mental and manual labor, social and natural worlds, than is experienced by the male worker in capitalism. The unity grows from the fact that women's bodies, unlike men's, can be themselves instruments of production: in pregnancy, giving birth or lactation, arguments about a division of mental from manual labor are fundamentally foreign.[21]

In light of these analyses of women's labor, some feminists have developed epistemologies that take as their models those women's activities in which the interconnectedness of theory and practice seem especially resonant.[22] Such projects are useful for understanding the deep significance of rejecting the theory/practice split. It is not sufficient to "rehabilitate" or reconceptualize the activities that have traditionally been termed "inquiry"; a deeper understanding of the relations between theory and practice urges us to explore "non-traditional" inquiry activities as well.

[B] The next aspect of Dewey's theory of inquiry to which I turn my attention is its recognition that inquiry is a relationship, an interactive relationship between inquirer and inquired. In this relationship, both inquirer and inquired undergo modification through the activity of inquiry. Gone is the glass wall that separates inquiring "subject" from inquired-into "object". On a traditional subject/object model of inquiry, the subject stands behind this wall, eliminating the possibility of interfering with their object of study, and also ensuring that they will remain untouched by it.

On Dewey's model, as suggested previously, the glass wall is removed, and objects on both "ends" of the inquiry relationship are free to influence and shape each other through the activity of knowing. Granted, both inquirer and inquired exist, in some respect, independently of each other; inquirers do not "make up" the world whole cloth. To say "I know," Dewey says, "does not mean that the self is the source or author of the thought and affection nor its exclusive seat," but that "[t]he self . . . identifies itself . . . with a belief or sentiment of independent and external origination."[23] The "object" of inquiry is not entirely the creation of the inquirer; nevertheless, through the process of inquiry, inquirer changes inquired, and vice-versa.

Human inquiry into the world might more properly be thought of as interaction within it. It is like " . . . the correspondence of two people who "correspond" in order to learn each one of the acts, ideas and intents of the other one, in order to modify one's own ideas, intents and acts . . . "[24] Our inquiry in the world is just one—albeit highly specialized—variety of interaction. "Interaction" is a general name for all sorts of relations that go on between all sorts of organisms and entities. The world, on this model, is a flexible fabric of interconnections, capable of being described and developed from myriad perspectives within itself.

In my earlier discussion of Dewey's elimination of the problem of realism. I suggest that his refutation of realism has two prongs. First, he exposes our tendency to make of reality what we wish it were, by attributing to it the qualities we'd like it to possess, and, second, he rejects the urge to speak of reality as in principle separate from inquirers. His treatment of that problem becomes clearer, now that his interactivist theory of inquiry is more fully elucidated.

The realist wishes to maintain the separateness and independence of the world, and also to sustain the related ontological separation between inquiring subject and inquired object. Dewey does away with the separation of observer and observed by placing inquirers squarely *in* the world and by making inquiry a species of natural activity. He never allows the foundations to be laid for a realist position.

Many contemporary feminists reiterate Dewey's rejection of the subject/object dichotomy, with its attendant separation of subject from object. Evelyn Fox Keller, for example, suggests thinking about the inquiry relation by recognizing that the "objects" of our inquiry are different from us, but that this fact does not necessitate severing "them" from "us."[25] We should recognize the obvious " . . . difference between self and other as an opportunity for a deeper and more articulated kinship. The struggle to disentangle self from other is itself a source of insight—potentially into the nature of both self and other."[26]

Keller suggests that a subject/object model of inquiry tends to make us see the rest of the world not as comprised of individuals with integrity, with things to "say for themselves," and with connections to us, but as a set of tools-for-use. This tendency is the result of two elements of the subject/object model, separation and domination/control. Conceived of as inquiring subjects, we are radically separated from the objects of our inquiry (remember the glass wall), over which we exercise considerable control; we put up the wall, we established the parameters of the experiment, and we will be the ones who will decide the uses to which our objects will be put. According to Keller then, this traditional model of inquiry is problematic not only because it separates subject from object, but also because it establishes the subject in a hierarchical and controlling relationship to the object.

One would expect that Dewey's interactive model of inquiry would also make him particularly sensitive to issues of control and manipulation. Specifically, one might well expect his rejection of the separation encoded in the subject/object model to bring him to reject as well the hierarchy that has come to inhere in it. It is such a move that can be found in Keller, for example. Keller, in analyzing and rejecting the subject/object model of inquiry, and the "static" conception of objectivity that emerges from it, shows that a genuine rejection of these notions also requires rejecting the control exercised by inquiring subject over the object of inquiry.[27]

But it is here that Dewey disappoints, by failing to take his criticism of traditional philosophy far enough. Ultimately, it appears that Dewey rejects the subject/object model *not* out of any particular concern about the manipulativeness that has come to be embodied in such a model, but because he thinks the model doesn't enable us to exercise as *much* control over "nature" as his reconstructed model would.

I would argue that our realization that the world is comprised of endlessly-changing interactions, that humans and our interactions are a part of this world, and that we and the things with which we interact affect each other in many ways, should lead us in a direction very different from the one Dewey ends up taking. To put it succinctly, I suggest that a deep understanding of the world as a flexible fabric of interconnections of which we are a part compels us to reject not only the rigid separation between subject and object, but also the control and domination used by inquiring subjects. This is not to say that we must "swear off" any use of power or force as inquirers—indeed to do so would be impossible. It is a fact of the matter that not all members of the world have the same powers, potentialities, capacities. But there is a difference in kind between acting as powerful subject over against a disempowered, disconnected object, and functioning in interactions as a participant who *has* certain powers.[28] It is this latter approach to power that I would have emerge in a reconstructed model of inquiry.

In the next few pages, I shall attempt to show why I believe that Dewey's view of the nature of the world and of inquiry should lead him to be more thoroughgoing in his rejection of the subject/object model than he actually is. In making this claim, I am not accusing Dewey of anything like simple logical inconsistency, or inability to follow a thought to its necessary conclusion. That is, there is nothing logically or causally necessary about rejecting the hierarchy of the subject/object model once you've rejected the separation. The two features are linked, conceptually and historically, in far more complicated ways. My contention here arises from my belief that the very thing that motivates Dewey's rejection of separation—namely, a careful consideration of the world in which we actually *do* find ourselves—should motivate a concomitant rejection of hierarchy. Furthermore, the sorts of epistemological, ethical and social goals Dewey apparently has cannot be realized without abandoning the hierarchy as well as the separation. In order to make these claims clearer, I'll say more about Dewey's position.

In his discussion of the relation between inquirer and inquired, as in his discussion of the relation between theory and practice, Dewey uses the sciences as his example of a set of activities that most clearly manifest the relation he advocates. The experimental method is for him the paradigm example of a method that recognizes our interconnection with the world. To experiment is to interact with one's surroundings, to vary conditions, to interfere with the flow of events in order to see what results. The experimental method gives the lie to the notion that the inquiring "subject" does not interfere/interact with their "object." Interaction is the very essence of experiment. As such, experiment seems to him most fully to embody his conception of inquiry as communication, and most fully to acknowledge his ontological assertion that we are situated *in* the world into which we inquire. But consider the way Dewey describes the communication, and discusses the nature of our situation.

In *Reconstruction in Philosophy,* Dewey describes Bacon as the "great forerunner of the spirit of modern life . . . "[29] Bacon is important, according to Dewey, because he sets the stage for a new logic of inquiry, a logic that doesn't simply rearrange "received truths", but " . . . teaches [the mind] to undergo a patient and prolonged apprenticeship to fact in its infinite variety and particularity: to obey nature intellectually in order to command it practically."[30] He refers with favor to Bacon's suggestion that we construct an "Empire . . . of Man over Nature, substituted for the Empire of Man over Man."[31] It is through experiment that such an Empire is being brought about: "Active experimentation must force the apparent facts of nature into forms different to those in which they familiarly present themselves; and thus make them tell the truth about themselves, as torture may compel an unwilling witness to reveal what he has been concealing."[32]

To date, our efforts at this task have enjoyed only scattered success: " . . . our science is not yet such that this command [over nature] is systematically and pre-eminently applied to the relief of human estate."[33] The reconstructive task in philosophy is to reconceptualize the individual inquirer "as the agent who is responsible through initiative, inventiveness and intelligently directed labor for recreating the world, transforming it into an instrument and possession of intelligence."[34]

These quotations show that Dewey may embrace the notion that inquiry into the world is interaction in it, but he does not by any means reject the traditional notion that the aim of inquiry is control over nature. In Keller's terms, he rejects the separation, and even the fixity of the static conception of objectivity, but not the element of control that has come to reside in this conception. Indeed, he seems wholeheartedly to embrace this extremely problematic notion.

My criticism here is not, then, a criticism of Dewey's "fondness for science," but rather a criticism of his *reasons* for being "fond" of it. Whether or not science does *in fact* hold the possibility of establishing an "Empire of Man over Nature," I question the desirability of building any such Empire. Furthermore, I question how such a building project can be compatible with the view that the real world is a set of complex interconnections which *includes* humans and our inquiry. Dewey's characterization of science as Man over Nature effectively removes humans—or men, at least—from that world, and sets them up as its rulers. That is, in holding onto the hierarchy of the traditional model, Dewey does not fully free himself from its separation either. Nature, for Dewey, still looks much like a tool for Man.

I am not suggesting that Dewey uncritically accepts all and any sort of control of nature that humans could dream up.[35] Indeed, in an introduction to *Reconstruction in Philosophy,* written twenty-five years after the original text, Dewey speaks grimly, if ambiguously, of the development of the atomic bomb.[36] His praise for technological developments that enable us to control (human and nonhuman) others is by no means without qualification.

Furthermore, he is keenly aware that the benefits of technology have not been visited equally upon all. "[T]he knowledge which regulates activity is so much the monopoly of the few, and is used by them in behalf of private and class interests and not for general and shared use."[37] Dewey's respect for science and its uses is indeed not uncritical.

But though he is critical of certain instances of control and domination, a question remains: on what *basis* does Dewey criticize developments like the bomb? Where does he place the responsibility for their development? The answer is that Dewey sees such developments not as emerging from the scientific method—an inquiry method he admires for its emphasis on human control over nature—but rather as resulting from the failure of moral and political thought to have made the same methodological advances that science has. Our destructive activities are not the consequences of science; they are the consequences of the inadequate moral and political theory the sciences are forced to serve. We need " . . . a generalized reconstruction so fundamental that it has to be developed by recognition that while the evils resulting at present from the entrance of 'science' into our common ways of living are undeniable, they are due to the fact that no systematic efforts have as yet been made to subject the 'morals' underlying old institutional customs to scientific inquiry and criticism."[38]

The experimental method, conceived of as a method for control of nature, is not the problem, according to Dewey. Indeed, "science is strictly impersonal; a method and a body of knowledge."[39] The activity of science—the actual doing of an experiment or proving of a theorem and the methodology employed—is neutral; it is not a proper subject for moral or social criticism. Given this view, it is not surprising that Dewey dwells only briefly on the problem of the usurpation of the means of production of science by the wealthy and the powerful; he sees this not as a problem inherent in the scientific activity he has described, but rather as one inherent in a political or social system that makes use of science. It is not science, but the uses to which science is put, that are often dangerous. Dewey does not explore the possibility that the science which has originated in this particular social setting might itself be shaped and colored by its origins.

In framing my criticism of Dewey, it must be emphasized that I am not arguing that science is the root of all evil, or that it is science alone that is responsible for the atom bomb, for example. I take his point that " . . . this destructive consequence [the bomb] occurred not only in a war, but because of the existence of war . . . "[40] Nonetheless, I think his conception of inquiry is shortsighted and even irresponsible, in that it fails to recognize any conceptual connections between, say, the control of "Nature" by "Man", and the control of the poor by the wealthy—by those who own technologies. That is, he fails to see that his model of science itself—like the penicillin and atomic weaponry that science engendered—has been developed in a social and political context. As such, it cannot be "neutral." It cannot even be separated clearly from that context; where does "science" stop and "politics" start? Furthermore, it is not at all clear how developing the experimental method so conceived, for use in the moral and social spheres, could ameliorate the problems there. Would the method charge us to obey *society* intellectually in order to command it practically? Such a goal would clearly run counter to Dewey's aim of destroying the "knowledge monopoly" that the wealthy and powerful exercise over the poor and disenfranchised.

Feminists have worked to show the interconnectedness of various kinds of power relationships, relationships of control. We have explored the connections between racism, sexism and classism, heterosexism and ableism, and the ways in which these structures of oppression shape our social realities. Feminists have also explored the relations between human oppressive structures, and humans' exploitation and destruction of the environment. We have attempted to show that conceptions of inquiry that emphasize separation and hierarchy in fact work to support and justify such controlling, exploitative activities. It is necessary, I would argue, to recognize the interconnections between all these sorts of structures of power if we are to work to undermine them. Just as we recognize the impossibility of "eliminating" sexism without eliminating racism, so too ought we recognize the importance of addressing and undermining the control and exploitation of nature in working to eliminate human oppression.

Dewey's model for inquiry has the potential to make the connection between the oppression and exploitation of nature at the hands of technology, and the forms of inquiry that produced that technology in the first place. I do not mean to suggest that the connection is an easy or "single-stranded" one. But in failing to make it, I would suggest that he has failed to realize the full implications of his own position. His failure lies in not recognizing that being a part of the world in which inquiry goes on impels[41] you to rid yourself of the hierarchical view that the world is an external "instrument" for your use. Even as Dewey rejects the distancing effect of the subject/object model, he embraces its emphasis on control of the world. This latter move, in turn, undermines the force of the former; his image of humans as having control over nature, reintroduces the image of humans as beings who are separate from the objects of our inquiry.

One way to make my point more clearly would be to consider it in terms of the theoretical underpinnings of various ecological movements. I think of Dewey's model as providing a solid foundation for what is sometimes termed as "managerial" conception of ecology—the ecological theory that considers humans to be the "stewards" of the rest of the world, put here to take care of it. Obviously, manager-minded ecologists "do good things"; it is not as if approaching the environment in this frame of mind will necessarily cause you to do more damage than you repair. But it is a model that maintains the notion that humans hold a special place in the scheme of things, and that we should take care of the natural world because it was "put there" for us. If we hurt it, in the end we hurt ourselves. If you destroy your tools, you won't be able to work as effectively.

There may seem to be only a subtle difference between this view of humans' relation to the environment, and a view that argues that we are not "special", we're just capable of bringing about more cataclysmic change than any other species. But I would argue that it is this latter view which has the potential to eliminate the sorts of destruction and oppression of which Dewey speaks with genuine concern, and not the former. Recognizing ourselves as parts of a complex and flexible fabric of interconnections compels us to see all forms of oppression and exploitation in relation to each other—and as elements that can weaken and destroy the fabric. Humans have the capacity to reflect on this fabric in a way that perhaps no other animal does. That may be one of our chief differences from others. But it is a difference in degree, not kind. It requires recognizing that human respect for the rest of the world cannot rest on some narrow conception of human self-interest. A human conception of inquiry must embody this recognition if it is fully to escape the destructive tendencies of subject/object thinking.

Conclusion

The intention of this chapter has been to show the promise Dewey's epistemology holds for feminist epistemologists, but also to show how Dewey himself failed to realize his own promise. I would argue that he is a significant figure in the history of attempts to get out from under the problems of modern philosophy. I would also rush to reiterate the fact that Dewey would be among the first to acknowledge the limitedness, the dated quality of his own work, and to embrace attempts to reformulate that work in light of new evidence, new ways of looking at the world, brought to light by the use of new conceptual tools. Indeed, I consider my project here to be very much in the spirit of Dewey's; it has been my aim to show how the reconstruction of philosophy that he plotted, while moving in the right direction, could not move far enough until such time as it took account of certain unaddressed problems with the scientific method.

Some of these problems are just what some feminist theorists are attempting to address. It is through our attention to the roles of gender, class and race in the construction of social and scientific reality that feminists are carrying on the crucial reconstruction of inquiry and of philosophy more generally. Attention to women's activities as sources of insight into the nature of knowing and the relation between theory and practice, and attempts to understand the conceptual links between oppressive, hierarchical epistemologies and oppressive social structures, mark two important ways in which that reconstruction is taking place.

Notes

1. This chapter has benefitted from exchanges with Stephen Kellert and with students in my American Philosophy class at Gustavus Adolphus College, particularly Nancy Carlson and Shel Silvernail, who wrote insightful critiques of Dewey. Thanks also to Bat-Ami Bar On for her helpful review comments.

2. For a useful overview of some of the issues currently being explored by feminist epistemologists, see "Male-Gender Bias and Western Conceptions of Reasons and Rationality," by Karen Warren, in the *APA Newsletter on Feminism and Philosophy* (88:2, 1989).

3. Nor would he think any such liberation was possible. Dewey is well aware of the way in which philosophical positions emerge from their historical contexts, and of the fact that no one can spring utterly free of such a context. In *Reconstruction in Philosophy,* for example, he says "Men cannot easily throw off their old habits of thinking, and never can throw off all of them at once. In developing, teaching and receiving new ideas we are compelled to use some of the old ones as tools of understanding and communication." (Boston: Beacon Press, 1948, p. 74). I quote this passage in order to make clear the fact that my aim in this essay is not to "blame" Dewey for his failings, but rather to suggest that he would have been the first to counsel us to understand his ideas as the products of a certain time and place, and, as such, subject to modification, reformulation, in the face of further exploration.

4. Dewey suggests that this hierarchy has existed in some form or another throughout the history of western philosophy, beginning with Plato, who posited a realm of Forms over against he physical world. The former, being fixed and unchanging, was knowable, but about the latter, which was subject to motion, to generation and decay, one could only opine. Modern philosophy may have discarded the notion of two separate "realms", but it did not, Dewey argues, lose the notion that there is a sharp distinction between unchanging-and-knowable substances, and changing-and-unknowable accidents. See his account in chapter 5, "Changed Conceptions of the Ideal and the Real," in *Reconstruction in Philosophy*, for a more detailed account of his position. See also *Experience and Nature*, (2nd. ed., New York: Dover, 1958, p. 124).

5. John Dewey, *The Quest for Certainty* (1929. New York: Perigee, 1980, p. 45).

6. *Experience and Nature*, p. 69.

7. Ibid., p. 54.

8. The description of the realism/anti-realism debate which follows is necessarily brief. Consequently, it cannot describe the many forms this debate has taken, or the many subtle variations on the realist and anti-realist positions that have been developed. However, my description does highlight what I consider to be a central element of the debate.

9. For a representative sampling of some of the work being done in the fields of epistemology, philosophy of science and ecofeminism, see the special issues of *Hypatia* on feminist philosophy of science, Vol. 2 No. 3, 1987 and Vol. 3 No. 1, 1988; and also the special issue of the *APA Newsletter on Feminism and Philosophy* on feminist epistemology, Vol. 88 No. 2, 1989. This last contains a useful literature overview and bibliography of feminist epistemology, compiled by Karen Warren.

10. *Experience and Nature*, p. 130.

11. Arthur Murphy, "Dewey's Epistemology and Metaphysics," in *The Philosophy of John Dewey*, ed. Paul Arthur Schilpp (Evanston: Northwestern University Press, 1939, pp. 203–4).

12. John Dewey, *Liberalism and Social Action* (1935, New York: Perigee, 1980, p. 32).

13. *The Quest for Certainty*, p. 79.

14. *Experience and Nature*, p. 314.

15. John Herman Randall, "Dewey's Interpretation of the History of Philosophy," in *The Philosophy of John Dewey*, p. 82.

16. William Gavin, "The Importance of Context: Reflections on Kuhn, Marx and Dewey," *Studies in Soviet Thought* 21 (1980), p. 22.

17. " . . . [T]he physical sciences [were born of] the crafts and technologies of healing, navigation, war and the working of wood, metals, leather, flax and wool . . . " (*Experience and Nature,* p. 128). " . . . [M]odern industry *is* so much applied science." (*Reconstruction in Philosophy,* p. 41).

18. It is important to note that Dewey, the philosopher of education, did recognize the value of using homemaking activities to educate children. However, this acknowledgment of the significance of such activities did not transfer into his epistemology. There, his attention focuses almost entirely on traditional "inquiry activities"—science being the most notable.

19. It is not only traditional women's activity which portrays this connection. Other sorts of manual labor—cabinetry, tool-and-die making, surveying—also no doubt manifest this conception. Indeed, it might be said that anything that would be done by the lowest class in Plato's *Republic* potentially displays an intimate connection between theory and practice. Of course Dewey realized this: as I've noted, he argues that modern science grew out of these activities.

20. Dorothy Smith, "A Sociology for Women," in *The Prism of Sex: Essays in the Sociology of Knowledge* (Madison: University of Wisconsin Press, p. 168).

21. Nancy Hartsock, "The Feminist Standpoint: Developing the Ground for a Specifically Feminist Historical Materialism," in *Discovering Reality,* ed. Harding and Hintikka (Boston: D. Reidel, 1983). Quoted in Alison Jaggar, *Feminist Politics and Human Nature* (Totowa, N.J.: Rowman and Allanheld, 1983, p. 373).

22. In addition to the works by Smith and Hartsock already noted, see, for example, Ruth Ginzberg, "Uncovering Gynocentric Science", *Hypatia,* Vol. 2, No. 3 (1987); Gail Stenstad, "Earthy Thinking," *Hypatia,* Vol. 3, No. 2 (1988); and my "Recipes for Theory Making," *Hypatia,* Vol. 3, No. 2 (1988).

23. *Experience and Nature,* p. 233.

24. Ibid., p. 283.

25. I have developed the similarities between Dewey and Evelyn Fox Keller with respect to this issue in "John Dewey and Evelyn Fox Keller: A Shared Epistemological Tradition," *Hypatia,* Vol. 2 No. 3 (1987).

26. Evelyn Fox Keller, *Reflections on Gender and Science* (New Haven: Yale University Press, 1985), p. 117.

27. For a discussion of the way that power and control came to be integral parts of the modern subject/object model, and of the modern conception of inquiry, see chapters 5 and 6 of *Reflections on Gender and Science.* While I would argue that Keller's account rests too heavily on the evidence of object relations theory, I believe her conclusion is significant, and could certainly be substantiated through the use of other models of analysis.

28. For an interesting exploration of the related difference between "power-over" and "power-from-within" in ethical behavior, see chapter 3 of Sarah Lucia Hoagland's *Lesbian Ethics* (Palo Alto: Institute of Lesbian Studies, 1988).

29. *Reconstruction in Philosophy*, p. 28.

30. Ibid., p. 36.

31. Ibid., p. 37.

32. Ibid., p. 32.

33. Ibid., p. 43.

34. Ibid., p. 51.

35. Indeed, if he had, I wouldn't be compelled to offer the sorts of criticism of Dewey that I do. It is precisely *because* he is deeply concerned about many of the ways humans control and manipulate other people and things that I find his support for "inquiry as torture" so deeply disturbing. Dewey seems to have other, "higher" epistemological and ethical aims in mind; my intention here is to show how those aims might have been realized.

36. *Reconstruction in Philosophy*, p. xxiv.

37. *The Quest for Certainty*, p. 80.

38. *Reconstruction in Philosophy*, p. xxiii.

39. John Dewey, *Philosophy and Civilization* 1931 (New York: Capricorn, 1963), p. 319.

40. *Reconstruction in Philosophy*, p. xxiv.

41. I refrain from using the stronger "requires" here, because my argument cannot support the claim that there is a causal or logical necessity between rejecting separation and rejecting hierarchy. Nevertheless, given certain sorts of epistemological and ethical aims, the compulsion to do so should be extremely strong.

Suggestions for Further Reading

Books

Bordo, Susan R. *The Flight to Objectivity: Essays on Cartesianism and Culture*. Albany, NY: State University of New York Press, 1987.

Brown, Wendy. *Manhood and Politics: A Feminist Reading in Political Theory*. Totowa, NJ: Rowman and Littlefield, 1988.

Clark, Lorenne M. G. and Lange, Lynda (eds.). *The Sexism of Social and Political Theory: Women and Reproduction from Plato to Nietzsche*. Toronto, Canada: University of Toronto, 1979.

Coole, Diana H. *Women in Political Theory: From Ancient Mysogyni to Contemporary Feminism*. Brighton, England: Wheatsheaf Books, 1988.

DiStefano, Christine. *Configurations of Masculinity: A Feminist Perspective on Modern Political Theory*. Ithaca, NY: Cornell University, 1991.

Elshtain, Jean Bethke. *Public Man, Private Woman: Women in Social and Political Thought*. Princeton, NY: Princeton University, 1981.

Elshtain, Jean Bethke (ed.). *The Family in Political Thought*. Emhurst, MA: University of Massachusetts, 1982.

Kennedy, Ellen and Mendus, Susan (eds.). *Women in Western Political Philosophy*. N.Y.: St. Martin's, 1987.

Krell, David Farrell. *Postponements: Women, Sensuality and Death in Nietzsche*. Bloomington, IN: Indiana University Press, 1986.

Lloyd, Genevive. *The Man of Reason: "Male" and "Female" in Western Philosophy*. Minneapolis, MA: University of Minnesota, 1984.

Lorraine, Tamsin E. *Gender Identity and the Production of Meaning*. Boulder, CO: Westview, 1990.

Mills, Patricia Jaqentowicz. *Woman, Nature and Psyche*. New Haven, CT: Yale University, 1987.

O'Faolain, Julia and Martines, Lauro (eds.). *Not in Gods Image: Women in History from the Greeks to the Victorians*. N.Y.: Harper and Row, 1973.

Okin, Susan Moller. *Women in Western Political Thought*. Princeton, NJ: Princeton University, 1979.

267

Shanly, Mary Lyndon and Pateman, Carole (eds.). *Feminist Interpretation and Political Theory*. Pennsylvania State University, 1991.

Schott, Robin May. *Cognition and Eros: A Critique of the Kantian Paradigm*. Boston: Beacon, 1988.

Schutte, Ofelia. *Beyond, Nihilism: Nietzsche Without Masks*. Chicago, IL: University of Chicago, 1984.

Tuana, Nancy. *Woman and the History of Philosophy*. N.Y.: Paragon House, 1992.

Essays

1. Descartes

Allen, Prudence. "Aristotelian and Cartesian Revolution in the Philosophy of Man and Woman." *Dialogue* 26 (1987): 263–270.

2. Locke

Butler, Melissa. "Early Liberal Roots of Feminism: John Locke and the Attack on Patriarchy." *American Political Science Review* 72 (1978): 135–150.

Clark, Lorenne M. G. "Women and Locke: Who Owns the Apples in the Garden of Eden?" *The Canadian Journal of Philosophy* 7 (1977): 699–724.

Squadrito, Kathy. "Locke on the Equality of the Sexes" *Journal of Social Philosophy* 10 (1979): 6–11.

3. Hume

Baier, Annette. "Good Men's Women: Hume on Chastity and Trust." *Hume Studies* 5 (1979): 1–19.

Baier, Annette C. "Hume, The Women's Moral Theorist" in Kittay, Eva Feder and Meyers, Diana T. (eds.). *Women and Moral Theory*. Totowa, NJ: Rowman and Littlefield, 1987, pp. 37–55.

Bar On, Bat-Ami. "Could There Be a Humean Sex-Neutral General Idea of Man?" *Philosophy Research Archives* 13 (1987–88): 367–377.

Battersby, Christine. "An Enquiry Concerning the Humean Woman." *Philosophy* 56 (1981): 303–312.

Burns, Steven A. MacLead. "The Humean Female." *Dialogue* 15 (1976): 415–424.

Marcil-Lacoste, Louise. "Hume's Position Concerning Women." *Dialogue* 15 (1976): 425–440.

4. Rousseau

Kaufman, Sarah. "Rousseau's Phallocratic Ends." *Hypatia* 3 (1989): 123–136.

Lange, Lynda. "Rousseau and Modern Feminism." *Social Theory and Practice* 7 (1981): 245–277.

Lange, Lynda. "A Feminist Reads Rousseau: Thoughts on Justice, Love and the Patriarchal Family" *Newsletter on Feminism and Philosophy* (June 1989): 25–28.

Lloyd, Genevive. "Rousseau on Reason, Nature, and Woman" *Metaphilosophy* 14 (1983): 308–326.

Okin, Susan Moller. "Rousseau's Natural Women." *Journal of Politics* 41 (1979): 393–416.

Rapaport, Elizabeth. "On the Future of Love: Rousseau and the Radical Feminists." *The Philosophical Forum* 5 (1973–1974): 185–205.

5. Kant

Blum, Lawrence A. "Kant's and Hegel's Moral Rationalism: A Feminist Perspective." *Canadian Journal of Philosophy* 12 (1982): 287–302.

Schott, Robin May. "A Feminist Critique of the Kantian Paradigm." *Newsletter on Feminism and Philosophy* (June 1989): 28–31.

6. Hegel

Blum, Lawrence A. "Kant's and Hegel's Moral Rationalism: A Feminist Perspective." *Canadian Journal of Philosophy* 12 (1982): 287–302.

Clarke, Eric O. "Fetal Attraction: Hegel's An-aesthetics of Gender." *Differences* 5 (1991): 69–93.

Easton, Susan M. "Hegel and Feminism." in Lamb, David (ed.) *Hegel and Modern Philosophy*. London: Croom Helm, 1987.

Landes, Joan B. "Hegel's Conception of the Family." *Polity* 14 (1981): 5–28.

Mills, Patricia Jagentowicz. "Hegel's Antigone." *Minerva* 17 (1986): 131–152.

7. Marx

Arneson, Richard J. "Marx's Comments on Women in the *1844 Manuscripts*." *Philosophy Research Archives* 6 (1980): 25–54.

Goldstein, Leslie. "Mill, Marx, and Women's Liberation." *Journal of the History of Philosophy* 18 (1980): 319–334.

Held, Virginia. "Marx, Sex and the Transformation of Society." *The Philosophical Forum* 5 (1973–74): 168–184.

Nicholson, Linda. "Feminism and Marx: Integrating Kinship with the Economic." in Benhabib, Seyla and Cornell, Drucilla (eds.) *Feminism as Critique: On the Politics of Gender.* University of Minnesota, 1987, pp. 16–30.

8. Nietzsche

Ainley, Alison. "Ideal Selfishness: Nietzsche's Metaphor of Maternity." in Krell, David Ferrell and Wood, David (eds.) *Exceeding Nietzsche: Aspects on Contemporary Nietzsche Interpretation.* London: Routledge, 1988, pp. 116–130.

Cocks, Joan. "Augustine, Nietzsche, and Contemporary Body Politics." *Differences* 3 (1991): 144–158.

Frisby, Sandy. "Woman and the Will to Power." *Gnosis* 1 (1975): 1–10.

Hatab, Lawrence J. "Nietzsche on Woman." *Southern Journal of Philosophy* 19 (1981): 333–346.

Kennedy, Ellen. "Nietzsche: Women as Untermensch." in Kennedy, Ellen and Mendus, Susan (eds.) *Women in Western Political Philosophy.* NY: St. Martin, 1987, pp. 179–201.

Oliver, Kelly A. "Woman as Truth in Nietzsche's Writing" *Social Theory and Practice* 10 (1984): 185–200.

Oliver, Kelly. "Nietzsche's Woman: The Poststructuralist Attempt to Do Away with Women." *Radical Philosophy* 48 (1988): 25–29.

Ormiston, Gayle I. "Traces of Derida: Nietzsche's Image of Woman" *Philosophy Today* 28 (1984): 178–188.

Schutt, Ofelia. "Nietzsche on Gender Difference: A Critique." *Newsletter on Feminism and Philosophy* (June 1989): 31–35.

Strong, Tracy B. "Oedipusas Hero: Family and Family Metaphors in Nietzsche." *Boundary* 2 (1981).

9. Dewey

Heldke, Lisa. "John Dewey and Evelyn Fox Keller: A Shared Epistemological Tradition." *Hypatia* 2 (1987): 129–140.

Laird, Susan. "Women and Gender in John Dewey's Philosophy of Education." *Educational Theory* 38 (1988): 111–129.

Seigfried, Charlene, Haddock. "Where Are All the Pragmatist Feminists?" *Hypatia* 6 (1991): 1–20.

Contributors

—— *Bat-Ami Bar On* is associate professor of philosophy and Director of Women's Studies at the State University of New York at Binghamton. Her detour into canonical commentary is motivated by a need to configure a relation between feminist philosophy and philosophy. Her primary focus is socio-political and ethical issues and theory, especially as these arise in relation to everyday kinds of violence and abuse. She is working on a book about these issues.

—— *Susan Bordo* is Joseph C. Georg Professor of Philosophy at LeMoyne College. She is the author of *The Flight to Objectivity: Essays on Cartesianism and Culture* (SUNY Press, 1987) and *Unbearable Weight: Feminism, Western Culture and the Body* (U. of California Press, 1993). She is also the co-editor (with Alison Jaggar) of *Gender/Body/Knowledge: Feminist Reconstructions of Being and Knowing* (Rutgers U. Press, 1989).

—— *Lisa Heldke* is assistant professor of philosophy at Gustavus Adolphus College, St. Peter, MN. She writes and teaches on pragmatist feminism and on the philosophy of food. Her dissertation, "Coresponsible Inquiry: Objectivity from Dewey to Feminist Epistemology" (Northwestern University, 1986), was her first attempt to explore the feminist implications of Dewey's epistemology. With Deane Curtin, she is the editor of *Cooking, Eating, Thinking: Transformative Philosophies of Food* (Indiana University Press, 1992).

—— *Jane Kneller* is assistant professor of philosophy at Grinnell College. She has written on Kant's aesthetics, on the German Enlightenment and early German Romanticism, and is currently editing a volume on Kantian social theory and contemporary issues.

—— *Lynda Lange* is a Canada Research Fellow, Department of Philosophy, University of Toronto-Scarborough. She is co-editor with L. M. G. Clark of *The Sexism of Social and Political Theory* (University of Toronto Press, 1979). Her present research concerns the political development of feminist theory, and especially its relation to democratic theory.

—— *Wendy Lee-Lampshire* completed her Ph.D. in May 1992, specializing in philosophy of mind, language, Wittgenstein and feminist theory and has since taken up a post at Bloomsburg University as assistant professor of philosophy. Her interests revolve around the interstices and connections between philosophy of mind, neurophysiology, biology, artificial intelligence and anthropology—connections fruitfully blurred in the texts of thinkers like Marx.

—— *Marcia Lind* teaches philosophy at Duke University.

—— *Sarah Bishop Merrill,* M.S., Ph.D., was a Fellow of the Center for Women in Government in 1986. She teaches philosophy at Kansas State University, and serves on the Women's Studies Governing Board. Her research and teaching is interdisciplinary, in both feminist social philosophy and applied and professional ethics.

—— *Margaret Nash* is assistant professor of philosophy at SUNY College at Cortland. She received her doctorate from the University of Mass. at Amherst in 1987. She has published articles on psychoanalytic theory and is currently working in the area of recent French philosophy and feminism.

—— *Amy Newman* teaches philosophy and women's studies at the Philadelphia College of Textiles and Science.

—— *Kelly Oliver* is assistant professor of philosophy at the University of Texas at Austin. She is the author of *Reading Kristeva: Unraveling the Double-bind.* Her book *Womanizing Nietzsche: French Readings of the Figure of Woman* and edited collection *Ethics, Politics and Difference in Julia Kristeva's Writings* are both forthcoming.

—— *Elizabeth Potter* is the Alice Andrews Quigley Professor of Women's Studies at Mills College. Her recent work includes "Making Genders/ Making Science: Gender Ideology and Robert Boyle's Experimental Philosophy," in *Making a Difference: Feminist Critiques in the Natural Sciences,* edited by Bonnie Spanier, forthcoming from Indiana University Press. She is completing *Gender Politics in Seventeenth-Century Science,* a book exploring the intersections of gender and the production of early modern atomic theory, especially Boyle's Law of Gases.

—— *Robin May Schott* is associate professor of philosophy at the University of Louisville. She is the author of *Cognition and Eros: A Critique of the Kantian Paradigm* (paperback publication: Penn State University Press, spring 1993), and has written articles on critical theory, contemporary feminist theory, and postmodernist theory.

—— *Ofelia Schutte* is the author of *Beyond Nihilism: Nietzsche without Masks* (University of Chicago Press, 1984) and *Cultural Identity and Social Liberation in Latin American Thought* (SUNY Press, 1993). Some of her recent articles appear in *Hypatia: A Journal of Feminist Philosophy, Social Theory and Practice, The Philosophical Forum,* and *The Owl of Minerva.* She teaches philosophy at the University of Florida, where she is affiliated with the Women's Studies program and the Latin American Studies Center. A recent Fellow at Radcliffe's Bunting Institute, her current research involves a new study on feminist ethics.

————— *Kristin Waters* holds a Ph.D. from the University of Connecticut, and has taught most recently at Bard College and Clark University. Among her published works are, "Abortion, Technology and Responsibility," in the *Journal of Social Philosophy* (winter 1986) and reviews for *Women's Studies International Forum*. Her most recent work explores issues in feminist ethics and epistemology.

————— *Cynthia Willett* is assistant professor of philosophy at the University of Kansas in Lawrence. Her publications include "The Shadow of Hegel's *Logic*" in *Essays on Hegel's Logic* (SUNY, 1990), "Partial Attachments: A Deconstructive Model of Responsibility" in *Ethics and Danger* (SUNY, 1992), "Tropics of Desire: Derrida and Freud" in *Research in Phenomenology* 1992). Her current research focuses on the origins of self and sociality.

Index

Abortion, 85–6
Aeschylus; *Oresteia,* 169
Abstract, 143, 167, 171, 174
Actuality, 159
Actualization, 162
Adversary, 156; agonistic, 169; conflict, 158, 169, 179
Agency, 117, 122
Alien, 161, 163
Alienation, 133–6, 190, 192–3
Anglicanism, 33–4, 37, 45
Anthony, Susan B., 41–2
Aporia, 169
Aristotle, xi, xvi, 7, 38, 70, 83, 117, 168, 174, 176; *Poetics,* 176
Art, 168
Artists, 146–7
Asceticism, 130–1, 133, 136
Ashley-Cooper, Anthony (the Earl of Shaftsbury), 34–5
Assimilation, 160, 164
Authoritarian; democracy, 98; equality, 95, 106
Autonomy, 111, 117, 120, 145

Bacon, Francis, xii, 5, 9–11, 15, 18
Bar On, Bat-Ami, vii, xi, 268, 271
Barthes, Ronald, 51
Beauty, 53, 55, 57–8, 78, 119, 121–2, 146, 231
Bergson, Henry, 9
Bias, Cultural, 59, 61–2
Birke, Lynda, 185, 191, 199
Bishop, Sarah Merrill A., vii, xv, 69, 272
Blackwell, Antoinette Brown, 123
Body, 203, 206, 208, 221–2, 225, 227
Bordo, Susan, vii, xv, 3, 267, 271
Bourgeoise, 141
Brown, Norman O., 13

Canon, xi, xii–iv, xvi, 51, 128
Capitalism, 185–6, 188–9
Categorical Imperative, 120, 124, 143, 145
Catholicism, 33
Catharsis, 167–70, 172–3, 175–9
Certainty/Chance, 248–9, 251
Cervantes, 53
Charles I, 29–30, 33, 43
Charles II, 33–6
Child, Children, 3, 149, 171, 195–6, 206
Childlike, 141–2, 145, 148, 151
Chodorow, Nancy, 18–20
Civil Society, 151
Cixous, Helen, 227, 239–41, 243–4
Class, 107, 141, 156, 187, 196
Clear and Distinct Ideas, 4
Cognition, 130–1, 145, 148, 167
Coherence, 29
Comedy, 169, 176, 180
Commodity, 133, 136
Community, 159, 170, 176–7
Consciousness, 158, 163, 170, 221; false-consciousness 24; self-consciousness, 158–60, 178
Courage/Cowardice, 141–2
Cromwell, 33

Darwin, Charles, Robert, 123
Death, 157–9, 162–4, 170, 178
Dehumanization, 162
Democratic Theory, 95–8
Deontology, 121
Derrida, Jacques, 201, 238
Descartes, 39; *Meditations on First Philosophy,* 4–8
Desire, 168, 171–3, 175–8
Devotion, 171–2, 174
Dialectics, 157–9, 161, 167, 170–3, 175–6, 178–80, 204, 220
Dichotomous/Dichotomy, 150, 167, 250